The
Scottish
Government
Yearbook
1980

Edited by
H. M. DRUCKER
*Department of Politics and Unit for
the Study of Government in
Scotland,
University of Edinburgh*

and

N. L. DRUCKER
*Department of Social Administration,
University of Edinburgh*

Paul Harris Publishing
Edinburgh

First published 1979
by Paul Harris Publishing
25 London Street
Edinburgh

ISBN 0 904505 707

The Publishers would like to acknowledge the financial assistance
of the Scottish Arts Council

Printed in Great Britain by The Shetland Times Ltd., Lerwick, Shetland

THE SCOTTISH GOVERNMENT
YEARBOOK 1980

CONTENTS

REFERENCE SECTION

*Reference section prepared with the assistance of
Richard Parry, Centre for the Study of Public Policy,
University of Strathclyde.*

PREFACE

The *Yearbook* is edited by H. M. Drucker and N. L. Drucker on behalf of the Unit for the Study of Government in Scotland at the University of Edinburgh. Additional copies of the *Yearbook*, back-copies of the three previous volumes, and further information about the Unit's activities can be obtained from the editors, at 31 Buccleuch Place, Edinburgh EH8 9JT, Scotland.

We are grateful to several previous contributors and other friends for suggestions for papers for this volume and for their helpful comments on drafts of papers received. We would welcome suggestions from our readers about subjects or authors for papers. We are indebted to the *Glasgow Herald* and to several other Scottish newspapers and broadcasting organisations for permission to reprint public opinion polls they originally sponsored. We also wish to record our thanks to Andrew Bolger for editorial assistance and to Helen Ramm for typing the text.

HMD
NLD
Edinburgh
June 1979

I

SCOTLAND:
BACK INTO THE CLOSET?

THE EDITORS

The *Scottish Government Yearbook 1980* is the fourth in our series. Since we published the 1979 *Yearbook* Scottish politics and government have undergone much change. All our previous *Yearbooks* were written when there was a prospect that a directly elected Assembly would sit in Edinburgh to control the Scottish Office. This prospect was the central political concern of Scottish government during the recent Parliament (1974-79) and this centrality was reflected in our volumes. This hope or spectre has now passed. The Scottish people did not vote for the Government's plans, embodied in the Scotland Act, in sufficiently large numbers on 1 March 1979 for the Act to be implemented. Further, in the subsequent General Election the British people returned to power the only party, the Conservative Party, which had campaigned for a "No" vote in the referendum. For these reasons devolution will not dominate the recently elected Parliament, nor will we have an elected forum for the discussion of Scottish politics for the next four or five years. However, there has been more to the change in Scottish politics than that.

The recent General Election saw a government elected in Westminster which lacked a majority in Scotland. More to the point, the Conservative Party had a safe majority in Parliament but only twenty-two of the seventy-one Scottish parliamentary seats. This means that the team of Scottish Office Ministers will have a weaker hand to play in the centre of power than their Labour predecessors. They will be taken less seriously in Whitehall and will find it more difficult to get Westminster's decisions taken seriously in Scotland. It is no criticism of the present Scottish Office team led by Mr George Younger to say that they will have much less leverage than did Mr Bruce Millan and his colleagues.

It was frequently said during the 1974-79 Parliament that

Scotland and Wales were taken seriously because Labour and Conservative leaders had been shaken by the rise of the Nationalist parties. This was a half truth. Certainly they were taken seriously for this reason, but both also benefited from the double fact that they had elected a majority of MPs to the Government party and that that party had only a small majority — later a minority — in the House of Commons. Scotland's success in demanding increasingly favourable treatment from the centre depended on the parliamentary weakness of a government beholden to Scotland. Had the General Election of February 1974 led to a large overall Labour majority it is safe to assume that nothing would have been done about devolution or about Scotland — for example, the Scottish Development Agency might well not have been created. Had the Labour Government elected in October 1974 with a bare majority won a large majority, the Government might well have treated its commitment to devolution as it treated its commitments to open government and a wealth tax. Because the present Government is secure in its parliamentary position and not particularly beholden to Scotland, it need do little for Scotland and Scotland is unlikely to figure prominently in British politics for the next few years.

This is a bleak prospect. It is not simply bleak in the sense that the future does not offer us great hope of advance. It is bleak in that the larger issues of Scottish politics may not be much discussed; and the major decisions affecting Scotland will be taken, once again, in private and in secret.

I

This year we publish three papers on the referendum. The first, by Ray Perman, analyses the campaign itself. The second, by Michael Brown, analyses the effects of the Press on that campaign. Perman points to the divisions within the "Yes" side as one reason for the victory of the "Nos". Divided, the "Yes" side certainly was. Devolution had become not just a political issue but a party issue and the "Yes" and "No" men of each party wanted to run their own show and not share credit or platforms with members of other parties. This had a more damaging effect on the "Yes" campaign than on the "No". The "Nos" appeared separately to say much the same things: the "Yes" had different messages. The Nationalist "Yes" people made the Scottish argument: devolution was important for Scottish self-respect and as a step to Scottish self-rule. The Labour (and Conservative) "Yes" people needed to distance themselves from this argument. For them the point was that devolution would lead to democratic control of the Scottish Office and, by making the government of Scotland more responsive to its people, guarantee the unity of the United Kingdom. The incompatibility of these two arguments hurt just because the Nationalists succeeded in getting their point across — and hence raised the fears of the anti-separatist majority — while the Labour democratic argument seems never to have penetrated at all. Many voters must have thought that only the SNP were in favour of the Government's Act. Michael Brown's careful analysis of the Press shows just why the "Yeses" were foolish to conduct so many campaigns: the Press was not going to give them enough space to develop these relatively sophisticated differences. Furthermore, he points to the fact that the "Nos" managed to dictate the issues on which the referendum campaign was fought, thus quite possibly neutralising the pro-devolution stance of the majority of the Scottish Press.

In our third paper on the referendum, Chris Baur argues that this form of popular consultation is in danger of being discredited. Indeed the various *ad hoc* arrangements came close to bringing the whole electoral process (and not least the electoral register) into disrepute. Is there any other advanced industrial state which would invoke such an untried and ill-considered device to adjudicate on an important constitutional issue? If the devolution referendum leads to a reconsideration of the electoral system and the role of referenda in British politics it will at least have accomplished some positive good.

The loss of face the Government suffered when the results were announced (particularly in Wales) led to the May 1979 General Election. Without the prospect of devolution the Government lost the support of the Nationalists of both Scotland and Wales. It did not take long for the Conservatives to put together the coalition of anti-Government House of Commons votes which brought the Government down. We are pleased to publish here, for the first time, an account of the crucial meeting within the SNP parliamentary group which led to their decision to put down a motion of no confidence in the Government. The divisions within the parliamentary group which James

Naughtie reveals in his piece are all too credible: few parties
are the monoliths they like to appear in public. But these divisions
within the SNP confirm the ineffective impression that party
gave throughout the 1974-79 Parliament.

In Scotland at the subsequent General Election, as Peter
Hetherington points out, Labour won the battle. It had all
the ammunition and the larger army. Thanks to its devolution
stand it could no longer be labelled anti-Scottish, and thanks
to the plans of the Conservatives it looked the better bet for
the people of the depressed parts of central Scotland. Labour's
problems will come in the longer term: will it be able to promise
devolution at a future General Election, having failed to carry
it through this time? Hetherington also points to the weakness
of the SNP campaign: this was quite a surprise after its success
in 1974. When the going got rough, the party faltered.

In many ways the biggest talking point of 1978-79 was
decline of the SNP. This can be overstated. Although its 17.3%
of the poll in the General Election was quite a comedown after
the 30% of October 1974, it is not a bad result on which to
build. The fact that the SNP was reduced to two seats is as
much a reflection of our electoral system as of its performance.
But these comments cannot hide the fact that the SNP failed
to live up to its boundless promise of 1974 and is now a much-
reduced party. However, the electoral failure of the party had
given its left wing the spur to open a campaign to move the
party away from its present right-wing bias. This struggle for
the soul of the party may have significant long-term consequences
for the future not only of the SNP, but also of Scottish politics
in general. The Labour Party has never seriously been challenged
for the votes of the working class. If it were to be challenged,
all sorts of interesting vistas would open up. But for the time
being the Left within the SNP remains very much a minority.

II

Perhaps the most significant long-term effect of the year's
political events will be a change in the focus of political debate
in Scotland. Because the recently elected Government has a
secure majority and because it has little stake in Scotland,
Scottish politics will be much less newsworthy than during the
last Parliament. The important battles will be fought out in
private. This change of emphasis poses a challenge for the

Yearbook. We began by wanting to illuminate the workings of Scottish administration and government; to bring light on the dark quarters. Now such light will be needed more than ever.

Our suspicion is that one of the most important arenas of Scottish politics over the next few years will be the Rate Support Grant negotiations. The present Government was elected on a promise to reduce public spending. It never hid its intent. But neither this Government nor its Labour predecessor (which also cut public spending, after being forced to by the IMF) has been willing to face the full consequences of its decision. Governments are inescapably tempted to make the local authorities take the blame for government decisions and make some of the hardest choices. This problem arises because local government employs large numbers of people in public services, many of whom, such as teachers, environmental health inspectors and firemen, are required by statute. Many of the salary and other costs of these public employees are paid for by the central government. Each year central government negotiates with local government over the level of central support for local services: these negotiations are the Rate Support Grant (RSG) negotiations. If central government brings down its Rate Support Grant, as this one has announced that it intends to do, local government is faced with the choice of cutting services and staff or raising rates — and probably will do a bit of both.

We have a Conservative government. The body with which it will negotiate the RSG is the Labour-dominated Convention of Scottish Local Authorities (COSLA). Scotland, unlike England, and unlike Scotland before the recent reform of local government, has just one body to negotiate with central government. Yet despite the fundamental importance of the issues to be decided, these negotiations will be conducted in private and will receive little Press coverage (though the losing side may leak the contents to the Press). If governments were less obsessed with secrecy, more could be known and public support for government might be encouraged. As it is, cynicism will grow.

Too little is known about the working of government in Scotland. Chris Allen in his trenchant analysis of the available literature makes the all too pertinent point that studies of administration tend to substitute details for analysis. Allen's own analysis of the failure of Scottish political science can hardly be accused of that — for all that this *Yearbook* has been consistently, and is again this year, aided by his lengthy bibliographies. We are, however, delighted to offer a paper this year by Colin Wiseman which goes some way to filling one of the most annoying gaps: lack of analytical studies about the Scottish Office. Wiseman's paper, "Policy Making of the Scottish Health Services at National Level", is, as far as we know, the first paper to analyse policy-making in the Scottish Office on the basis of first-hand observation.

Wiseman's picture of the Scottish Home and Health Department operations is not entirely flattering. His main concern is that long-term policy-making in the department hardly exists: too much time is consumed by responding to emergencies as they arise. The department is a GP to an elderly, much scared patient. Wiseman would have it perform a more considered, more rational, less harassed role. There are, of course, many objections to Wiseman's view. Perhaps the most fundamental is that one cannot plan when one doesn't know what one is planning for. Since our culture lacks a generally agreed definition of health it is hardly fair to blame Civil Servants for failing to make us healthy. The other main objection is constitutional. Wiseman wants greater public control of and accountability by the Health Service in Scotland. His chart (fig. 1) gives away the present game: in it the Secretary of State and the Ministers are shown to be but one pressure group amongst many. Wiseman's chart is, we do not doubt, accurate: it is also shameful in a country that purports to be a democracy.

Wiseman's paper about policy-making in the SHHD differs in intent and compass from Mary Macdonald's paper about the Scottish Office in the last twenty-five years. In 1957, as part of the new Whitehall series on British Ministries, George Allen & Unwin published a description of the Scottish Office by Sir David Milne. Sir David was, at the time, the Permanent Under-Secretary of State (i.e. the chief Civil Servant) in the Scottish Office. Despite its age and the considerable changes which have occurred in the operation of the Scottish Office since 1957, Sir David's is still the standard work on the subject. During 1978, when it looked as if the devolution legislation would be implemented, the Scottish Office approached us with the offer of a paper from the inside which would update Sir David's book on the eve of the Office's anticipated transformation. We agreed to publish such a piece and the Scottish Office put Mary Macdonald (a retired Assistant Secretary from the Scottish Office) and a research assistant, Adam Redpath, onto writing it for us. We publish their paper here. We think its account of the changes made will provide a useful baseline for future studies of the Scottish Office during this period of rapid change. Any analysis of the change must begin with an accurate picture of what has been done.

With the record straight it is possible to see where future research ought to begin. We need to know more about the relations between the Scottish Office and the Whitehall Ministries. Outsiders commonly assert that the Scottish Office lamely follows the lead given in England. On detailed technical matters this assertion may be difficult to contradict, but on more general policy lines this outsiders' perception is hotly contested from within the Scottish Office and by Miss Macdonald in her paper. We need studies of certain policies to see how this relationship works. We also need to know more about the internal workings of the Scottish Office, particularly about the question of the co-ordination of the several departments of the Scottish Office. The degree of departmental pride of people in the SDD, for instance, leads one to suspect that co-operation is not what it seems — and Wiseman's paper lends some support to this suspicion. We need to know more about it. There are questions about the relationship between the Scottish Office and the large number of QUANGOs which operate under its auspices. The accountability of these QUANGOs, as well as the degree and manner of Scottish Office influence and control of them, is a neglected field. Raymond Williams has recently written a most useful critical piece about the operations of the Arts Council, of which he is a member (*Political Quarterly*, Spring 1979). We need something similar for Scottish bodies.

It is no secret that the relationships between the Scottish Office and the local authorities are not always smooth — but why not, and can anything be done about it? In her paper Miss Macdonald shows that the Scottish Office has divested itself of many small executive responsibilities — such as running farms — in recent years. One can't help wondering what happens to the Civil Servants who used to perform these tasks or to supervise those who performed them. Can they be fitted into the quite different work of the rest of this large government department or not? There is also the related question of precise Scottish Office control of local government. Miss Macdonald points out that the departments have been divesting themselves of these controls too. This is certainly commendable, but is it not then a bit odd that the Scottish Office continues to employ so many professional Civil Servants, such as Inspectors of schools (we have as many as England and Wales together), architects and nurses? What do these professional staff do if they do not advise on very precise detailed execution of policy?

We are likely to have a new parliamentary Select Committee to shadow the Scottish Office. Surely someone will investigate the work of this committee and compare it with some of the other parliamentary Select Committees? How much difference does the personality and the political weight carried by the Secretary of State for Scotland make? We harbour the suspicion that life is easier for Labour Secretaries of State because their party owes more to Scotland. But is it this sort of calculation of the weight of the administrative machine which wins arguments in Whitehall? We are asked by the Scottish Office to believe that it has a closer understanding of our needs and resources than the English Ministries have of their clients. Is this true?

In suggesting that these questions remain to be answered we are not simply blaming the Scottish Office. The point made by Chris Allen about the feebleness and patchiness of academic work is relevant here. Our impression is that the Scottish Office is actually rather good, and certainly much better than it used to be, at providing access (to people like Mr Wiseman, for example) though it is still very touchy about what gets published.

We must not, however, become obsessed with investigating the workings of the machine. It is the product which matters most of all, and this year we continue our series about the social and economic policies of government in Scotland with three papers on specific areas of policy-making. The first is a proposal by Mike Adler and Edward Woznick for an entirely new way of settling debt. This is a serious human and social problem in Scotland. A good proportion of our prisoners are in jail for the failure to pay debt. Other features of the debt collection system are also most unsatisfactory and humiliating to the people involved. Adler and Woznick call the present judicial basis of the system into question given that the facts of the case —

how much is owed, and whether the debt is admitted — are rarely in question. They propose a new system for Scotland which, if adopted, would put us ahead of other countries in this area where we now lag.

John Godfrey and Norman Godman contribute a paper to this year's *Yearbook* which makes proposals in another area of government policy: the Scottish fishing industry. Their proposal for a Common Fisheries Policy is the first we have published which puts Scottish policy into a European context. But as Godfrey and Godman show, it no longer makes sense for any one nation to try to have its own fishing policy. International co-operation is needed if we are to retain a fishing industry and the fish on which it is dependent.

G. A. Mackay contributes the third paper on public policy — in this case energy policy. This is a matter not directly for government but for a number of QUANGOs — the electricity supply boards, the National Coal and Gas Boards and the nuclear power industry. Mackay notes that an increased emphasis on indigenous fuels, particularly coal with its high use of skilled manual labour, is desirable on social grounds. He also argues that the increasingly public debate about energy needs and energy usage which has marked Scottish discussion over the past few years is an encouraging sign which has led to slower but better policy decisions. Once again the danger of secret and private policy-making is emphasised.

This danger and the prospect that Scottish politics and Scottish public life might go back into the closet from which it emerged in the late sixties is the biggest threat posed to us. Our first *Yearbook* was subtitled, in a paraphrase of the Government's then infamous devolution White Paper: "Our Changing Scotland". If Scotland goes back into the closet we might title next year's book "Our Unchanging Scotland". But there are already some signs that we will not have to do this. The pessimists have been heard too often lately. Despite the failure of the devolution legislation, public life in Scotland changed during the 1974-79 Parliament in ways which will bring about further changes. The most important administrative change was the creation of the Scottish Development Agency (SDA) and with it the admission by British government that Scotland's economy could not be wholly run from London. The long-term implications of this admission and the large sums of government money

B

now being used to back it up are considerable. Moreover, the creation of a highly viable government agency in Scotland will only serve to increase the demand for some form of directly elected Scottish body to scrutinise the Scottish Office.

At the same time, and notwithstanding the pain of the process, the politics of Scotland have changed considerably in the last five years. The Labour Party has now recovered its commitment to elective devolution and in some respects looks no less nationalist than the SNP. This reconversion by the party which holds the majority of Scottish seats and governs most major Scottish towns is more important than is often realised. The traumas of conception and rebirth belie the health of the bairn, and her importance. Three of the four political parties in Scotland which hold seats in Westminster are committed to devolution. Together these parties won 68% of Scottish votes at the 1979 Election and they hold forty-nine of Scotland's seventy-one parliamentary seats.

Again, during the course of the recent Parliament there was a steady stream of government agencies which felt compelled to open up Scottish branches or create semi-autonomous Scottish regions. A recent example of such devolution of administrative power was the creation of the Scottish Council of the Council of National Academic Awards (CNAA). This devolution is a small step but it is a sign of the way things are moving.

Finally, there was the devolution legislation and referendum. For all that the "No" side won the day on March 1, they did not win all of the arguments. The democratic accountability argument put by some in the "Yes" camp — which would have been so much more effective had John Mackintosh lived — was never countered by the "Nos". Even the No-dominated Conservative Government will want to do something about this. If they don't, they make it easier for their enemies to do something really radical next time the wheel turns and the Conservatives are out of power.

2

THE STUDY OF SCOTTISH POLITICS:
A BIBLIOGRAPHICAL SERMON

C. H. ALLEN
Lecturer in Politics, Edinburgh University

Each issue of this *Yearbook* has carried a lengthy bibliography on the previous twelve months' writing on Scottish
government and politics. Yet its length is deceptive, for in all
too many fields there is remarkably little work: like its teeth,
the study of Scotland's politics is most notable for gaps. The
reasons ultimately lie in the nature of the Scottish political
system and in its political culture, for most of what is written
on Scotland is written from Scotland. This brief article tries to
identify those reasons, once the extent of the gaps in the
literature has been established.

I. Pathology

Scotland has for many years been accepted as a politically
distinct area of the United Kingdom, no less in terms of its
political behaviour and consciousness than its institutions. Yet
in all of these areas of study there are extensive and surprising
gaps, together with a narrowness of conception and vision, that
makes a full understanding of the Scottish political system
and the tendencies within it very hard to achieve. James Kellas's
valiant and pioneering attempt at such an understanding (Kellas
1975) shows both the extent and the intractability of this
problem.

We may start by considering the major *formal institutions
of government* of Scotland: Parliament, the Scottish Office and
its appointed bodies, and local government. The distinctively
Scottish elements of Parliament are reasonably broadly covered,
with useful accounts of the Scottish Committees (Burns 1960;
Edwards 1972) and an impressive thesis by the subsequently
prolific Michael Keating, on Scottish MPs (Keating 1975; summary versions Keating 1977, 1978; see also Mishler and Mughan

1978). Where we are still ill-served, despite the efforts of this *Yearbook*, is in assessment of the effect of these elements on the process of law-making. Received ideas are easier to come by than evidence, as Robin Cook points out in one of the few articles on the background to a Bill and its enactment or failure (Cook 1977; see also Cope 1977 and Gibson 1978).

The Scottish Office, though the most influential institution in Scotland, remains among the least analysed. Hanham (in Wolfe 1969), Breckenridge (1969) and Kellas (1975) provide stock brief accounts, but suffer from the pervasive superficiality and blandness of the official descriptions, which substitute detail for any hint of self-criticism (Royal Commission on Scottish Affairs 1954; Milne 1957; Kilbrandon 1973; Select Committee on Scottish Affairs 1968/9, 1969/70; Haddow 1964; McGuiness in MacKay 1979). Much the same can be said for the few pieces on the Secretary of State, which are hardly more informative on the office than are the occasional references in the memoirs of other Ministers (see Ross 1977 and, for a general historical account, Pottinger 1979). Academic commentary has thus remained limited to an inconclusive debate on the significance of the separate administration of Scotland (Mackintosh 1964; Keating 1976), limited comparison of the Scottish Office with other Ministries (Hood 1978), and general surveys which raise more questions than they can hope to answer (Kellas 1975; Keating 1979b). Individual Scottish departments are even more rarely discussed, apart from the evidence to Kilbrandon and the Select Committee on Scottish Affairs; for the SDD and SEPD see Scottish Council (1970).

Attached to the Scottish Office, and responsible for the execution of more of its powers (and the spending of more of its budget) than is the case for any other Ministry, are hundreds of appointed bodies (see Haddow in MacKay 1979, and Hogwood 1979 for general accounts). Few of them publish even annual reports, and those that do are too often discussed only in those reports or in brief newspaper features. There are short accounts of the new Health Service structure (D. Hunter 1976; Levitt 1976), but only one assessment (Hunter, forthcoming) that raises issues of accountability and participation. Similarly, only Williams' thesis on the early years of the HIDB (Williams 1973; see also Thompson 1978) does this for the major economic agencies, though they are prolific and informative producers of documents and have attracted several critical assessments of their activities (e.g. Carter 1973; Bryden and Houston 1977; Radice 1978; Davies 1978; Lotz 1969). In other important fields — such as education and the New Towns — there are at best the annual reports, and in housing some brief commentaries on housing associations (e.g. Edinburgh Housing Research Group 1977).

Perhaps the most documented of Scotland's formal institutions is local government, with the Wheatley Report (1969) and its volumes of evidence at one end, through the reports and commentaries on the new structure (e.g. Paterson 1973; Peggie 1976; Midwinter 1978), to the massive output in the planning field, much of which is very informative (for general surveys see S. McDonald 1977 and Planning Exchange material such as Howat 1976). Problems begin to arise though when one moves away from the essentially descriptive (or prescriptive) areas of structure, output and finance to that of the assessment of local government. The parties have produced interesting but brief criticisms, especially the Conservatives (see Scottish Conservative Local Government Review Group 1977), but there is very little on the internal workings of local government and its politics (Young 1977; Turpie 1977), on central-local relations (Page 1978), or on such major topics as region-district relations or the Convention of Scottish Local Authorities itself (here one must rely on David Scott's solid pieces in *The Scotsman*). Community councils, the newest and least significant part of local government, have had disproportionate attention, largely because of Scottish Office funding of research and the enthusiasm of Councils of Social Service. For their rationale and structure, see SDD 1974, SCSS 1974, and Rowe 1975; for more critical assessment, see the work of Mike Masterson (in e.g. Scottish Office 1978a, Strathclyde Area Survey 1978), Scottish Office 1978b, Clarke 1977, and the SCSS's *Community Council News.*

In much the same fashion that analysis of the legislative process is scarcer than description of legislative institutions, so the slim material on policy-making stands in sharp contrast to the plentiful discussion of policy problems.* Kellas bravely

* The extensive literature in this field, from all manner of sources, testifies to the activity of the Scottish political system, if not its self-consciousnses.

attempts a description in his text book and in more tentative papers on education and regional policy (Kellas 1975, 1977a, 1978b); there is an unusual and useful paper on the role of economists in government (Coats 1978), and both Hunter (forthcoming) and Williams (1973) touch on this question in their accounts of the NHS in Scotland and of the HIDB. But apart from a number of case studies of local planning decisions (Rodger 1978; Burton and Johnson 1976; Mutch 1977) there is nothing substantial, though a major study of educational policy, administration and policy-making is well under way at Edinburgh University.

Parties, Pressure Groups and Political Action

Of all the parties active in Scotland, only one has anything near a full treatment: the Scottish National Party. The minor parties (with one exception) have at best the odd article or pamphlet devoted to them, or brief mentions in volumes of political reminiscence (most of which are concerned with pre-war politics). For the Communist Party see Reid (1976) and Denver (1972), and for the smaller Left organisations Thompson in MacDougall (1979) and Williamson (1978). There is no general account of Fascist organisations or activity (though Scotland has been relatively free of these), nor of extreme nationalist or sectarian organisations (though the Press has had material on all these).

More surprisingly, considering their historical and contemporary importance, there are no major studies of either the Liberal Party or the Labour Party in Scotland, though both Kellas (1975) and Harvie (1977) have short commentaries, as does Breckenridge (1969). By contrast, the shortlived Scottish Labour Party has a monograph (Drucker 1977a) and a number of articles (e.g. Nairn 1977b), while the Conservatives, thanks largely to their own industry and perhaps the stimulus of a declining vote, have a fairly substantial literature, of which the most useful is Chris Wyke's undergraduate thesis (Wyke 1978; see also Urwin 1966; Kernohan and Wright 1973; Lang and Henderson 1975; Ward 1977).

Nationalist parties, especially the SNP, have been far more generously treated. There are major books on nationalism in the UK (Coupland 1954; Nairn 1977a; Birch 1977) as well as on Scotland alone (Hanham 1969; W. Wolfe 1973; Webb 1976;

Harvie 1977; Brand 1978; Williamson and Kerevan forthcoming). To these we may add a series of theses, mainly by Americans (Haworth 1968; Bain 1973; Drieux 1974; Gallo 1974; Reich 1978; Grasmuck 1978) and a wide range of articles and pamphlets. These latter range from general accounts, often repeating each other (Burrell 1957; Mackintosh 1967; Maclean 1970; Schwartz 1970; Kellas 1971; Begg and Stewart 1971; Esman 1975), through largely sociological description and interpretation (Brand 1968; Brand and McCrone 1975; Mullin 1977; Hanby 1977; Miller 1977b; Dickson 1978), to attempts at a more general interpretation of UK nationalisms (Lazer 1977; Rawkins 1978; Birch 1978; Rose 1976, 1978). It is churlish to complain that this is not enough, but the sociological material remains incomplete and unconvincing (see the discussion in Brand 1978) and there is little beyond Brand and Roger Mullin's undergraduate dissertation (Mullin 1977) on the organisation and interior working of the party, on policy-making, patterns of recruitment and growth at national or local level, and on the SNP in local government (though some of the material on local politics is relevant here).

Pressure groups are almost as important in British politics as the parties; but in Scotland they are as sketchily covered as the equally numerous (and equally unaccountable) appointed bodies. Studies of the Labour movement confine themselves almost entirely to its history to 1926 or 1939, though there are studies of the Scottish TUC (Craigen 1975) and the Glasgow Trades Council (Liddell 1978), together with a dissertation on the EEC referendum and the Scottish Labour movement (Purves 1978). Other organisations fare no better: the Educational Institute of Scotland and the NFU are mentioned — but only in relation to the European Communities — in Kellas (1977b), W. Grant (1978) and Massie (1979), and there are short general surveys in Kellas (1975) and Gibson (1977). Such major economic interest groups as the Scottish Council (Development and Industry) and the Scottish CBI have been discussed only in terms of their position on devolution, in a set of rather repetitive articles on devolution and interest groups (Kellas 1976; Drucker 1977b; Dalyell 1977; Heald and Keating 1979; Drucker and Brown forthcoming). The Churches, despite their far greater influence on and activity in Scottish politics, have not been studied at all (a thesis was begun at Glasgow by L. Benskin), though they and several other groups are mentioned in the *Yearbook* series on legislation (Cope 1977; Cook 1977; Gibson 1978), and from time to time in Press features. As for more secretive or sinister influences, as with the Orange Order and other sectarian groups, even this last source often fails us (but see R. Mackay 1975).

A little more information on pressure-group membership and its political importance can be gleaned from the material on parties already mentioned, and that on local politics, which is full of neglected and often fascinating studies. One block of material covers elections with exhaustive accounts of the recent local elections by Bochel and Denver (1975, 1977a, 1977b, 1978) and a number of constituency-based studies of local and national elections, notably Chrimes (1950, Glasgow), Wood, (1971, Edinburgh), Goulstone (1974) and Chalmers (1978, Dundee), and Dyer (1975) and Lang (1973, Aberdeenshire). Discussions of the recruitment, institutional ties and behavious of councillors form a second block (though there is very little in the way of reminiscence; see McKensie 1976 on Dundee). Apart from the material just cited there are a pair of studies apiece on councillors in Edinburgh (McGregor 1973; Elliott et al. 1977) and Glasgow (Brand 1973; Fowe 1970), and on New Town or nationalist councillors (Grant 1970; Morris 1968). Studies of local political behaviour again focus on the major cities: Mackintosh (1966) and Brand (1976) on Edinburgh, Budge et al. (1972) and Rollo (1971) on Glasgow (the latter focusing on Irish politics), and Brand (1976) on Aberdeen. Rural politics is dealt with only in Dyer (1975) and Howatson (1976), and somewhat indirectly in two interesting accounts of local campaigns: the "Save the Argylls" campaign in Argyll (Allan 1974) and that to make Fife a Region (Ballantine 1975). Research on Highland politics is in train, but the Borders remain untouched, as do the Western Isles and Orkney and Shetland, despite the considerable interest in other aspects of these areas; for discussion of these areas we must rely on the weekly newspapers and the *New Shetlander*.

Political Behaviour and its Bases

The main contrast in this field is between the relatively large number of studies of electoral behaviour and the dearth of material on any other aspect since the pioneering Glasgow-based work of Budge and Urwin (1966). Electoral sociology is covered by Miller (1977a) (see also Cornford and Brand in N.

Wolfe 1969, and of course Kellas 1975), and there are more specialised articles on the influence of religion (Bochel and Denver 1970) and age (Mercer 1974), and on the 1974 elections (Jaensch 1974; R. J. Johnson 1977). The basis of support of particular parties is less surely covered, and there is nothing for Scotland alone which is comparable to the general UK study of Crewe et al. (1977), though some conclusions can be drawn from the careful and detailed analyses of nationalist support in Miller (1977b) and Kellas (1971). Kellas and Fotheringham (1976) offer some sociological interpretation of Labour support and there are a few brief accounts of the sociology of nationalism (see above), none entirely convincing. Several of the studies of the SNP try to explain the growth of nationalist attitudes, as opposed to SNP votes, notably Brand (1978); for particular factors see Brooks (1973) (relative deprivation), Grasmuck (1978) (underdevelopment and oil) and Reich (1978) (ethnicity). Other forms and areas of political consciousness remain the province of more literary or journalistic attention, though there is data in one of the Kilbrandon research papers, and the opinion polls (especially those in *The Scotsman*).

Scottish political culture resembles that in England in its covert racism and its devaluing and subordination of women (E. Hunter 1979; Maxwell 1977a; for material on the political participation of women see Mullin 1977; Lewenhak 1973; Masterman 1978). In other ways it is said to differ, being on the one hand more romantic, intellectual, internationalist, democratic (or even radical), and egalitarian (see e.g. Kellas 1968; Kennedy 1976; Nairn 1976b), but on the other hand parochial, authoritarian and didactic (Nairn 1968, 1977a, 1977c; Smout 1977; and for commentary Maxwell 1976 and 1977b). Unfortunately, given the intrinsic importance and interest of the field, the material cited is longer on polemic than evidence. Often the argument is based on reasonable but unexamined assumptions that Scottish political culture is formed by a combination of its social institutions (essentially the educational and legal system and the Kirk) and the history of political (and cultural) subordination to England. Attractive though this model is it remains essentially untested, despite the existence of a large amount of material casting doubt on the egalitarian and other credentials of the Scottish educational and legal systems, and on their differences from the English ones.

Constitutional Reform

This background of, at best, uncertainty about the general nature of the Scottish political system, and, at worst, of ignorance about many of its specific features, has tended to distort the vigorous and extensive discussion of alternatives. The literature on devolution and on independence has shifted steadily away from justification of proposed change (as e.g. in Mackintosh 1968; Kilbrandon 1973; Cornford 1975; Paton 1968) towards an increasingly pragmatic and technical discussion of constitutional detail and policy issues. As the recent referendum campaign showed, there is still little presentation or debate of the arguments for devolution in terms of the structure and behaviour of the Scottish political system. There is a certain irony in that, since Kilbrandon, the best general accounts of the justification for devolution have been produced for Wales (Osmond 1977; also useful on the history of government proposals) and for the UK (Bogdanor 1979, also useful for the arguments against devolution, and for comparative material on Northern Ireland*).

The specifically Scottish literature, though closely bound to the Scotland Act and its predecessor, has considerable value. Part of it describes the political background to and histories of the various proposals, reports, White Papers and Bills, with Keating and Bleiman (1979) and Drucker and Brown (forthcoming) the most comprehensive. Also useful are Bogdanor (1979), Dalyell (1977), Kellas and Owen (1977), Jordan (1979), Kerr (1977), Naughtie (1978), and Heald and Keating (1979).

Another substantial body of work has been concerned with assessment and criticism of the recent government proposals and Bills**. For general assessments see Drucker and McAllister (1976), Gunn and Lindley (1977), Mbadinuju (1976), Christie (1976), Thomson (1977) and again Dalyell (1977). Particular problems raised included the financing of a devolved legislature (Heald 1976 and 1977; Wilson 1976; Nevin 1978), the electoral system (Chapman 1976; Proctor 1977), and various constitutional problems, including the future of Scottish MPs and that of

---

* on which see also Brett (1970), Arthur (1977), Birrell (1978).

**Apart from those mentioned, there were a great many papers produced by the parties, professions and other bodies, most of which can be consulted in the Depository of the Unit for the Study of Government in Scotland.

Shetland (Bogdanor 1978; N. Johnson 1977; Calvert 1975; Sharpe 1978; Judge and Finlayson 1975; Mishler and Mughan 1978; Nevis Institute 1978; and Grönneberg 1978).

Lastly, and in some ways marking a return to the earlier justificatory literature, there has been discussion of the politics of an Assembly and a devolved Scotland, with the most comprehensive being MacKay (1979) and the Fabian "Radical Agenda for Scotland" series (see e.g. Keating 1979a; Craig and Gilmore 1979; Booth 1979); briefer contributions include Kellas (1979) and Bonney (1978).

Though less prolific than the devolution literature, that on independence is no less substantial in range and quality. While there is little on the rationale of independence there are major contributions on several important issues. The most discussed have been economic questions, with the early debate on economic viability (McCrone 1969; Simpson 1969; Economist Intelligence Unit 1969; McCormick 1970) now modified by the existence of North Sea oil revenues (E. D. Brown 1978; Smallwood and Mackay 1976; Labour Party Scottish Council 1976). The shape of economic policy and management in an independent Scotland has been the subject of several SNP policy documents, not all consistent with each other, plus various pamphlets produced by the Fletcher Society (Slesser 1976; Shirley 1977; Stevenson 1977) and a rather circumspect volume of papers (MacKay 1977). Less optimistic than these is the recent collection on the economic and political constraints on an independent Scotland, a relatively neglected topic (Carty and McCall Smith 1978).

A similar pattern occurs with literature on the politics of independence. There are again SNP policy documents, including a draft constitution and an outline of the structure of an independent government, some discussion of possible routes to independence (McCormick 1976; Madeley 1977) and of legal or constitutional issues (J. P. Grant 1976), and a modest but far from uncritical collection of the nature of an independent Scotland (Kennedy 1976; MacRae 1977; Nairn 1976a; Maxwell in Carty and McCall Smith 1978; Maxwell 1979).

In addition to the pattern of patchy coverage, the great bulk of writing on Scottish politics tends to be descriptive rather than analytical, and concerned far more with the activity and problems of governing Scotland than with the rest of the political system. This narrowness of conception also leads to a fundamentally uncritical literature, manifest for example in studies of government, concerned as they principally are with identifying defects of detail and possible minor reforms (as with material on the structure of local government, endlessly chewing over the issues of how many tiers there should be, or of the proper structure of management, but rarely with the questions of popular participation or accountability). It is also manifest in the discussion of constitutional reform, even when this amounts to the radical step of independence. Little of the devolution literature (with the notable exception of Osmond 1978 and Bogdanor 1979) discusses at length either its systemic justification or implications, or takes seriously the objections not only to the Scotland Act but to the very notion of devolved legislatures as a means of solving contemporary defects of unitary states. Similarly, independence is all too often presented in wholly uncritical terms (except by Nairn, and by Maxwell), producing an image of an independent Scotland as a Caledonian Erewhon (or, in some cases, a social democratic paradise) somehow freed of all the major problems afflicting the United Kingdom by the simple device, in the late Neil Williamson's phrase, of "rearranging the furniture".*

Writing on Scotland's politics, unlike studies of its literature and history, also tends to be parochial, in the sense that it does not treat Scotland comparatively, either in terms of related systems, institutions, processes and issues occurring elsewhere (e.g. Quebec, Catalonia, etc.), or in terms of other parts of the United Kingdom. For all the likening of an independent Scotland to a small Scandinavian state, it is hard to find more than the most superficial and uncritical comparison with, for example, Norway. Where Scottish Nationalism has been discussed in a comparative context, it has been by a Scot long resident outside Scotland (Nairn), a Canadian specialising in Welsh Nationalism (Rawkins), or a variety of English and American analysts of contemporary nationalisms or UK politics (e.g. Rose, Birch). At a more mundane level, with the exception of Edward Page (and indirectly the Wheatley Commission Report) there are no substantial studies comparing English and Scottish local government, the operations of the Scottish and Welsh Offices, or the various regional sections of the major

* In his review of Mackay 1977, in *West Highland Free Press* 17/6/77.

UK parties. Devolution in the rest of Britain or elsewhere in the world, well established though it is, has only given rise to a very modest comparative literature bearing on Scotland's problems, concerned entirely with Northern Ireland and with the financing of devolved legislatures and services.

II. Diagnosis

The several causes for this condition can be considered under three main heads: the nature and difficulties of the producers of material, the nature of the Scottish political system, and that of its main antagonists: the SNP and the revolutionary parties.

Producers

Virtually all the literature on Scottish politics is produced by journalists, scholars and officials in government or voluntary organisations. Freelance writers, playwrights and others have produced very little, with the obvious exception of MacDiarmid and John McGrath (Maxwell 1977b). So also have politicians: indeed the only major participant contributions are the memoirs by Tom Johnston (Secretary of State for Scotland 1941-45), Willie Wolfe of the SNP, and Wendy Wood of the Scottish Patriots, none of which are all that helpful. There is nothing to compare with the series of memoirs and biographies of pre-war figures, especially those in the Labour movement. Part of the reason lies in the paradox that the more successful a Scottish Minister or MP is in representing Scotland, the less likely he is to achieve prominence elsewhere (as with Willie Ross) and thus the smaller the market for an account of his life. Another part lies in the nature of the post-war decades: the period 1945-60 represents the nadir of modern Scottish politics, unlikely to inspire anyone to reminiscence, let alone autobiography (though Chris Harvie is working on the 1945-51 period).

The voluntary sector (mainly the parties and pressure groups) has shown a remarkable expansion in the last ten years, both in overall numbers and in the size of their staffs, especially research staffs (erratic though the number of the latter can be). Nonetheless they are still understaffed, and their overworked officers have multiple responsibilities. Spread thinly over several areas, they rarely have time to treat questions lying outside their immediate concerns. As a result, though there are articles concerning pressure-group activities, devolution and the legislative process by party and group officers, they are rare and brief (see e.g. Peter Gibson's articles mentioned above).

Government, both central and local, is of course a prolific employer and producer, and sponsors a considerable amount of research, not all of it concerned with technical matters or policy options. Scottish Office departments have, for example, commissioned research on both community and schools councils, while (more indirectly) the Royal Commission on Legal Services in Scotland has encouraged some research into that influential but virtually unstudied institution, the Scottish legal profession. The bulk of research originating in or sponsored by central government is, though informative and often invaluable, necessarily parochial and narrowly conceived. Local government sponsorship tends to be for research of more immediately practical application (see, for example, the long list of publications of the Planning Exchange), and the various authorities collect a considerable amount of data: the regional reports and their supporting volumes begin to represent a fourth Statistical Account of Scotland.

The media in Scotland are to a large extent specific to the area (see Kellas 1975; Hutchison 1978), especially the newspapers. The broadcasting services, while borrowing extensively from the "national" network, all produce specifically Scottish news and current affairs programmes, of varying quality. The two commercial television companies generally offer hackneyed, dreary and mediocre current affairs programmes, shallow in their approach, thin on information and analysis, and utterly stereotyped in format. Even with its limited resources, STV's "Ways and Means" ought to be at least as informative, investigative and argumentative as — say — Tyne-Tees' modest farming programme "Farming Outlook". The BBC offerings are considerably better but suffer from problems common to the entire Scottish media: limited staff, lack of comparative examination of Scotland, and repetition and superficiality both in choice of subjects and their treatment, frequently dictated by current preoccupations and prejudices.

About 80% of all newspapers read in Scotland are edited there, so that the bulk of political information presented to

Scots is domestically produced. Unfortunately it is often trivial, biased, governed by fashion, didactic and uncritical. Very few Scottish papers concern themselves with political analysis and even these vary in quality and scope. In the North there are three weeklies with excellent local coverage and commentary, and which remain the best sources in their areas: *The Shetland Times, The Orcadian* and the *West Highland Free Press.* Central Scotland, like the Borders, is less well served: only the *Glasgow Herald* and *The Scotsman* offer serious coverage, both the *Daily Record* and *Scottish Daily Express* having become more and more limited to occasional coverage of issues or events like elections, the referendum, or the improprieties of West of Scotland local government. The *Herald,* while it still carries occasional substantial series (on, for example, land ownership, the Scottish Office, or politics after devolution), has recently carried fewer and fewer feature articles on Scotland as a matter of course. By contrast, *The Scotsman* has not only generously covered Scottish political issues in its news pages, but has managed to combine a broad series of features on foreign affairs with domestic features qualitatively superior to all other Scottish papers in scope and depth. The only papers to begin to rival it are the *Guardian* and *The Financial Times,* largely thanks to their past and current reporting staffs.

Part of *The Scotsman's* strength lies in its relatively large staff of reporters and feature writers, and its willingness to take outside contributions. Despite this its news material tends to be uncritical and descriptive, often consisting of marginally edited press releases, and its features tend to contain more opinion than analysis. There is very little investigative journalism on political issues, and rather more of discursive essays, interesting in themselves but with little new information or analysis and often dictated either by the loyalties of the authors or by what appears — or what the Press have made to appear— to be of current importance*. This absence of investigative political journalism and the substitution for it of Press releases and informed opinion is a general characteristic of the Scottish media. The result is a substantial degree of ignorance and even self-deception especially in the areas of devolution and nationalism, where fluctuations in the fortunes of the SNP, the rise

---

* See also Drucker (1977a), and Kerr in Hutchison (1978).

and significance of the Scottish Labour Party, and the prospects of devolution have all been misjudged.

Academics are freer from the constraints of numbers and deadlines, but equally governed by fashion and personal preference. Although Departments of Politics are generally smaller in Scottish universities than is the case in England, there are several dozen lecturers and graduate students working on Scottish politics, enough to make it possible to consider the formation of a Scottish Political Studies Association. Since there are relatively few such academics outside Scotland (perhaps ten at any one time) it is the work of domestic academics that displays the gaps, overconcentration on certain topics, and narrowness illustrated above. Fashion, as much as their inherent interest or significance, has dictated the preponderance of attention to elections, nationalism, devolution and independence, while the tendency to focus on problems of government rather than on the analysis and comparison of systems is common to the profession in general. Thus a recent survey of work on central-local relationships in British government concludes that it has been marked by a lack of concern with the "dynamic process of central-local relationships", a lack of comparative work, and an emphasis on descriptive case studies rather than theoretical work (Barker 1979).

Equally important may be questions of finance and career considerations (though no research is available on these matters). The main source of research funds for the study of Scottish politics is the Social Science Research Council. There is no evidence of discrimination against Scottish academics in the making of grants (the reverse, if anything, in recent years) but the SSRC's methods of allocating grants, and its rules, have a major influence on research on politics in Scotland as they do on research generally. The SSRC has over the years shown a marked preference for large, methodologically orthodox projects, in areas considered important by its subject committees, and run by academics who have successfully administered previous SSRC grants. Not only has this led to the neglect of certain areas of research (see e.g. Moore 1978), but it does not correspond to the needs of most academics, as a recent SSRC report (Jones 1979) points out:

"Too often it appears as if SSRC arrangements are appropriate only for huge projects, indeed team enterprises with supporting

research staff and secretaries, involving great sums of money.
The nature of the grant application form, the same for both
large and small grants, and the checklist of points for appli-
cants and referees to consider seem predisposed to projects
that contain already worked out specific hypotheses to be
tested, employ sophisticated methodological techniques and
involve exercises of quantification. What the junior academics
often require is assistance tailored to help them explore around
a topic, for example, small grants for travel, subsistence, a
research assistant, and especially time off for a short period."

This is particularly important given the difficulty of obtaining
sabbatical leave, and the rising teaching loads of many aca-
demicals.

It is however difficult to prove that this has contributed
directly to the patchiness of research on Scotland, since career
considerations may also be significant. Until relatively recently
social science academics in most Scottish universities have not
seen themselves as permanently resident in Scotland, but rather
as geographically downwardly mobile. For that reason, as well
as the poor quality and lack of theoretical interest of earlier
work on Scottish politics (and sociology), they have tended to
concentrate on UK or European politics, political theory and
international relations, all in demand furth of Scotland. The
effects of lessened mobility and the increasing general realisation
in other universities of the importance of "regional" politics
have only recently been felt (and then mainly in the study
of nationalism and devolution).

Intimately connected to production of material is the
question of how it is published: perhaps a lack of suitable
outlets helps account for the imbalance, clusters and gaps I
have noted? This argument would hold for the 1950s and 1960s,
when the scope for having any material on Scottish politics
published, whether by academics, participants or journalists,
was extremely limited. In the last decade, however, academics
have found increasing access to existing journals and presses,
and a large variety of new outlets have come into existence.

Scottish publishers, hitherto largely visible through a bizarre
combination of maps, medical and legal textbooks, thrillers
and children's comics, have flourished recently (see Kinnimont

C

in Hutchinson 1978). Several have published material on Scottish politics (Edinburgh Student Publications Board, Paul Harris, Q Press, Molendinar, Thuleprint, etc.), and appear willing to continue. Apart from the *Yearbook* and two new biannual journals (the *Scottish Journal of Sociology* and the *Nevis Quarterly*), several academic institutions publish a series of occasional papers*, as do the Planning Exchange in Glasgow and the Fletcher Society in Edinburgh. At the graduate student level, access to studentships for research on Scottish politics and society has become easier and there are a large number of dissertations and projects in progress, though mainly concerned with nationalism and planning. Even allowing for the relative recency of this flowering of opportunity, then, the pattern of production by academics would seem to reflect more choice than constraint.

For others it is a different story. Journalists and those active in politics or government are relatively restricted, for apart from *The Scotsman* which has its own large and productive staff, there are only occasional opportunities to contribute to weeklies and monthlies, which tend in any case to rely on the same contributors and offer limited space. Journals of political commentary, so common elsewhere, are rare in Britain and non-existent in Scotland. There is nothing comparable to the Welsh *Planet***, and the experience of *Seven Days* and of *Question,* which published a great many valuable pieces among a quantity of rubbish, suggests it is currently impossible to achieve an

* They are: Paisley College of Technology: Local Government Unit
Strathclyde University: Centre for the Study of Social Policy
Strathclyde University: Fraser of Allander Institute
Edinburgh University: Unit for the Study of Government in Scotland
Heriot-Watt University: Scottish Centre of Political Economy
There are also series covering economic and planning topics from Glasgow University and Dundee, while Aberdeen University produced a series on oil and the Scottish economy, and now houses the Institute for the Study of Sparsely Populated Areas, which produces regular material on "marginal regions".

** Though there once was briefly, in the shapes of *Calgacus* and *Scottish International.*

adequate readership for such periodicals in Scotland*. As a result there are very few extended commentaries by Scottish political journalists, politicians and others (though the *New Edinburgh Review* and the *Yearbook* regularly carry such material), and little opportunity for freelance investigative journalism.

The Scottish Political System

A second set of reasons for the sad state of the study of Scottish politics lies, I suggest, in the nature of the Scottish political system itself. While its main features are to be found in the British system in general, and of course in Northern Ireland and Wales, Scotland is unique in the degree of their overall importance and in the pervasiveness of their influence. The Scottish system is marked by six main features: centralisation, administrative primacy, exclusiveness, secrecy, corporatism, and authoritarianism. These features influence commentary on the system and its components in several ways. Thus the highly centralised nature of the administration itself and the overwhelming importance in Scottish government of administrative action produce what one may call a "bureaucratic illusion": that politics in Scotland is, and hence its study should be, all about administration, and in particular, the Scottish Office and the regional authorities (but not, of course, the councillors). Political issues come to be treated as problems in government and from the standpoint of government.

The exclusiveness of the system lies in the restriction of influence over decision-making to a small body of fairly senior Civil Servants and MPs, and a large but still modest group of

*Which is not to deny that both periodicals also suffered from problems of organisation and editorial idiosyncrasy. *Question,* edited from Edinburgh by Peter Chiene and with many nationalist contributors, was published some thirty-four times between October 1975 and August 1977, when its sales fell below 1,000 and the Scottish Arts Council refused support (see Ascherson in *The Scotsman,* 28/12/77, p.7). *Seven Days,* edited by Brian Wilson from Glasgow and with mainly Labour movement contributors, lasted even less time: seventeen issues from October 1977 to March 1978, and an odd one in May 1978. *Seven Days* was more journalistic and investigative than *Question,* drawing perhaps on the experience of *Glasgow News,* a splendidly indiscreet weekly edited by Brian Barr and others, and surviving some seventy-four issues, during 1971-74.

persons regularly consulted or involved in the various boards, committees and commissions established by the Scottish departments and their appointed bodies. While the latter group include a small proportion who owe their selection to having been elected to these or other bodies, or who regard themselves as representing a general interest, the bulk of the membership consists of persons with a professional or sectional interest, accountable only to those who appointed them.

Exclusiveness helps to maintain the fourth general characteristic of the system (and in particular of the Scottish Office and the appointed bodies): its secretiveness. Ironically, while there has been growing complaint against and debate over the lack of open government in Britain as a whole, such criticism is less frequent in Scotland, though Neal Ascherson has railed against "the Scottish tradition of rule by sanctified oligarchy, the Elect owing respect to Heaven but little to the reprobate mass stumbling and sinning outside the locked doors" *(The Scotsman,* 3/5/77). Information is denied as a matter of course, especially when it concerns the reasons for Ministerial decisions or administrative action, while the Scottish Information Office is merely the purveyor of Ministerial speeches and circulars and of factual material on matters lying within its remit. The combination of exclusiveness and secrecy reduces the available primary material for commentary and inhibits investigative journalism in particular. As far as academic research is concerned, the Scottish Office naturally encourages work on policy options, but also discourages research into the functioning of departments and into decision-making in general. Where access is granted to material bearing on these questions, then the Official Secrets Act, if nothing else, inhibits discussion of its contents and implications. This situation also affects individual Civil Servants, drawing the following saddened comment from the editors of the first *Yearbook:*

> "There is too great a reluctance — stemming from the legal inhibitions of the Official Secrets Acts and the informal conventions which surround them — for insiders in central government to write about what they see around them. Of course, no practising politician or official can be expected to write in a detailed way about either his day-to-day existence or his colleagues, but there is a happy medium between this and a description of the organisation chart."

"Corporatism" I use in its more recent sense (see e.g. Osmond 1978) to cover two increasingly important institutional aspects of the Scottish system. The first is the large and growing importance of appointed bodies, especially in the areas of economic management and of high public spending: the Scottish Development Agency and the Highlands and Islands Development Board, the Scottish Special Housing Association, New Town Development Corporations, the NHS in Scotland, are all examples. Appointed bodies show the general features of the Scottish system to an enhanced degree, and are particularly hard to bring to account which is perhaps why they are popular with governments. Where they are studied at all it is almost always entirely in terms of the bureaucratic concerns of structure, efficiency and output, and not in terms of accountability and democratic control, or their general role in the Scottish system (see Hogwood 1979, *The Scotsman* 5-6/12/78).

The second aspect is the tendency to incorporate private bodies (mainly voluntary associations) into not merely the process of consultation over policy or action, but into both policy-formulation and implementation. While this has been most apparent at the United Kingdom level with, say, the TUC or CBI, it occurs in Scotland with the professions in general, especially the teaching professions, and with bodies like the Scottish Council (Development and Industry) (especially over attraction of industry) and a wide range of single-issue pressure groups and welfare-orientated bodies. Two consequences of importance flow from this involvement. Firstly, the body concerned — or more properly its officers, who increasingly tend to be appointed and not elected — come to value this involvement for personal and institutional reasons, and to wish to retain it. In the process they may become less critical of government and more oriented towards administrative viewpoints and questions. Secondly, the body may become less internally democratic and research-orientated, and less self-critical. In both cases, the nature of commentary originating from such bodies also changes in the general directions I have indicated. This process can equally well occur with academics, singly or in groups, since the "implementation" element here occurs in taking part in drafting consultative or even policy documents; the effect is the same.

The whole set of features and the generally authoritarian

30 SCOTTISH GOVERNMENT YEARBOOK 1980

cast of Scottish government have wider implications, through their effect on the intellectual climate, on the operations of local government (which closely resembles those of central government), and even on the parties. There is space only to discuss the last of these, in the shape of the SNP and the revolutionary parties.

The Left, and the Nationalists

The parties most critical of the current Scottish political system are those with Marxist or nationalist ideologies. Yet their contribution to the understanding of the system they wish to eradicate is sadly small. The Communist Party, despite its relative strength in Scotland and its attention to Scottish history and economics, produced nothing on Scottish politics between John Gollan's *Scottish Prospect* (1947) and a few chapters in Gordon Brown's remarkable *Red Paper on Scotland* (G. Brown 1975). Since then their main contribution has been a few shallow pieces in *Scottish Marxist* and a handful of articles in the party monthly on devolution and the national question. Part of the reason lies in the ambivalent attitude of the Communist Party as a whole towards intellectuals and its long practice of favouring historical rather than contemporary political analysis, but even allowing for this their work on Scotland is notably thin. The smaller revolutionary groups have tended to concentrate on mutual exposés and on brief analyses of nationalism (see Drucker 1977a; Williamson 1978), though a book-length study of nationalism and socialism is in press (Williamson and Kerevan).

All this is in marked contrast to the Left aligned with non-revolutionary parties, most obviously in the work of Tom Nairn which, however rhetorical and repetitive it may be at times become, is of fundamental importance. Lack of numbers and sectarian concerns may excuse the smaller groups, but the Communist Party's neglect of the study of contemporary Scotland is harder to explain, though its internal difficulties, declining social base and support, and its preoccupation with electoral and trade union matters are contributing factors.

One of the more obvious features of classical European nationalism, or of contemporary nationalism in Quebec or even Wales, is the tremendous impetus it gave or gives to intellectual life. Not only did the movements themselves produce a wide range of material, but supporters and opponents have engaged in a much higher level of intellectual activity and production than before. Yet in Scotland this is not so; or more accurately it has ceased to be so compared to the pre-war period, or even the 1940s. There is very little production by the SNP itself: a thin handful of policy documents lacking in intellectual justification or even at times coherence, no general attempts to justify independence, and a determinedly non-intellectual monthly magazine. Intellectuals attached or sympathetic to the SNP have fared little better, producing two short volumes touching on the ideology and principles of nationalism, and two on Scotland after independence — but no analysis of Scotland as it is now. Plaid Cymru, with far less support and fewer resources, does much better.

The reasons for this lie in the SNP being a very British party, resembling its rivals in many ways. One aspect is its concentration since 1960 on organisation and on electoral mobilisation together with the success of that activity; another is the relative conservatism of the party leadership and the absence within the SNP until very recently of an organised radical and intellectual wing. Both are reflected in two features of SNP policy: its acceptance of the nature of the Scottish political system, and its neglect of culture. The implication in many SNP policies, and especially those dealing with economic and social policy, is an independent Scotland characterised by a high degree of centralisation, little internal democracy, and the development of corporatism. The concept of participation by workers, tenants etc. is present in many policy documents as well, but more as an eclectic addition than as an integral part of the rationale of the policy. The relative lack of interest of the SNP in literary, cultural and intellectual matters shows not only in policy documents, but in the general materialist tenor of party propaganda and in party activity itself: the *Sunday Post* as well as the Queen would be jealously guarded in an independent Scotland.

III. Prognosis

I have argued, or at least asserted, that examination of the Scottish political system is biased towards descriptive accounts of government and its structure, activity and problems, towards reform, and towards the institutional study of nationalism. The

reasons I attribute partly to general characteristics of the study
of politics in Britain, partly to characteristics of the staff of
of politics departments and of the media in Scotland, and finally
to the overall influence of the Scottish political system. In the
absence of any marked change in that system and in the other
factors, the prospects for any change in the overall pattern
are poor.

Some of the gaps listed will be filled in the coming years,
not least because of the increased interest in Scottish politics
and opportunities to publish mentioned above. Thus in the local
government field, projects on local-central relations, COSLA
and the Scottish Office, and on the contribution of parties to
local government activity, are all likely to begin in 1979-80.
The most important influence, however, might have been the
existence of a devolved legislature. The politics of an Assembly,
the new institutions involved, and the possibilities for comparative research, would have attracted a great deal of academic
interest. Less surely, an Assembly would have had some potential
for changing the Scottish political system, the character of
Scottish politics and the level and character of information
available, all of which would have encouraged more wide-
ranging and critical work on politics. The defeat of the referendum campaign, like the decline of the SNP, closes off this
path (or right of way?) for the moment, but need not have
entirely negative effects.

It was among those who analyse, discuss and try to influence
the Scottish political system that many of the most convinced
devolutionaries were to be found. If they respond not with
demoralisation but by a reconsideration of their arguments and
an attempt at a fuller understanding of Scottish politics, then
the constricted patterns of existing study will be partly eased.
Similarly, if the SNP respond to their defeats not by reiterating
existing strategy and policies but by a move to a more radical
nationalism, then the effect on its intellectual life could be
dramatic. None of this would, of course, alter the underlying
bias in work in Scotland; but it would help to redress its effects.

BIBLIOGRAPHY

Allan, G. F. 1974 "The 'Save the Argylls' Campaign." Ph.D. thesis, University of London.

Arthur, P. 1977 Devolution as administrative convenience: Northern Ireland. *Parliamentary Affairs* 30:1 (1977), pp. 97-106.

Bain, D. 1973 "The SNP 1966-70." M.Sc. thesis, University of Strathclyde.

Ballantine, R. R. 1975 "The 'Save Fife' campaign: a case study of a county's fight against local government reform proposals." B.Phil. thesis, University of Dundee.

Barker, A. 1979 Central-local government relationships in Britain as a field of study. London: Social Science Research Council, 48pp.

Begg, H. M. & Stewart, J. A. 1971 The nationalist movement in Scotland. *Journal of Contemporary History* 6:1 (1971), pp. 135-52.

Birch, A. H. 1977 *Political integration and disintegration in the British Isles.* London, 183pp.

1978 Minority nationalist movements and theories of political integration. *World Politics* 30:3 (1978), pp. 325-44.

Birrell, W. D. 1978 The mechanics of devolution: Northern Ireland experience and the Scotland and Wales Bill. *Political Quarterly* 49:3 (1978), pp. 304-21.

Bochel, J. M. & Denver, D. T. 1970 Religion and voting. *Political Studies* 18:2 (1970), pp. 205-19.

1975 *The Scottish local government elections 1974.* Edinburgh: Scottish Academic Press, 176pp.

1977a *The Scottish district elections 1977.* Dundee: the authors, 110pp.

1977b The district council elections of May 1977. *The Scottish Government Yearbook 1978.* Edinburgh: Paul Harris, pp. 129-50.

1978 The regional council elections of May 1978. *The Scottish Government Yearbook 1979.* Edinburgh: Paul Harris, pp. 140-57.

Bogdanor, V. 1978 Devolution and the constitution. *Parliamentary Affairs* 31:3 (1978), pp. 252-67.

1979 *Devolution.* Oxford: Oxford University Press, 246pp.

Bonney, N. 1978 The Scottish Assembly: a proving ground for parliamentary reform. *Political Quarterly* 49:2 (1978), pp. 191-99.

Booth, S. 1979 *The Scottish Executive: departmental and ministerial structure.* Glasgow: Council of Scottish Fabian Societies.

Brand, J. 1968 These are the Scotnats. *New Statesman* 17/5/1968, pp. 648-50.

1971 The politics of fluoridation. *Political Studies* 19:4 (1971), pp. 430-39.

1973 Party organisation and the recruitment of councillors. *British Journal of Political Science* 33:4 (1973), pp. 473-86.

1976 Support for democratic procedures in Scottish politics. *Political Studies* 24:3 (1976), pp. 296-305.

1978 *The national movement in Scotland.* London: Routledge & Kegan Paul, 330pp.

Brand, J. & McCrone, D. 1975 The SNP from protest to nationalism. *New Society* 20/11/1975, pp. 416-18.

Breckenridge, G. B. 1969 "The government of Scotland." Ph.D. thesis Duke University.

Brett, C. E. B. 1970 Lessons of devolution in Northern Ireland. *Political Quarterly* 41:3 (1970), pp. 261-80.
Brooks, R. A. 1973 "Scottish nationalism: relative deprivation and social mobility." Ph.D. thesis, Michigan State University, 317pp.
Brown, E. D. 1978 It's Scotland's oil? Hypothetical boundaries in the North Sea, a case study. *Marine Policy* 2:1 (1978), pp. 1-21.
Brown, G. (Ed.) 1975 *The Red Paper on Scotland.* Edinburgh: Student Publications Board, 368pp.
Bryden, J. & Houston, G. 1977 *Agrarian change in the Scottish Highlands.* London: Martin Robertson, 152pp.
Budge, I. et al. 1972 *Political stratification and democracy.* London: Macmillan, 322pp.
Budge, I. & Unwin, D. 1966 *Scottish political behaviour.* London: Longman, 148pp.
Burns, J. H. 1960 The Scottish committees of the House of Commons. *Political Studies* 8:3 (1960), pp. 272-96.
Burrell, S. A. 1955 The Scottish separatist movement: a present assessment. *Political Science Quarterly* 70 (1955), pp. 358-67.
Burton, A. W. & Johnson, R. 1976 *Public participation in planning: a review of experience in Scotland.* Glasgow: Planning Exchange, 63pp.
Calvert, F. (Ed.) 1975 *Devolution.* London: Professional Books, 201pp.
Carter, I. 1973 Six years on: an evaluative study of the HIDB. *Aberdeen University Review* 45 (1973), pp. 55-78.
Carty, T. & McCall Smith, S. 1978 *Power and Manoeuvrability.* Edinburgh: Q Press, 185pp.
Chalmers, R. 1978 "Labour Party politics in Dundee." M.A. thesis, Edinburgh University, Dept. of Politics, 88pp.
Chapman, J. 1976 *Scottish Assembly elections: a report to the committee.* Edinburgh: Scottish Campaign for a Representative Assembly, 21pp.
Chrimes, S. B. (Ed.) 1950 *The general election in Glasgow, 1950.* Glasgow: Jackson, 189pp.
Christie, D. 1976 Our changing democracy. *Scots Law Times* 5/3/1976, pp. 65-70.
Clarke, C. 1977 Community councils: power to the people? *British Political Sociology Yearbook* (Ed. by C. Crouch) 3. London: Croom Helm, pp. 110-42.
Coats, A. W. 1978 The changing role of economists in Scottish government since 1960. *Public Administration* 56 (1978), pp. 399-424.
Cook, R. F. (1977) Parliament and the Scots conscience: reforming the law on divorce, licensing and homosexual offences. *The Scottish Government Yearbook 1978.* Edinburgh: Paul Harris, pp. 99-112.
Cope, E. 1977 Consultation or confrontation? The campaign to save the Scottish Colleges of Education. *The Scottish Government Yearbook 1978.* Edinburgh: Paul Harris, pp. 88-98.
Cornford, J. (Ed.) 1975 *The Failure of the state.* London: Croom Helm, 198pp.
Coupland, R. 1954 *Welsh and Scottish nationalism.* London: Collins, 426pp.
Craig, C. & Gilmore, S. 1979 *Women and the Scottish Assembly.* Glasgow: Council of Scottish Fabian Societies.
Craigen, J. M. 1975 "The STUC (1897-1973): a study of a pressure group." M.Litt. thesis, Heriot-Watt University.

Dalyell, T. 1977 *Devolution: the end of Britain?* London: Cape, 321pp.
Davies, J. R. 1978 The industrial investment policy of the SDA. *Quarterly Economic Commentary* (Fraser of Allander Institute), Oct. 1978, pp. 34-46.
Denver, D. T. 1972 "The Communist Party in Dundee." B.Phil. thesis, University of Dundee.
Dickson, T. 1978 Class and nationalism in Scotland. *Scottish Journal of Sociology* 2:2 (1978), pp. 143-62.
Drieux, J. P. 1974 "Le Scottish National Party 1945-70." Ph.D. thesis, University of Reims.
Drucker, H. M. 1977a *Breakaway: the rise and fall of the Scottish Labour Party.* Edinburgh: Student Publications Board, 157pp.
1977b Devolution and corporatism. *Government and Opposition* 12:2 (1977), pp. 178-93.
Forthcoming with G. Brown *The politics of devolution and nationalism.* London: Longman and Manchester: Manchester University Press.
Drucker, H. M. & McAllister, R. (Eds.) 1976 Our changing Scottish democracy. *New Edinburgh Review* 31 (1976).
Dyer, M. C. 1975 "The politics of Kincardineshire." Ph.D. thesis, Aberdeen University.
E.I.U. 1969 *The economic effects of Scottish independence.* London: Economist Intelligence Unit.
Edinburgh Housing Research Group 1977 *The lid off: The Housing Corporation and housing associations in Edinburgh.* Edinburgh: the group.
Edwards, G. E. 1972 The Scottish Grand Committee 1958-70. *Parliamentary Affairs* 25:4 (1972), pp. 303-25.
Elliott, B. et al. 1977 *Property and politics: Edinburgh 1875-1975.* Edinburgh: Edinburgh University Dept. of Sociology, 36pp.
Esman, M. 1975 *Scottish nationalism, North Sea oil and the British response.* Edinburgh: Edinburgh University, Waverly Paper 6:1, 85pp.
Fowe, J. C. 1970 "Councillors and party activists in Glasgow and Rutherglen." M.Sc. thesis, University of Strathclyde.
Gallo, M. M. 1974 "The politics of nationalism in Scotland." Ph.D. thesis, University of Connecticut, 326pp.
Gibson, P. 1977 The rise of pressure groups in Scotland. *Question* 31(1977), pp. 3-4.
1978 How Scotland got the Housing (Homeless Persons) Act. *The Scottish Government Yearbook 1979.* Edinburgh: Paul Harris, pp. 36-47.
Goulstone, P. 1974 "Political stratification in Dundee: a study of councillors." B.Phil. thesis, University of Dundee.
Grant, J. P. 1976 *Independence and devolution: the legal implications for Scotland.* Edinburgh: Green, 233pp.
Grant, W. P. 1970 "Aspects of community conflict: councillors and activists in two Scottish new towns." M.Sc. thesis, Strathclyde University.
Grant, W. 1978 Industrialists and farmers: British interests and the European Community. *West European Politics* 1:1 (1978), pp. 89-106.
Grasmuck, S. L. 1978 "Uneven regional development and Scottish nationalism: activists, ideology and North Sea oil." Ph.D. thesis, University of Texas (Austin).

Gronneberg, R. (Ed.) 1978 *Island futures*. Sandwick: Thuleprint, 79pp.
Gunn, L. & Lindley, P. 1977 Devolution: origins, events and issues. *Public Administration Bulletin* 23 (1977), pp. 36-54.
Haddow, D. 1964 The administration of development. *Public Administration* 42 (1964), pp. 241-52.
1978 Appointed and *ad hoc* agencies in the field of the Scottish Office. *The Scottish Government Yearbook 1979*. Edinburgh: Paul Harris, pp. 115-26.
Hanby, V. 1977 Current Scottish nationalism. *Scottish Journal of Sociology* 1:2 (1977), pp. 95-110.
Hanham, H. J. 1969 *Scottish nationalism*. London: Faber, 250pp.
Harvie, C. 1977 *Scotland and nationalism*. London: Allen & Unwin, 318pp.
Haworth, J. C. 1968 "The National Party of Scotland." Ph.D. thesis, Syracuse University, 303pp.
Heald, D. 1976 *Making devolution work*. London: Fabian Society, 56pp.
1977 *Giving the Scottish Assembly financial teeth*. Glasgow: Scottish Council of Fabian Societies.
Heald, D. & Keating, M. 1979 *The impact of the devolution commitment on the Scottish body politic*. Political Studies Association annual conference, Sheffield, 26pp.
Hogwood, B. W. 1979 *The tartan fringe: quangos and other assorted animals in Scotland*. Glasgow: Strathclyde University, Centre for the Study of Public Policy.
Hood, C. C. 1978 *The Scottish Office in the UK context: some quantatative comparisons*. Glasgow: Political Studies Association Workgroup on UK Politics, 27pp.
Howat, B. 1976 *Policy planning and the first regional reports in Scotland*. Glasgow: Planning Exchange, 17pp.
Howatson, W. 1976 Labour and a rural seat. *Question* 9 (1976), pp. 11-12.
Hunter, Drummond 1976 The reorganised health service: a Scottish perspective. *Our changing Scotland* (Ed. by M. G. Clarke & H. M. Drucker). Edinburgh: Student Publications Board, pp. 26-37.
Hunter, David, forthcoming "Decision making in the NHS in Scotland." Thesis submitted for Ph.D., University of Edinburgh.
Hunter, E. 1979 *Scottish woman's place*. Edinburgh: Student Publications Board.
Hutchison, D. (Ed.) 1978 *Headlines: the media in Scotland*. Edinburgh: Student Publications Board, 112pp.
Jaensch, D. 1976 The Scottish vote 1974. *Political Studies* 24:3 (1976), pp. 306-19.
Johnson, N. 1977 *In search of the constitution*. Oxford: Pergamon, 239pp.
Johnson, R. J. 1977 The electoral geography of an election campaign: Scotland in Oct. 1974. *Scottish Geographical Magazine* 93:2 (1977), pp. 98-108.
Jordan, G. 1979 *The committee stage of the Scotland and Wales Bill 1976-77*. Edinburgh University, Waverley Papers: Scottish Government Studies 1, 42pp.
Judge, D. & Finlayson, D. 1975 Scottish MPs: the problems of devolution. *Parliamentary Affairs* 28:3 (1975), pp. 278-92.
Jones, G. W. 1979 *Central-local government relationships*. London: Social Science Research Council, 183 leaves.

Keating, M. 1975 "The role of the Scottish MPs." Ph.D. thesis, Glasgow College of Technology.

1976 Administrative devolution in practice. *Public Administration* 54 (1976), pp. 133-45.

1977/78 *A test of political integration in the UK: the Scottish MPs.* Glasgow: Strathclyde University Centre for the Study of Public Policy, 33pp; and in *Legislative Studies Quarterly* 3:3 (1978), pp. 409-30.

1979a *The structure of the Scottish Assembly.* Glasgow: Scottish Council of Fabian Societies, 15pp.

1979b *The Scottish Office: some issues for discussion.* Political Studies Association: Scottish/English Local Government Conference, 14pp.

Keating, M. & Bleiman, D. 1979 *Labour and Scottish nationalism.* London: Macmillan.

Kellas, J. G. 1968 *Modern Scotland.* London: Pall Mall, 284pp.

1971 Scottish nationalism, *The General Election of 1970* (Ed. D. Butler & M. Pinto-Duchinsky). London: Macmillan, pp. 446-62.

1975 *The Scottish Political System.* Cambridge: Cambridge University Press (2nd edition), 250pp.

1976 Political reactions to 'Our changing democracy'. *Our Changing Scotland* (Ed. M. G. Clarke & H. M. Drucker). Edinburgh: Student Publications Board, pp. 62-71.

1977a *Decentralisation and devolution: policy making in education and regional development.* Berlin: European Consortium on Political Research conference.

1977b The effect of membership of the European Community on representative institutions in Scotland. *The British People, their voice in Europe* (Ed. Hansard Society). Farnborough: Saxon House.

1978a *Policy making in Scottish education.* Political Studies Association Workgroup on UK politics, 11pp.

1979 Politics in a devolved Scotland. *Nevis Quarterly* 2 (1979), pp. 5-10.

Kellas, J. G. & Fotheringham, P. 1976 The political behaviour of the working class. *Social Class in Scotland* (Ed. A. A. MacLaren). Edinburgh: John Donald, pp. 143-65.

Kellas, J. G. & Owen, R. 1977 *Devolution and the political context in Scotland.* Washington: American Political Science Association annual meeting, 44pp.

Kennedy, G. (Ed.) 1976 *The radical approach.* Edinburgh: Palingenesis, 109pp.

Kernohan, R. D. & Wright, E. 1973 The Scottish Tories. *Swinton Journal,* Autumn 1973.

Kerr, J. 1977 The failure of the Scotland and Wales Bill. *The Scottish Government Yearbook 1978.* Edinburgh: Paul Harris, pp. 113-19.

Kilbrandon 1973 *Report of the Royal Commission on the Constitution.* London: HMSO (Cmnd. 5460), 2 vols., plus volumes of written evidence, and minutes of evidence.

Labour Party (Scottish Council) 1976 *Analysis of the economics of separation.* Glasgow: the Council.

Lang, R. 1973 *West Aberdeenshire in the General Election of 1970.* Aberdeen University: St. Machars Papers 2, 84pp.

Lang, I. & Henderson, B. 1975 *The Scottish Conservatives: a past and a future.* Edinburgh: Conservative Political Centre in Scotland, 20pp.

Lazer, H. 1977 Devolution, ethnic nationalism and populism in the UK. *Publius* 7:4 (1977), pp. 49-69.
Lewenhak, S. 1973 Women in the leadership of the STUC 1897-1970. *Journal of the Scottish Labour History Society* 7 (1973), pp. 3-23.
Levitt, R. 1976 *The reorganised NHS.* London: Croom Helm, pp. 216-30.
Liddell, P. 1978 "The role of the Trades Council in the political and industrial life of Glasgow 1858-1976." M.Sc. thesis, Strathclyde University.
Lotz, J. 1969 Regional planning and development in the Highlands and Islands of Scotland. *Canadian Public Administration* 12:3 (1969), pp. 372-86.
McCormick, N. (Ed.) 1970 *The Scottish debate.* London: Oxford University Press, 160pp.
1976 The mandate question. *Question* 12 (1976), pp. 8-9.
McCrone, G. 1969 *Scotland's future.* Oxford: Blackwell, 111pp.
McDonald, S. T. 1977 The regional report in Scotland. *Town Planning Review* 48:3 (1977), pp. 215-32.
MacDougall, I. (Ed.) 1979 *Essays in Scottish labour history.* Edinburgh: John Donald, 265pp.
MacGregor, G. M. 1973 *The background of Edinburgh town councillors.* Aberdeen University, St. Machars Papers 1, 44pp.
MacKay, D. (Ed.) 1977 *Scotland 1980.* Edinburgh: Q Press, 211pp.
Mackay, D. (Ed.) 1979 *Scotland: the framework for change.* Edinburgh: Paul Harris, 196pp.
Mackay, R. 1975 Protestant extremists in Scotland. *Calgacus* 2 (1975), pp. 7-10.
McKensie, A. 1976 *Nothing but the truth.* Dundee.
Mackintosh, J. P. 1964 Regional administration: has it worked in Scotland? *Public Administration* 42 (1964), pp. 253-75.
1966 The city's politics. *Third Statistical account of Scotland.* Edinburgh (Ed. D. Keir) Glasgow: Collins, pp. 109-19.
1967 Scottish nationalism. *Political Quarterly* 38:4 (1967), pp. 389-402.
1968 *The devolution of power.* Harmondsworth: Penguin, 207pp.
Maclean, I. 1970 The rise and fall of the SNP. *Political Studies* 18 (1970), pp. 357-72.
MacRae, T. 1977 *Norway: a model for Scotland's future.* Edinburgh: Fletcher Society, 30pp.
Madeley, J. T. S. 1977 Patterns of subordination and strategies of separation: Norway and Scotland compared. *Journal of Conflict Research Studies* 1:1 (1977), pp. 58-69.
Mansbach, R. W. 1973 The SNP: a revised profile. *Comparative Politics* 5:2 (1973), pp. 185-210.
Massie, A. 1979 Scotland and Europe: the representation of Scottish interests. *Nevis Quarterly* 2 (1979), pp. 34-46.
Masterman, E. M. 1978 *Women in elected positions in Scotland.* Dundee, for the European Consortium for Political Research meeting, 24pp.
Maxwell, S. 1976 Can Scotland's myths be broken. *Question* 16 (1976), pp. 5.
1977a Women in Scotland. *Question* 29 (1977), pp. 4-5.
1977b Politics and culture. *Question* 25 (1977), pp. 4-5.
1979 Implications of prospective independence: the problems of state power. *Nevis Quarterly* 2 (1979), pp. 11-20.

Mbadinuju, C. C. 1976 Devolution: the 1975 White Paper. *Political Quarterly* 47 (1976), pp. 286-96.

Mercer, G. 1974 Party affiliations of adults and adolescents in Scotland. *Political Studies* 22:2 (1974), pp. 210-14.

Midwinter, A. 1978 The implementation of the Paterson Report. *Local Government Studies* 4:1 (1978), pp. 23-38.

Miller, W. L. 1977a *Electoral dynamics.* London: Macmillan.
  1977b The connection between SNP voting and the demand for Scottish self-government. *European Journal of Political Research* 5:1 (1977), pp. 83-102.

Milne, D. 1957 *The Scottish Office.* London: Allen & Unwin, 232pp.

Misnler, W. & Mughan, A. 1978 Representing the Celtic fringe: devolution and legislative behaviour in Scotland and Wales. *Legislative Studies Quarterly* 3:3 (1978), pp. 377-408.

Moore, R. 1978 Sociologists not at work. *Power and the state* (Ed. G. Littlejohn et al.) London: Croom Helm, pp. 267-302.

Morris, D. S. 1968 "Scottish Nationalist councillors." M.Sc. thesis, Strathclyde University.

Mullin, R. 1977 "Women in the SNP." M.A. thesis, Edinburgh University Sociology Department.

Mutch, W. E. S. 1977 The expansion of Turnhouse, Edinburgh Airport. *Public participation in planning* (Ed. W. R. D. Sewell & J. T. Coppock.) London: Wiley, pp. 43-58.

Nairn, T. 1968 The three dreams of Scottish nationalism. *New Left Review* 49 (1968), pp. 3-18.
  1976a Scotland the misfit. *Question* 13 (1976), pp. 3-4.
  1976b The 'Radical approach'. *Question* 10 (1976), pp. 8-11.
  1977a *The breakup of Britain.* London: New Left Books, 368pp.
  1977b The SLP. *Planet* 37/38 (1977), pp. 14-17.
  1977c The new exiles. *Question* 25 (1977), pp. 7

Naughtie, J. 1978 The Scotland Bill in the House of Commons. *Scottish Government Yearbook 1979.* Edinburgh: Paul Harris, pp. 16-35.

Nevin, E. (Ed.) 1978 *The economics of devolution.* Cardiff: University of Wales Press, 160pp.

Nevis Institute 1978 *The Shetland Report.* Edinburgh: the Institute, 3 volumes; shortened version published by the Institute, 223pp.

Osmond, J. 1977 *Creative conflict.* London: Routledge & Kegan Paul, 305pp.

Page, E. 1978 *Why should central-local relations in Scotland be any different from those in England?* Glasgow: Strathclyde University Centre for the Study of Social Policy, 46pp.

Paterson, I. V. 1973 *The new Scottish local authorities.* Edinburgh: HMSO, 127pp.

Paton, H. J. 1968 *The claim of Scotland.* London: Allen & Unwin, 279pp.

Peggie, R. E. G. 1976 The new local authorities. *Our changing Scotland* (Ed. M. G. Clarke & H. M. Drucker.) Edinburgh: Student Publications Board, pp. 17-25.

Pottinger, G. 1979 *The Secretaries of State for Scotland 1926-76.* Edinburgh: Scottish Academic Press, 214pp.

Proctor, J. H. 1977 Party interests and the electoral system for the proposed Scottish Assembly. *Political Quarterly* 47:2 (1977), pp. 186-200.

Purves, A. 1978 "Scottish labour and British entry: Labour movement attitudes to the European Community at Scottish and UK levels 1960-1977." M.Phil. thesis, Edinburgh University, 180pp.

Radice, H. 1978 *The SDA and the contradictions of state entrepreneurship.* Stirling: Stirling University Discussion Papers in Economics 59, 24pp.

Rawkins, P. M. 1978 Outsiders as insiders: the implication of minority nationalism in Scotland and Wales. *Comparative Politics* 10:4 (1978), pp. 519-34.

Reich, G. G. C. 1978 "Symbols and sentiment in Scotland." Ph.D. thesis, Washington University, 365pp.

Reid, J. 1976 *Memoirs of a Clyde-built man.* London: Souvenir Press, 166pp.

Rodger, J. J. 1978 "Inauthentic' politics and the public enquiry system. *Scottish Journal of Sociology* 3:1 (1978), pp. 103-27.

Rollo, D. A. T. 1971 "Comparative aspects of Irish politics in Boston and Glasgow." M.Litt. thesis, Edinburgh.

Rose, R. 1976 *The United Kingdom as an intellectual puzzle.* Glasgow: Strathclyde University Centre for the study of Public Policy, 31pp.

1978 *From steady to fluid state: the unity of the Kingdom today.* Glasgow: Strathclyde University Centre for the Study of Social Policy, 38pp.

Ross, W. 1977 Approaching the Archangelic: the office of Secretary of State. *The Scottish Government Yearbook 1978.* Edinburgh: Paul Harris, pp. 1-20.

Rowe, A. 1975 *Democracy renewed.* London: Sheldon Press, 119pp.

Royal Commission on Scottish Affairs *Report of the Royal Commission of Scottish Affairs 1952-54.* Edinburgh: HMSO (Cmd 9212), 126pp.

Schwartz, J. F. 1970 The SNP: non-violent separatism and theories of violence. *World Politics* 22:4 (1970), pp. 496-517.

Scottish Conservative Local Government Review Group 1977 *First report.* Edinburgh: Scottish Conservative Central Office, 44pp.

Scottish Council 1970 *Economic development and devolution.* Edinburgh: Scottish Council Research Institute, 66pp.

S.C.S.S. 1974 *Topic 2: community councils.* Edinburgh: Scottish Council of Social Service, 27pp.

S.D.D. 1974 *Community councils: some alternatives for community council schemes in Scotland.* Edinburgh: Scottish Development Department, 46pp.

Scottish Office 1978a *Community councils research project: interim reports 1976-78.* Edinburgh: Scottish Development Department Central Research Unit, 62pp.

1978b *Community councils in Scotland: an analysis of the approved community council schemes.* Edinburgh: Scottish Development Department Central Research Unit, 38pp.

Select Committee on Scottish Affairs 1968/69 *Minutes of evidence session 1968/69.* London: House of Commons (HC Paper 397 (1968/69)), 406pp.

1969/70 *Minutes of evidence session 1969/70.* London: House of Commons (HC Paper 267 (1969/70)), 553pp.

Sharpe, T. 1978 The constitutional consequences of Mr Smith. *Scolag Bulletin* 18 (1978), pp. 56-58.

Shirley, R. 1977 *Taxation in an independent Scotland.* Edinburgh: Fletcher Society, 43pp.

Simpson, D. 1969 *Scottish independence: an economic analysis.* West Calder: Scottish National Party, 16pp.

Smallwood, C. & Mackay, D. 1976 The economics of independence. *Our changing Scotland* (Ed. M. G. Clarke & H. M. Drucker). Edinburgh: Student Publications Board, pp. 98-107.

Smout, C. 1977 The Scottish identity. *The future of Scotland* (Ed. R. Underwood). London: Croom Helm, pp. 11-21.

Slesser, E. M. 1976 *Scotland and energy.* Edinburgh: Fletcher Society, 19pp.

Stevenson, D. 1977 *Scotland's responsibilities in international aid and co-operation.* Edinburgh: Fletcher Society, 43pp.

Strathclyde Area Survey 1978 *Community Councils in Scotland.* Glasgow: the Survey, 72 leaves.

Thompson, F. G. 1978 *The Highlands and Islands Advisory Panel: a review of its activities and influences.* Stornoway: the author, 50pp.

Thomson, W. 1977 Scottish Devolution. *Marxism Today* 21:4 (1977), pp. 100-105.

Turpie, L. 1977 Opposition in local government. *Scottish Government Yearbook 1978.* Edinburgh: Paul Harris, pp. 51-60.

Urwin, D. W. 1966 Scottish conservatism. *Political Studies* 14:2 (1966), pp. 144-62.

Ward, J. T. 1977 In search of Scottish conservatism. *University of Strathclyde Gazette* 7:2 (1977).

Webb, K. 1976 *The growth of nationalism in Scotland.* Glasgow: Molendinar, 147pp.

Wheatley 1969 *Report of the Royal Commission on Local Government in Scotland.* London: HMSO (Cmnd 4150).

Williams: A. 1973 "The HIDB 1965-70." Ph.D. thesis, Glasgow University, 332pp.

Williamson, N. 1978 Ten years after: the revolutionary left in Scotland. *Scottish Government Yearbook 1979.* Edinburgh: Paul Harris, pp. 61-77.

Williamson, N. & Kerevan, G. forthcoming *Devolution and the politics of nationalism.* London: Macmillan.

Wilson, T. 1976 Devolution and public finance. *Three Banks Review* 112 (1976), pp. 3-29.

Wolfe, N. (Ed) 1969 *Government and nationalism in Scotland.* Edinburgh: Edinburgh University Press, 205pp.

Wolfe, W. 1973 *Scotland lives.* Edinburgh: Reprographia, 167pp.

Wood, S. M. 1971 "Political participation." Ph.D. thesis, Edinburgh University.

Wyke, C. 1978 "Recent reforms in the Scottish Conservative and Unionist Party." M.A. thesis, Edinburgh University (Politics Department), 133pp.

Young, R. 1977 *The search for democracy.* Milngavie: Heatherbank Press, 133pp.

D

3

THE YEAR AT WESTMINSTER: THE SCOTLAND ACT BRINGS DOWN THE GOVERNMENT

THE CRIMINAL JUSTICE (SCOTLAND) BILL

JAMES NAUGHTIE

The Scotsman

I

After the Referendum

Scotland was, once again, the fulcrum on which the political year turned at Westminster. On one side of the balance was the need for the Labour Party to continue the tortured progress of devolution to which they had committed themselves. On the other was the survival of the Government. In the end, neither aim was achieved and the whole structure collapsed, leaving the Royal High School in Edinburgh an empty shell and the Callaghan Government tottering into an early election which in its heart it knew it could not win.

So the story of devolution at Westminster after the referendum is the story of what might have been. Had the referendum result been decisive the Commons would probably have given reluctant support to the Scotland Act, even without a 40% vote. The Government could have eased devolution from the centre of the stage and slipped through the summer to an October election which James Callaghan believed gave him at least an even chance of blocking Mrs Thatcher's progress to Downing Street.

If the "No" side had won, the problem would have been still been simple. Politically it would have been easy to drop the hot potato and, while it would have outraged the SNP, the Government's authority would not have been challenged as a result. But neither course was open to the Labour leadership.

When 32.9% of the electorate voted "yes" the loyalty of Labour's devolution converts was strained to its limit, and the morale of the dedicated opponents of the Assembly rose to new heights. Within days of the resumption of Parlament, Eric Moonman, the Labour MP for Basildon (who was to lose his seat in the Election on May 3) was whipping the anti-devolutionists into strategy meetings to put pressure on Michael Foot, Lord President and Leader of the Commons. They urged him to move forward immediately with the repeal of the Scotland Act. Most Labour devolutionists maintained a polite and embarrassed silence.

Within a month of the referendum the Government had fallen, the first time since 1924 that a Prime Minister had been sent to the Queen with his resignation after losing a vote of confidence. The problem which exercised Callaghan's mind in that month was one of timing.

Although the Scotland Act had been amended by Messrs Cunningham, Dalyell et al to force repeal if the 40% requirement was not met, the length of time the repeal order could lie on the table before the fateful vote was unrestricted. Indeed one of the most celebrated backstairs confrontations of the early devolution days was a chance meeting between George Cunningham, architect of the 40% vote, and John Smith, then the Devolution Minister. Just after the anti-devolutionists' triumph in inserting the clause, which they believed would kill devolution, Smith pointed out that if less than 40% of the electorate voted "yes" the Government could, firstly, let the repeal order lie for a long time and, secondly, could whip its supporters to vote down its own order. In retrospect this all seems painfully obvious, but at the time — long before the referendum — Cunningham was shocked, and furious. That realisation was later to become a near nightmare for him and his followers as the Government wriggled to find a way out of the impasse.

When the result came through, Callaghan decided to play for time. There is a school of thought which holds that a quick vote in the week after the referendum might have won the day. But although many suggested this would have been the best tactic, it was not a genuine option at the time. Such was the consistency of the wet blanket which extinguished all devolution fervour on March 1 that the Government Whips would have had the devil's own job in persuading their recalcitrant MPs into the lobby to vote down the repeal order. And they told the Cabinet so. A defeat at that stage would have done no good — even if we assume a lukewarm Government commitment to devolution — because it would almost certainly have precipitated a vote of confidence which the Tories, with the support of SNP MPs looking for electoral benefit, would have won.

So the Government's best hope was to gain time to catch its breath. Yet in the end the Government choked, in a particularly humiliating way, and the reason had more to do with the dangers of political bluffing than the merits or otherwise of devolution. Indeed, it now seems likely that the demise of the Edinburgh Assembly and the collapse of the Government came about because of a political blunder by Callaghan, the old master. Whether it was caused by a lack of nerve or political misjudgement or sheer exhaustion (or by a combination of all three) we cannot tell. But the fate of the Government was sealed at a meeting in Foot's room at the Commons on the night before Callaghan made his statement on the future of the Scotland Act on 22 March — the "wait and see" announcement which brought on the vote of confidence. Before looking at the events of that day it is worth going back to the days immediately after "Black Friday" when the referendum results came in.

Immediately after the results, it was fairly clear that the game was up. *The Scotsman's* banner headline on 3 March was "Callaghan fighting for survival: plans for Assembly gravely wounded", and that was no overstatement. Within hours of the result one prominent Scots Labour MP was wondering aloud whether he could vote for radical constitutional change in the face of the electorate's verdict. Yet he had been one of the most enthusiastic supporters of the Assembly. By Sunday a survey for the television programme "Weekend World" suggested that a minimum of twenty-four Labour MPs would rebel against any attempt to vote down the repeal order. David Steel, the Liberal leader, was "far from certain" that the Act should be saved. So the portents were bad.

Mrs Thatcher, the Tory leader, warned the Government that they would be bending the Constitution if they tried to prolong the devolution business. This statement illustrated her concern. She could see in the collapse of a measure which was unpopular (at least at Westminster) a chance for her long-awaited vote of confidence, but she had to tread carefully.

Nothing would be worse for party morale than for her to rush into the ring, throw down a censure motion and then find herself on the losing side. She had to be sure of her moment. She feared that any successful delaying tactic by the Government would leave her looking weak, apparently unwilling to challenge Labour to a vote of confidence. She also had to worry about the SNP, necessary partners in any successful confidence vote.

Their line, early on, was predictable and clear. "A Yes is a Yes is a Yes", they said. No one need worry about the 40%, indeed it would be treacherous even to consider it. As usual there were two camps. A kamikaze squad wanted an immediate challenge to the Government, in the hope of reaping rewards in an early election. Another group wanted to turn every screw on the Government, without opening the trap door, even if it meant some kind of amendment which would get a modified Bill through, although this view (at that time or since) has never been properly clarified. Publicly the SNP said: "either we get our Assembly now or there is an election". So Callaghan's most sensible course, faced with SNP threats against no action, and Tory threats against an attempt to vote down the repeal, was to play for time and, so the story went, call the SNP bluff.

In the middle distance, of course, was the Government's other problem — the so-called winter of discontent after the failure of the 5% pay policy. As a result of his blunder in not seizing the opportunity of an election in October 1978 (largely because of the promptings of Michael Foot) and his miscalculation about the reception of his pay policy by rank-and-file trade unionists, Callaghan feared an early election. October 1979 was the goal, but this soon became June as the Parliamentary pressure on the Government increased week by week and they began to run out of legislation. It was a question of winning not a few more months, but a few more weeks.

Against this background, which moved into vivid close-up after the referendum, the safest policy seemed to be what came to be known as "the Frankenstein solution". This, appropriately, was one of the last additions to the devolution patois which had grown up over a decade and included such favourites as "Dalintober Street", "The Secretary of State's governor general powers" and, of course, "the West Lothian question". "Frankenstein" actually began life as Dracula but a newspaper got the allusion all wrong, and Frankenstein it stayed. The idea was that the Act could be preserved in suspended animation, even through a General Election, to be revived (under a Labour government) with a surge of energy which would startle the world and grant the beast virtual immortality.

The Scottish Council of the Labour Party played along towards this general aim. The meeting of its executive after the referendum regretted the result, but stopped short of a ringing call to the Government to push the Act through whatever the consequences. The message was clear: they made Callaghan well aware of their support for the Act and their belief in its electoral value but left the wheeling and dealing to him. At the same time the National Council of the SNP said they would ask their MPs to bring the Government down if the Act were not pushed through.

When Callaghan said in the Commons on March 6 that "of course" the repeal orders would be brought forward, he knew that the Labour antis were being numbered at anything up to 40. Warnings had come from the Whips that there was no sign of slackening in their opposition to the very idea of voting against the repeal. David Steel was having difficulty holding Liberals behind the Act. Richard Wainwright had already said bluntly that he would vote against it.

Frankenstein was to be created through all-party talks. Such talks were the devolutionists' way out. In the early days after the referendum it appeared to be working. The SNP and the Liberals calmed their rhetoric, and seemed content to help Callaghan to play along until after the Budget. This would have suited the Prime Minister well because by then the defeat of devolution would pale into insignificance beside the treasured prize of a June election, far away from the winter's slough of despond.

At Labour's annual Scottish conference on March 12, little miracles were worked and there was no call — officially — for a three-line Whip against rebels. Clearly the calculations of the party managers had reached Perth. There comes a time when three-line Whips start to lose their sting, and the fag end of a Parliament is just such a time.

While Labour in Scotland were agonising about their many internal divisions, the SNP, through George Reid, MP for East Stirlingshire and Clackmannan, announced that they would delay a censure vote only if the Scotland Act were put to the test within three weeks. They presented a tough line, although it later crumbled privately when they considered in detail the likely consequences of an early election. Talks, Reid said, could take place after the vote. In this he was echoing Mrs Thatcher's line and preparing the way for the alliance which would ditch the Government. With the Liberals committed to an early election — as they had been since October — the opposition line-up began to look formidable indeed. Frankenstein was the only answer, but he had what could be called a credibility problem.

No one was particularly happy about ducking a decision on devolution. Even the Assembly's enthusiastic supporters in the Labour Party felt uncomfortable about the ploy, since it reeked of smoke-filled rooms. Some of them wanted to face execution bravely. Apart from anything else there was the question of what the Scottish people would think. Most of them were supposed to believe either that a simple majority was enough and the Act should be put to the Parliamentary test or that there was no mandate for such a constitutional change and the whole thing should be shelved, with the possibility of some kind of second-best devolution for those who were philosophically committed to it. Frankenstein made sense at Westminster, but nowhere else, and that was his greatest weakness.

In the middle of March the pressures on the Government began to increase. Donald Stewart, the SNP leader, met Callaghan in the Prime Minister's room and told him bluntly that there had to be a vote, and quickly. The SNP seemed to have decided that an early election, on balance, would be better for them than one in the autumn, although it was a fine judgement to say the least. They could see no political advantage in talking with Callaghan and nourishing Frankenstein.

D-day was to be Thursday March 22 when Callaghan would make his statement on the future of the Act, a statement which would probably have been delayed even longer had it not been for the sudden burst of SNP activity that week. On Thursday morning the Cabinet met and, with the knowledge that the Chief Whip could not guarantee a majority to keep the Act alive, played along with the Prime Minister for more time. Much more interesting was what had happened the previous night.

On Wednesday March 21 the SNP had held their weekly party meeting at Westminster and discussed their attitude to the Act. Stewart had already made his position clear to Callaghan and he was not prepared to change his stance. He told colleagues that if he backed down no one who mattered at Westminster would take his word for anything again. He was determined to continue to tell the Government that unless a vote on repeal was promised by the end of the following week the SNP would put down a motion of no confidence, one which everyone knew would finally lure Mrs Thatcher into the fight.

But by this stage some SNP MPs were wondering about the wisdom of killing off the Act so quickly. All but one of them believed that there was no hope of getting it through, even with a three-line Government Whip. They were well aware of the feelings of their Labour enemies. Some wanted simply to keep the argument alive, while there was still an Act to cling to, and others believed that it would do them no harm in the eyes of the electorate if they were seen to give Labour another chance and wait, confidently, for Labour to come up with nothing. In that position, some of the MPs believed they would be poised to hold electoral ground that seemed to be fast slipping away.

Two MPs were missing from that meeting. The nine present discussed various possibilities and it was clear that Stewart was facing opposition. Some of the MPs wanted to give the Government more time (even if it was only to let them fail dramatically). No dates were fixed, but the deadline of the following week was beginning to stretch. It was put to the vote and the MPs came down 5 - 4 to have an open-ended look at Callaghan's statement if he named a date, even if that date was beyond the previous deadline of ten days. Stewart let it be known that he might find it necessary to resign as leader if the party failed to carry out its threat to bring down the Government.

Late that evening, Stewart and Andrew Welsh, his Chief Whip, went along the corridor to Michael Foot's room, where the Lord President was already convinced that the Government would face a confidence vote within a week or two. Despite all the ambiguous statements from the SNP, senior Ministers were sure that anything less than a speedy vote (which they knew they would lose) would have the SNP Whips rushing to the table office with their censure motion, closely pursued by breath-less Tories. They did not know that the SNP Parliamentary group was splitting at the seams over devolution.

So Foot, who already knew what Callaghan intended to say the next day, was not surprised when Stewart said that they needed a firm date. He did not name a date, concealing the weakness in his position which had opened up earlier. Foot saw Callaghan. It seems that by this stage the Prime Minister was irritated by the whole business. His instinct was to get on with it, whatever the consequences. Looking at the alterna-tives it was clear that the Government would stand a better chance of surviving a confidence vote and humiliating Mrs Thatcher than carrying devolution. Better to have a confidence vote without the disastrous split which a vote on the Scotland Act would reveal in the Labour ranks, and which would lead to an even more dangerous censure debate.

The Callaghan statement set a time limit of the end of April for all-party talks on improving the Scotland Act. Immediately Stewart rose to denounce him. "The Prime Minister is not prepared to face the outcome of an early vote on this," he said. "He is prepared to treat the Scottish people with con-tempt rather than face an early election." No one in the party could accept the Prime Minister's statement — it was too vague — and the motion of no confidence duly went down within an hour, followed shortly afterwards by Mrs Thatcher's own motion. Perhaps the most suitable comment on the episode was made by Willie Ross, the former Scottish Secretary of State, in his last Commons intervention. "Is the Prime Minister aware that I wish him well," he said, "but I hae ma doots?"

So the Commons moved towards the confidence vote, through the wheeling and dealing with the Welsh Nationalists over compensation for slate-quarrymen, the vague hints to Ulster Unionists, and the arm-twisting of Frank Maguire, the maverick Republican. In the end the Government lost by one vote, with one Labour MP missing sick. They nearly made it.

That vote ended Callaghan's hopes of a summer election, and so his chances of keeping power. Yet how different it could have been. If he had promised a vote on the Scotland Act on the day before the Easter recess he would have split the SNP. Perhaps a confidence motion would have gone down any-way, but it would probably have had some names missing. In those circumstances the Tories would have held back, and he could have held on for a few weeks. That was all he wanted. But he seems to have been convinced that the SNP were solid. Perhaps they would have closed ranks in any case, but it would have been a delicate manoeuvre. Yet because of the insipid statement their unity was never put to the test. If the statement had offered something more tangible it would, of course, have offended the Labour antis but that would scarcely have mattered. It would have given the Government that breathing space which they needed to prepare for a dangerous election.

Yet maybe justice was done. By the end of the process, devolution had become little more than a symbol of the Government's troubles, and a lever for the Opposition. As soon as the results came in, Westminster knew that the scheme was dead. The Prime Minister's mistake was that he did not realise that the SNP might after all have helped him to prolong the agony, and postpone the funeral.

:   :   :   :

After the election the Conservative Government moved quickly to repeal the Act. On a long, hot night in June, MPs voted 301 - 206 to throw it out. At the same time, Mr George Younger, the Secretary of State for Scotland, announced that all-party talks on devolution would start soon. The Labour Party argued that the Act should stay on the statute book while the talks went on, but the Government were determined to clean the slate. Mr Malcolm Rifkind, a Scottish Minister (who had campaigned for "Yes" in the referendum) talked at the end of the debate about the beginning of a new phase of devolution. It was clearly to be non-legislative, and the young and ill-starred Scotland Act, with the Assembly it created, was just an unpleasant memory.

II

The Criminal Justice (Scotland) Bill

One of the casualties of the vote of confidence which brought down the Labour Government was a Bill which focused the law and order debate in Scotland, and showed that in some respects Labour Ministers were trying to trump their Tory opponents in the rush to strengthen the police and claim credit for reducing crime. The Criminal Justice (Scotland) Bill had just finished its dramatic committee stage when the Government fell, and to no one's surprise it was not one of the pieces of agreed legislation rushed through before the Election.

It was a stern Bill. Tucked away in a host of procedural reforms was a proposal to allow police officers to question a suspect at a police station for four hours without having to make an arrest. It also proposed an extraordinary power giving sheriffs and judges the right to conduct trials in the absence of the accused.

Its tough measures were attacked on the Labour side by civil libertarians — principally Donald Dewar (Garscadden) and Neil Carmichael (Kelvingrove) — and by Conservatives who claimed that the Bill did not go far enough in strengthening the power of the police.

The long sessions of the Scottish Standing Committee, in which the Bill was discussed line by line, revealed splits in both parties. Ronald King Murray, the Lord Advocate, and Harry Ewing, an Under-Secretary, found themselves under constant attack from Dewar and Carmichael for infringing personal liberty.

On the Tory side, the troops were led by Nicholas Fairbairn, later to become Solicitor General for Scotland. He argued, most of the time, for stronger powers, (backing for example, greater powers of search for the police and the creation of a new offence of "vandalism) but also, as a practising advocate, attacked some of its powers as "a horrific breach in the laws of natural justice". This did not always please Teddy Taylor, who sat on the Committee and called consistently for more powers in the Bill.

The Government suffered two memorable defeats. In the first Peter Doig (then MP for Dundee West) used his chairman's casting vote to support a Tory amendment giving the police wide powers of search. In the second the "draconian" power given to a judge to expel an accused from a courtroom and continue a case in his absence was thrown out by an alliance of Tories and Dewar, Carmichael and Gordon Wilson, the SNP member of the Committee.

Yet for all the confusion the lines were fairly clearly drawn. The Conservatives argued, among other things, for the return of the birch. Among those voting for the proposals were two MPs later to become Ministers, Malcolm Rifkind and

Hamish Gray, as well as Mr Fairbairn. They failed in attempts to oblige judges to give minimum sentences for murderers, to reduce the number of jury challenges, to introduce a general crime of vandalism and, of course, to bring back corporal punishment.

Throughout the committee stage they were attacked for proposing bogus solutions to problems and Mr Taylor, inevitably, was described as Ayatollah Taylor. In return the Tories united behind a standard Right-wing claim that Labour members cared more for criminals than for their victims.

Perhaps the most interesting feature of the long debates was the Government's concern to steal the Conservative claim to speak on law and order. Mr Ewing said he was a member of the law and order party: they had increased the number of policemen in Scotland by 1000 since coming to office, he said.

In this race to be tougher with lawbreakers the scene was set for the Tory law reforms certain to be introduced during Mrs Thatcher's first administration. With the exception of the birching proposals, which Mr Taylor admitted reluctantly were not official party policy, their views on curbing crime can be expected to be enshrined in law. It seems likely that the Criminal Justice (Scotland) Bill, for all its bitter battles, was only a preliminary skirmish.

4

THE DEVOLUTION REFERENDUM CAMPAIGN OF 1979

RAY PERMAN
The Financial Times

No one can now deny that the Scottish referendum on devolution, held on March 1, 1979, was a significant political event. On that day Scottish voters were asked "Do you want the provisions of the Scotland Act 1978 to be put into effect?" 1,230,937 voted "Yes", 1,153,502 voted "No" and 1,362,783 did not vote all (more detailed results are given in the reference section). This indecisive result led within a month to the defeat of the Labour Government in a vote of confidence in the House of Commons — the first such defeat for fifty years — and a General Election. So we can expect the referendum campaign to attract continuing interest from political scientists and historians, and this will certainly be a good thing. It is still too early to take an objective view of why the campaign developed the way it did and why the Scottish people, who had apparently been heavily committed to seeing some form of legislative Assembly being set up in Edinburgh, did not turn out to vote in sufficient numbers to ensure that their wishes were fulfilled.

I make this qualification at the beginning of this chapter because, although I shall attempt to be impartial and in fact took no part in either side in the campaign, what I write must necessarily be subjective if it is to be anything more than a meaningless rehearsal of speeches and handouts. Some of my conclusions have already been published in articles in *The Financial Times* and have been challenged, notably by Mr Adam Ferguson of the "Scotland Says No" organisation (*The Daily Telegraph,* March 11, 1979).

My argument is that, despite beginning with the advantage that opinion polls had consistently over many years shown Scottish voters two-to-one in favour of devolution, the "Yes" side failed to win a sufficient majority in the referendum because it was hopelessly divided and its arguments and its efforts were often contradictory, because it underestimated the strength of the opposition and because it made several tactical blunders.

The devolution referendum was important, not only for its immediate political effect, but also because it confirmed the place of the referendum in British politics. The precedent had been set by the referendum on membership of the European Economic Community in 1975, but the Scottish devolution referendum (and the similar one held in Wales on the same day) and its campaign, differed significantly. Firstly, a simple majority of those voting was not sufficient to decide the outcome, as it had been in the EEC referendum; and, secondly, neither the groups campaigning for a "Yes" vote nor those on the "No" side were able to find sufficient common ground to unite them under all-party umbrella organisations. Whereas in 1975 there had been two sides, offering a clear-cut choice, in 1979 there were at least six bodies pressing the electorate to vote "Yes" or "No".

The idea of holding a referendum was first mooted in the autumn of 1976 when the Labour Government's first attempt at devolution legislation, the Scotland and Wales Bill, was making its faltering way through Parliament. Who originally made the suggestion is not clear, but it was taken up by Mr Michael Foot, Leader of the Commons, as a way of persuading dissident Labour MPs to support the Bill. When the second measure was introduced, as the Scotland Bill, the referendum idea was revived with the same intention and in fact a number of Labour MPs (such as Mr Robin Cook, Edinburgh Central) who were opposed to devolution were prepared to vote for the Scotland Bill on the understanding they would be free to campaign against it in the referendum. The date for the vote was announced in the Queen's Speech on November 1, 1978. The Prime Minister told the Commons that March 1, 1979 had been chosen to allow the referendum to be held on the new electoral register which would be published in mid-February and was therefore likely to be reasonably accurate when the vote was held. This was important because a clause inserted into the Scotland Act (as it had then become) against the Government's wishes required 40% of the whole electorate to vote in favour of devolution before the Act could be put into effect. Opponents of this clause (the "Cunningham Amendment", after Mr George Cunningham, Islington South, who proposed it) argued, with justification, that the older the register, the harder it would be to clear this hurdle, since as time went on and people died or moved away from places in which they were registered, the register would increasingly overestimate the size of the total electorate. But the long delay between the announcement and the referendum itself also gave the two sides plenty of time in which to prepare themselves.

The pre-Christmas period was spent mainly in internal organisation, sorting out who was going to campaign with whom, forming local groups, raising funds, booking meeting halls, poster spaces, newspaper advertising and so on. On the "Yes" side (that is, campaigning for devolution, since the referendum question asked whether the Scotland Act should be put into effect) the main campaigning groups were to be the Labour Movement Yes Campaign, the Scottish National Party, the Yes for Scotland group, the Alliance for an Assembly, the Liberals and the Communists, although other groups emerged during the campaign, such as the Conservative Yes group and several student organisations. The "No" side was slightly less fragmented, with Scotland Says No, Labour Vote No and the Conservative Party No campaign.

This fragmentation, particularly among the "Yes" groups, crucially affected the campaign and the way the issues were presented. It resulted mainly from the fact that the different groups had different reasons for supporting the devolution legislation. The Labour Movement — the Labour Party, Co-operative Party and Scottish Trades Union Congress — supported the establishment of an Assembly with limited powers over domestic affairs as a way of answering the demand from Scots for more say in their own affairs without going as far as setting up an independent state as demanded by the SNP. In three by-elections in 1978 Labour had used devolution as an effective counter to the Nationalists' demand for indepen-dence. The Nationalists, on the other hand, supported the Assembly only as a step on the road to independence. This divergence of view led Labour to refuse to take any part in a joint campaign with the SNP: "We will not soil our hands," said Mrs Helen Liddell, secretary of the Scottish Council of the Labour Party.

This schism was the most damaging to the "Yes" cause. It led to wasteful duplication of effort, particularly at local level, where SNP branches and the committees set up by all but a handful of Labour constituency parties worked in parallel delivering leaflets, arranging meetings and canvassing. But it also meant there were occasional public arguments between the two groups and it gave the "No" campaign an effective argument against the Assembly: there was an obvious contradiction between Labour urging a "Yes" vote against separation and the SNP urging a "Yes" vote as a means to independence.

There were lesser splits in other parts of the "Yes" campaign. Scotland Says Yes, supposedly an all-party group led by Lord Kilbrandon, who had chaired the Royal Commission on the Constitution which had recommended an Assembly for Scotland, was boycotted by Labour because it contained Nationalists. Although it did have a Conservative as its organiser, its leading lights were the Nationalists Mrs Margo MacDonald and Mr George Reid MP and the leader of the breakaway Scottish Labour Party, which advocated independence for Scotland, Mr Jim Sillars MP. This close identification with nationalism was too much for Mr Alick Buchanan-Smith, the Conservative MP who had resigned from the Shadow Cabinet over his support for devolution. He formed his own cross-party group, the Alliance for an Assembly and was joined by the Liberal MP Mr Russell Johnston and the Labour MP Mr Donald Dewar. The Liberal and Communist Parties contributed at local level to the efforts of Scotland Says Yes, but also ran campaigns of their own.

The effectiveness of the "Yes" argument was weakened still further by the split within the Labour Movement itself. There had always been a difference of opinion, even in Scotland, over the importance of the devolution policy to Labour, but the party leadership was unprepared for just how much this was to counter the success of the official "Yes" campaign. The split ran through the party from the six of thirty-nine Scottish Labour MPs who openly urged a "No" vote, to the unions, councillors and constituency parties. The Labour Vote No group, chaired by Mr Brian Wilson, one of the ablest of the younger Labour candidates, was effective chiefly in frustrating the "Yes" campaign at local level by persuading activists not to take part, in seeking publicity and in taking a very bold initiative in the Court of Session to stop party political broadcasts during the campaign which would have been three (Labour, Liberal and SNP) to one (Conservative) in favour of devolution. The official Labour leadership also underestimated Mr Tam Dalyell (West Lothian), the most persistent anti-devolution MP. It regarded him as so fanatical as not to be taken seriously, but he addressed a phenomenal number of meetings with the same simple arguments (the nature of which I will discuss later) and by the end of the campaign there was evidence that they were going home.

Labour Vote No did not formally co-operate with Scotland Says No, but there was not the same antipathy between the groups that existed between Labour and the SNP and in fact at least one member of the Labour No campaign, Mr Robin Cook, appeared on a Scotland Says No platform. The "Yes" groups also underestimated the effectiveness of Scotland Says No. This organisation had its origins in a loose group called Keep Britain United, formed in 1976 by Iain Sproat (Conservative MP for Aberdeen South) to campaign within the Conservative Party against its then official policy of setting up a legislative Assembly for Scotland. The following year it was broadened to include the Confederation of British Industry, some Chambers of Commerce and some individual Labour Party members like Mr Archie Birt, a party activist from Gourock, and Mr Danny Crawford, Scottish executive member of the building workers' union UCATT. The name was changed to Scotland is British and the group campaigned effectively against the two devolution Bills. It was relaunched as Scotland Says No at the end of November 1978 with many of the same people involved, but also some new faces, including its joint chairmen, the Very Rev Andrew Herron, a former Moderator of the General Assembly of the Church of Scotland, and Lord Wilson of Langside, a former Labour Minister, and its full time campaign manager, a former Conservative agent, Mr Hew Carruthers.

Scotland Says No was well organised. It raised money quickly (about £80,000, mostly from companies), produced eye-catching leaflets and other propaganda, booked advertising space in virtually every local and national newspaper in Scot-

E

land and organised local campaign groups. Its contacts in management not only donated money, but also distributed leaflets. The Clydesdale Bank sent Scotland Says No material to its branch managers and some other firms put them in pay packets. Although they decided not to join forces, the two main "No" groups remained friendly and Scotland Says No attempted to avoid duplication of effort by leaving what might be called "subversive" work among Labour activists to Labour Vote No. The larger group also kept a record of Labour No public meetings and gave information on them when asked.

The position of the Conservative Party in the campaign was equivocal. Its official policy still favoured some form of devolution, although there were varying degrees of enthusiasm among the leadership, but the party was against the Scotland Act. Some prominent members, like Mr Teddy Taylor, then MP for Cathcart and shadow Scottish spokesman, wanted the party to campaign all-out on its own behalf against the Act, but at a private conference early in 1979 the decision was taken to take part only as a supporter of Scotland Says No and allow proponents of devolution, such as Mr Buchanan-Smith and Mr Malcolm Rifkind, MP for Edinburgh Pentlands, to follow their consciences and campaign for the Act. In the event, although Mr Taylor and other individuals put a lot of effort into the campaign, the contribution of the party machine, the Central Office staff in Edinburgh and local agents and elected officers, was muted. Very little party money was spent on the campaign and many local parties did nothing more than distribute the Scotland Says No leaflet supplied to them free of charge by Central Office.

These, then were the main actors in the campaign. The period between the Queen's Speech and Christmas was taken up with internal organisation, there was a lull for the Christmas and New Year holidays and then most of the groups began their campaigns. The exception was the Labour Movement, which decided to wait until the second week in February and conduct a short, sharp campaign of General Election length. It was decided that this would be more effective than a longer campaign, which would tend to make people bored with the whole question, but as a tactical ploy it failed. The start given to Scotland Says No enabled it to put its arguments first and stake out the ground for the campaign. When Labour began to put its case it never effectively gained the initiative. Considering that Labour had the advantage of a virtual monopoly on well-known names, it was a major coup by Scotland Says No to be able to dictate the issues on which the campaign was to be fought.

The Scottish National Party also started its campaign in January after a special one-day conference which adapted the existing policies for an independent Scotland to the limits of the Assembly. Thereafter a large part of the SNP campaign consisted of publicising these policies. The argument was that if people were going to vote for an Assembly, they had a right to know what the parties were proposing it should do. However, this was putting the cart before the horse and deflected effort from actually winning support for the devolved legislature. Yes for Scotland began its campaign in a slightly different fashion, describing at various Press conferences what the Assembly would be able to do, for women, for example, or for the social services or education.

The issues in the campaign were by this time already fixed and from my observations of canvassing and the questions asked at public meetings they varied remarkably little throughout the campaign. They were whether or not the Assembly would lead to the break-up of the UK, whether it would mean more bureaucracy and more government and whether it would cost more. To hear these expressed by genuinely undecided voters was to hear how effective the "No" campaign had been. They were almost invariably expressed in a negative way. When a canvasser on the doorstep — where most contact with the voters takes place — meets a person who tells him the Assembly will lead to the break-up of the UK, it is extremely difficult to argue that on the contrary it will help to prevent the break-up of the UK, particularly when the SNP are campaigning in favour of an Assembly as a step towards independence. Similarly the canvasser confronted with the basic statement that the Assembly will cost more and mean more bureaucracy finds it difficult to put over the much subtler argument that by actually controlling the bureaucracy the Assembly will be able to reduce cost.

The "democratic" argument, that the Assembly was essential to make the Civil Servants in the Scottish Office more accountable and more responsive to public opinion, was to many "Yes" campaigners the strongest justification for devolution. But it was never established as an issue in its own right, merely as a counter to the "extra cost, extra bureaucracy" argument of the "No" side. Another drawback for the "Yes" canvassers was that the Assembly, as proposed under the Scotland Act, had no economic powers, whereas (as opinion polls during the subsequent General Election campaign showed) the main preoccupations of Scottish voters were prices and jobs. "Yes" canvassers that I watched found it difficult to give electors reasons for turning out to vote for a Parliament which would not be able to deal with their pressing concerns.

For the "Yes" campaign to be effective, it needed to confront these issues head-on, but it did not. Instead it persisted in putting what to many voters seemed like irrelevant points. These were not only the finer details of what an Assembly might do, but the complete red herrings of the 40% rule and the "No" campaign's funds. "Yes" speakers (and it was difficult in the last days of the campaign to listen to Mr Jim Sillars or any one of a number of SNP speakers who did not dwell on both at length) seemed to believe that railing against the unfairness of the Cunningham Amendment, or repeating the unsubstantiated allegation that Scotland Says No was financed by "English Gold" or big business (or both) would produce a wave of popular indignation that would sweep people to the polls to vote "Yes". It did not. Towards the end of the campaign the "No" side also got on to this side track, spending much of its time accusing the "Yes" campaign of deliberately spreading the false impression that an abstention was equivalent to a "No" vote.

The "Yes" side was not without its successes, for example in getting genuine support from shop stewards through the Confederation of Shipbuilding and Engineering Unions. Most unions, except UCATT, paid lip service to the "Yes" cause. Some, like the Transport and General Workers, went much further, producing a full-colour broadsheet and encouraging its officials at all levels to take part in the campaign. But practical help was in short supply. The "Yes" majority in Strathclyde seem to owe something to the work of stewards in their workshops. However, the "No" side produced two coups late in the campaign. Dr Herron managed to persuade the Church of Scotland not to issue a pastoral message in favour of devolution. Although many ministers had already read the message from their pulpits, the effect of Dr Herron's action was to confuse the position of the Church, which had been a long standing supporter of devolution. The second was persuading Lord Home, a former Conservative Prime Minister and a man with great influence among Conservatives in Scotland, to speak out against the Assembly. Coming from the man who had produced the Conservative devolution proposals, his speech was surprising. He said that the Scotland Act had five fundamental defects including its lack of tax-raising powers and system of election, and ought to be rejected. This was precisely the opposite view to that taken by Mr Buchanan-Smith and Mr Rifkind, who attempted to undo the damage by launching a separate Conservative "Yes" campaign in the last week. They argued that the Act had many shortcomings, but ought to be supported and once implemented could be amended. System Three polls in the *Glasgow Herald* showed that although in the last week of January 39% of Conservative supporters were intending to vote "Yes", against 45% "No" and 16% undecided, by the last week in February the proportion intending to vote "No" had risen to 71%, with 19% "Yes" and 10% undecided.

The Conservatives had a motive for campaigning against the Act which was nothing to do with the government of Scotland. They knew that a defeat for the legislation, which had occupied most of two sessions of Parliament and was central to the Government's policy, would severely damage Mr Callaghan's Administration, although they cannot have foreseen how effectively the strategy would work. Some leading members of the then Shadow Cabinet, including Mrs Margaret Thatcher, the leader, and Mr Francis Pym, who had been devolution spokesmen, wanted to come to Scotland to campaign for a "No" vote. They were dissuaded by Mr Taylor who believed that the appearance of too many English politicians would be counter-productive. Similarly Labour knew that it was fighting for more than a principle. The SNP was split on its enthusiasm for the measure. The "moderate, gradualist" wing such as Mr George Reid and Mrs Margo MacDonald, saw the Assembly as an essential step towards independence. A minority in the party, notably Professor Neil MacCormick, believed it to be possibly an end in itself. But other influential figures in the party including Mr Gordon Wilson, then deputy parliamentary leader, and Mr Douglas Henderson, then MP for East Aberdeenshire, believed devolution to be a distraction to the main task in hand and therefore campaigned half-heartedly for the Scotland Act.

The difficulty both sides encountered in getting enough active workers to undertake persuasive canvassing meant that the campaign was largely fought out in the press and on television. Of the Scottish nationals, *The Scotsman* and the *Daily Record* were strongly in favour of a "Yes" vote and the *Glasgow Herald* and *Sunday Mail* moderately in favour. On the other side the *Scottish Daily Express,* which had once been rabidly pro-devolution, was equally fervently anti by the time it came to the referendum. So was its sister Sunday newspaper and the *Sunday Post*. Of the London papers, *The Observer,* the *Guardian* and *The Financial Times* were moderately pro and the *Daily Mail* and *The Daily* and *The Sunday Telegraph* were anti. (*The Times* and *The Sunday Times* were not published). Most of the papers (and all the broadcasting organisations) attempted to be fair to both sides in their news coverage. The exceptions were the *Record,* which gave much more space to the "Yes" arguments than "No" ones, and the *Express,* which mainly treated "Yes" arguments with derision and went so far on one occasion as to suppress the main findings of an opinion poll it had itself commissioned (leading its story instead with a report of ludicrously unrepresentative straw polls among students and school children).

In the last days of the campaign the opinion polls predicted the result with reasonable accuracy. After so many years of discussing devolution it is perhaps understandable that many ordinary voters were tired of it. The result is difficult to interpret and is likely to be the cause of controversy for years to come: approximately one-third of the electorate voted "Yes", one third "No" and the remaining third was not sufficiently motivated by either side to vote at all.

I shall end with a short footnote on Orkney and Shetland. We cannot go into the reason in detail, but it should be pointed out that the referendum campaign in the northern isles was largely fought on different issues than in the rest of the country. Shetlanders, particularly, wanted a Constitutional Commission to examine their status within the UK and had been promised one in the event of an Assembly being set up for the rest of Scotland. However, the parliamentary manoeuvering that went on during the committee stage of the Scotland Bill confused many Shetlanders and they were unsure whether they should vote "Yes" or "No" in order to get the Commission. And so on March 1 only 27% of those who voted, voted "Yes" in Shetland and only 28% in Orkney. These proportions were far below those in the rest of the country — their nearest rivals being the Borders Region, and Dumfries and Galloway in both of which only 40% of the electorate favoured the Act. Yet who would have supposed, even a year before, that devolution far from commanding the support of 40% of the electorate would be endorsed by only 40% of those voting in some parts of the country? It is this reversal which I have tried to explain in this chapter.

5

THE SCOTTISH MORNING PRESS
AND THE DEVOLUTION REFERENDUM OF 1979

MICHAEL BROWN

*Journalist and Graduate Student,
Department of Political Science, Dundee*

Introduction

A distinctive daily and Sunday Press is published in, or for, Scotland. This Press, hereafter referred to collectively as the "Scottish morning Press", regards itself as the guardian and recorder of Scottish political interests. Most of the papers took up positions on the question of a Scottish Assembly as proposed by the Scotland Act 1978 and regarded the campaign leading up to the referendum on 1 March 1979 as a major news story. This article sets out to describe the salient characteristics of the Scottish morning Press, to describe the way it handled the referendum, and to assess the possible effects of Press activity.

The Scottish Morning Press: Its Existence and Composition

Past commentators on Scottish affairs have tended to ignore the existence of a Scottish Press or have noted and described it without identifying its role. Writers on the development of nationalism invariably draw a connection with Scottish literature but usually exclude the mass literature which is actually read by most of those who make a nationalist revival possible, concentrating instead on minority literary tastes. There has recently been some attempt at redress. As one writer has warned:

> "Nobody can appreciate Scottish culture unless he reads (even if he cannot understand) the *Sunday Post* which is read by a staggering 77 per cent of the adult population of Scotland".[1]

The most recent *Royal Commission on the Press* found a higher percentage of morning paper readers among Scots than among other Britons.[2] Moreover, different papers were read in Scotland from elsewhere in the UK. Penetration by the London Press is less extensive in Scotland, the readership of popular

Sundays is totally different and only the British quality Sundays maintain their market share, thanks to the lack of indigenous competition. Roughly four out of every five morning papers read in Scotland are published specifically for the Scottish morning market.

The Scottish morning Press consists of nine titles: two quality dailies, circulating throughout Scotland; two popular tabloids covering the same area; two regional dailies covering respectively the Dundee and Aberdeen areas and their hinterlands, and three Sunday papers.

The papers and their stance on devolution can be summarised as follows:

The Quality Dailies

The Scotsman. Owned by the Thomson Organisation. Published in Edinburgh. Circulation 90,000. Traditionally in favour of some form of Home Rule or federalism. Critical of aspects of the Scotland Act but campaigned ardently for "Yes" vote.

The *Glasgow Herald.* Owned by George Outram & Company, itself owned by Scottish & Universal Investments (SUITS) which, throughout the referendum campaign, was the object of a takeover bid (subsequently successful) by Lonrho. Published in Glasgow. Circulation 115,000. Formerly anti-devolutionist and always referred to "assembly" with a lower case "a". After conversion of SUITS' then chairman, Sir Hugh Fraser, to Scottish nationalism in 1974, attacks on nationalists were muted. Latterly supported devolution though with more resignation than zeal.

The Popular Tabloids

The *Scottish Daily Express.* Owned by Express Newspapers, owned in turn by Trafalgar House Investments. Formerly pro-devolutionist. Founder Lord Beaverbrook had flirted with early Scottish Nationalism. Expressions of Scottishness intensified when publication moved to Manchester in 1974. Following Trafalgar House take-over, switched to militant anti-devolution line.

The *Daily Record.* Part of Mirror Group Newspapers, owned by Reed International. Published in Glasgow. Circulation 700,000. Pro-Labour but favoured devolution even before Labour Party convinced. Enthusiastic "Yes" campaigner.

The Regional Dailies

The *Courier & Advertiser* (Dundee). Owned by D. C. Thomson, a private local company. Circulation 135,000. Traditional, old-fashioned paper. Has consistently opposed devolution.

The *Press & Journal* (Aberdeen). Owned by Thomson Organisation. Circulation 115,000. Low interest in devolution. Generally adopted stance of unenthusiastic neutrality.

The Sundays

The *Sunday Post*. Ownership as Dundee *Courier*. Published in Glasgow. Circulation undisclosed but believed to be over one million. Was suspicious of the devolution proposals but believed some sort of change necessary. Had difficulty in reconciling strong Scottish consciousness with innate conservatism.

The *Sunday Mail*. Ownership as *Daily Record*. Published in Glasgow. Circulation 800,000. Most nationalist of the Scottish press. Fervent and colourful "Yes" campaign.

The *Scottish Sunday Express*. Ownership as *Scottish Daily Express*. Published in Manchester. Little interest in Scottish affairs and little attention given to devolution — and that very hostile.

The Scottish Morning Press:

Coverage of the Referendum Campaign

The coverage of the referendum campaign has been studied for the seven months commencing on 1 August 1978, when the Royal Assent was granted to the Scotland Bill and ending on 1 March 1979 when a referendum was held in Scotland in which voters were asked whether they wished the Scotland Act to be implemented, an argument which was presented chiefly in terms of whether an Assembly should be set up in Edinburgh. Those in favour of an Assembly secured a narrow majority but failed to win the support of 40% of the electorate which would have ensured its establishment automatically.

The definition of such a period is inevitably arbitrary but the inclusion of earlier periods was beyond the scope of this study. The limited evidence available suggests that popular feeling on devolution remained relatively constant during the legislative stages but changed significantly during the period under consideration.

The Scottish morning Press covered the referendum campaign in different ways, not only in terms of political advocacy but also in terms of the extent and style of coverage. Indeed the approaches adopted were so varied that the tendency to regard the Scottish Press as homogeneous deserves to be questioned. This is in itself a finding worth emphasising here and testing in further studies of the British Press.

Space Allocated

There was a great variation in the space allocated to the referendum. The traditional measure of space is the column inch. The papers surveyed had a wide range of page sizes, column width and type faces, making valid comparison difficult, and space allocated has therefore been expressed as a percentage of the total editorial space available in each paper. Editorial space is defined as being all the space in the paper other than advertisements and advertising features. Table A shows the percentage of editorial space in each paper allocated to the referendum month by month.

Two extremes are recorded. *The Scotsman* is pre-eminent in its coverage with 3.5%. In February this rose to a remarkable 13%: in a typical twenty-page *Scotsman* this would mean between a page and a page and a half devoted to the subject. On some days the figure was well above that. At the other extreme the contribution of the *Scottish Sunday Express* is negligible at 0.2% and, being statistically worthless, will be omitted from much of the ensuing discussion and tables. The other papers cluster round the 1% mark. If the papers are ordered by allocation of space and their referendum stance noted, an interesting pattern emerges. Table B shows that support for devolution is associated with higher coverage.

The Build Up of Coverage

Table A also demonstrates the build-up of coverage which predictably increases as referendum day approaches. But the pattern of build-up varies with different papers. Table C, which expresses Table A in index form, shows this more clearly. *The Scotsman, Glasgow Herald* and *Dundee Courier* all stepped up coverage in November when the referendum date was announced. All the press except the regionals stepped up coverage in January 79, and all nine papers stepped up coverage in February. For the *Press & Journal* this was the only significant acceleration.

TABLE A

Coverage devoted to the referendum expressed as percentage of total editorial space in each paper.

month	S'man	G.Her.	D.Rec.	SDE.	DC.	P&J.	SP.	SM.	SSE.
Aug 78	1.16	0.36	0.23	0.05	0.36	0.11	0.17	0.29	0.00
Sept	1.31	0.36	0.31	0.00	0.21	0.12	0.12	0.00	0.49
Oct	0.69	0.32	0.35	0.01	0.05	0.03	0.28	0.00	0.00
Nov	2.39	0.67	0.31	0.19	0.62	0.40	0.30	0.18	0.00
Dec	1.49	0.64	0.27	0.06	0.65	0.25	0.23	0.12	0.00
Jan 79	4.46	1.58	0.60	1.51	0.69	0.33	0.59	1.97	0.00
Feb*	12.98	5.04	4.67	4.44	2.50	4.41	3.56	5.00	1.06
Seven month period	3.51	1.28	1.01	0.84	0.68	0.79	0.71	1.12	0.21

*Feb includes edition of March 1.

TABLE B

Papers, by space allocation to referendum over whole period, with assembly stance

Paper	% space	Stance
Scotsman	3.51	strongly pro
Glasgow Herald	1.28	pro
Sunday Mail	1.12	strongly pro
Daily Record	1.01	strongly pro
Sc. Daily Express	0.84	strongly against
Press & Journal	0.79	neutral
Sunday Post	0.71	sceptically neutral
Dundee Courier	0.68	strongly against
Sc. Sunday Express	0.21	against

TABLE C

Growth in coverage of the referendum. 100 in each case equals February percentage of total editorial space for that paper. This table presents table A in index form.

month	S'man.	G.Her.	D.Rec.	SDE.	DC.	P&J.	SP.	SM
Aug 78	9	7	5	1	14	2	5	6
Sept	10	7	7	0	8	3	3	0
Oct	5	6	7	0	2	1	8	0
Nov	18	13	7	4	25	9	8	4
Dec	11	13	6	1	26	6	6	2
Jan 79	34	31	13	34	28	7	17	39
Feb	100	100	100	100	100	100	100	100

TABLE D

Readers' letters as percentage of total items on referendum

Paper	Total items N	Letters %
Scotsman	834	49.3
Glasgow Herald	300	47.7
Daily Record	161	9.3
Sc. Daily Express	163	30.7
Dundee Courier	211	63.5
Press & Journal	218	30.7
Sunday Post	59	5.1
Sunday Mail	30	6.7

TABLE E

Readers' letters on referendum, by orientation, as percentage of all letters carried on all subjects, N.

paper	letters, all topics N	total ref letters %	pro devo %	anti devo %	other devo %
Scotsman	2018	20.4	9.1	5.1	6.2
G.Herald	1720	8.3	2.9	3.4	2.0
D.Record	1428	1.1	1.0	*	0.0
S.D. Express	1090	4.6	0.9	3.6	*
D.Courier	1534	8.7	4.6	2.7	1.4
P&J	188	35.6	15.4	14.9	5.3
S.Post	369	0.8	0.0	0.3	0.5
S.Mail	260	0.8	0.4	0.0	0.4

*less than 0.05%

TABLE F

Distribution, by types of coverage, of all referendum items, other than readers' letters

paper	total items N	page one lead %	other P.1 %	inside news %	leader comment %	feature/ diary %	column/ forum %
Scotsman	423	2.36	8.27	65.24	9.45	12.29	2.36
G.Herald	157	4.45	12.73	46.49	13.37	14.01	8.91
D.Record	146	2.05	2.05	24.65	4.10	65.06	2.05
S.D.Express	113	6.19	10.61	48.67	6.19	25.66	2.65
D.Courier	77	5.19	6.49	62.33	20.77	2.59	2.59
P&J	151	1.98	15.23	66.88	2.64	10.59	2.64
S.Post	56	0.00	1.78	5.35	5.35	83.92	3.57
S.Mail	28	3.57	0.00	17.85	3.57	67.85	7.14

The Style of Coverage

While it is customary and useful to compare coverage in terms of space allocated, such a method fails to reveal the different forms of coverage which can be employed. During the seven-month period a count was kept on all referendum items appearing in the press. "Item" here includes news stories, feature articles, letters, opinion columns and so on. As Table D shows, readers' letters constitute a sizeable proportion of the items occurring in some papers. All the papers, except the *Press & Journal,* carry large numbers of letters. Letters on the referendum made up nearly half the total items occurring in *The Scotsman* and the *Glasgow Herald* and over 60% in the Dundee *Courier.* In *The Scotsman* a fifth of all letters carried concerned devolution, a considerable proportion given the other Scottish, British and foreign issues which receive attention. Despite lively readers' pages the tabloids and Sundays carried few letters on the referendum. Most of these carried in the *Express* were in response to a competition for anti-devolution letters in which first prize was £100! The absence of referendum letters from the *Sunday Post* is interesting in the light of the finding of the recent Royal Commission on the Press that the letters page was the paper's most popular feature. As Table E shows, there was no consistent connection between editorial slant and the dominant view expressed by letters. The predominant view reflected editorial stances in the pro-Assembly *Scotsman* and the anti-Assembly *Express* and went against editorial preference in the pro-Assembly *Herald* and anti-Assembly *Courier.* The category "other" in Table E consists of letters dealing with devolution or referendums elsewhere, those failing to express a preference, and those which were simply obscure.

The distribution of items other than readers' letters is shown in Table F. The "page one lead" is the main front-page story and provides a useful indication of editorial priorities. A number of the *Express* leads were not news but campaign exhortations. On several occasions the *Herald* led on polls it had commissioned. There is obviously more scope for "other page one" news in papers such as the *Press & Journal* which carry a large number of front-page stories. The tabloids rarely carry more than two. The Dundee *Courier* carries only advertising on the front page: for the purpose of this study the main news page was regarded as page one. "Inside news" refers to all other news reports including occasional back-page news. The *Herald* is here under-represented since it ran each day's referendum news into one long item while *The Scotsman* ran each topic separately. If allowance were made for this practice the *Herald* would probably join the regionals and *The Scotsman* with inside news around the 60% mark.

The *Sunday Post* rarely treated the referendum as hard news and confined most reporting to impressionistic accounts in its Parliamentary diary column. The papers differed widely in the use made of this diary-type coverage which interpreted and analysed aspects of the news. In the *Daily Record* much material regarded as ordinary news by other papers was treated in this manner. Most papers devoted feature space to detailing the issues, background, implementation and possible consequences of the referendum. Only the Dundee *Courier* failed to make significant use of this category of journalism whose growth has been identified as the major change in newspaper content over recent decades[3]. Most papers made use of the contributed article or column by outsiders. The *Glasgow Herald* in particular has long made use of this device and along with the *Courier* and the *Sunday Post* sometimes paired contributors with opposing views on the same page. Most contributors were partisan to the referendum debate but some use was made of outside experts, to discuss either particular aspects of devolution or the political significance of the referendum.

The Scotsman, the *Herald* and the *Courier* carry several leading articles or "editorial comment" articles every day and made frequent pronouncements on devolution and the referendum. The other papers usually carry only one editorial, not necessarily every day. The *Sunday Post's* "As We See It" column is less a reasoned statement of editorial opinion than an anecdotal rumination on events.

The various members of the Scottish morning Press thus allocated varying percentages of their editorial space to devolution and the referendum, built up their coverage at different speeds, and employed widely differing editorial techniques to cover the subject. It remains to examine the aspects of devolution which were covered.

The Agenda of Referendum Coverage

The agenda of issues covered by the Press fell into three distinct categories: the campaign itself; the details of the devolution proposals; and the anticipated consequences of devolution going ahead — or not. The *campaign* attracted the usual horse-race excitement of an election. Initial speculation on the date of the referendum was followed by speculation on the result. Several papers carried opinion polls and they were all eager to report each other's findings. There were novel features in the referendum campaign related to the requirement that 40% of the Scottish electorate must vote "yes" if a motion repealing the Scotland Act were not to be laid before Parliament, and to the fact that the campaign groups cut across traditional party allegiances.

The 40% requirement aroused much controversy — about the justice of the rule and about the allowance made for inaccuracies on the register — and much speculation about whether the requirement would be met. The splits in the Labour and Conservative Parties over devolution and the fact that neither Labour faction would work with members of other parties produced not only a surfeit of campaign groups but a wealth of activities and feuds to report. Political personalities found themselves in unlikely and newsworthy alliances; there were predictable allegations of deceit and trickery and one instance of infiltration when the press talked hopefully but vainly of a Scottish Watergate. The financing of the campaign brought some sharp Press exchanges and the wealthiest group — "Scotland says No" — was accused on occasion of using Arab money and (probably more damagingly) funds from England. The unusual alignments posed problems for the broadcasting authorities with their statutory requirement to be impartial. The Press, unhindered by such requirements, followed the ensuing disputes and court cases with enthusiasm.

The party leaders were scrutinised and when Mr Callaghan came to Glasgow campaigning for the Assembly, five of the six dailies led their front pages with the story. It is worth recording that this was the first time in the seven-month period that so many dailies agreed on a devolution lead. The Press, thrown by the odd campaign alignments and suspecting a lack of public enthusiasm for the subject, tended to fall back on the familiar fare of journalism. This search for personalities rather than abstract issues led both sides to list well-known names in politics, industry, sports and entertainment who supported them, prompting one terse and weary three-word letter to *The Scotsman:* "Who *is* Lulu?"

One intriguing sideshow was the conflict between the papers. Since its move to Manchester in 1974 the *Scottish Daily Express* had been sensitive to any questioning of its Scottishness. With its switch to an anti-Assembly stance the sensitivity was heightened. The pro-Assembly *Record* challenged the right of the *Express* to claim to speak for Scotland. The *Express* replied that the Record was English owned; its editor was even an Englishman! Much energy — and front-page space — was spent in late January on the subject, bringing a rare knock-about element to Scottish journalism though little enlightenment to the readers. In more restrained vein *The Scotsman* drily reported the failure of the *Express* to publish a poll it had commissioned on the referendum. The poll had shown a surprisingly strong "yes" vote.

The *details* of devolution were dutifully reported. All the Press at some point or other listed the substance of the Scotland Act, what was devolved and what would be retained by Westminster. Much space was given to pictures of the hall prepared for the Assembly, the cost of preparation was discussed and there was some speculation on its use in the event of the Assembly failing to materialise. The events leading up to the Assembly were recounted: the *Herald* had a useful account going back a few decades, the *Record* and *Sunday Mail* delved farther, and more selectively, into ancient Scottish history.

The Consequences

Much Press coverage tended to view the referendum vote as an end in itself but there was some speculation on the aftermath of devolution. The "No" campaigners hammered on the themes that the Act was a bad piece of legislation, it would mean more bureaucracy and higher taxes, and might lead to the break-up of Britain. The papers in Dundee and Aberdeen also suggested an Assembly would be dominated by the central belt and hence the Socialists. The force with which this negative case was put pushed the "Yes" campaigners on the defensive. That the Act was bad they sometimes conceded — "But the

F

best you'll get". That Britain could break-up was conceded implicitly, for why else were those seeking Scottish independence backing the Assembly? On the positive side the "Yes" campaigners could argue that democracy would be brought nearer the people who would be given more control over government.

These however were abstract notions: there was a noticeable failure on the part of "Yes" campaigners to present a vivid and attractive image of post-Assembly Scotland. *The Scotsman* did run a series of leaders, "Agenda for the Assembly", which described what the Assembly might do. Several papers based articles on the newly published collection of essays *Framework for Change*[4], among them Neal Ascherson's humorous and human description of the Assembly at work. The *Glasgow Herald* and the *Press & Journal* touched on relations between the Assembly and a range of interests — the arts, industry, the regions — but these were far from frequent. For the most part the "Yes" campaigners were more concerned to rebut the grim future forecast by opponents than present their own version. It was left to the pro-Assembly Press to try to put some life into the idea.

The Effects of Press Coverage: An Assessment

Conventional election studies are accustomed to recording the allegiance and activities of the Press during the campaign. The implication is that the Press is in some way important but the issue is rarely taken beyond this point[5]. Political activists and journalists frequently question the role of the Press but while often asserting its irrelevance they behave as though it was important.

The problem is a complex one. It is worth emphasising that in a modern mass society few people can witness politics at first-hand and even those politically active cannot survey the entire political environment unaided. The mass media are not a sideshow to events: they are the major means of observing most events and are often influential in shaping them. For the ordinary elector the mass media are a major means of surveying the political world, either directly or through discussion with those who have used the media.[6] Moreover in a modern society the media themselves are actors on the scene with their own interests to pursue.[7]

The political effects of mass media are still imperfectly understood. We are emerging from a period of pessimism during which it was often suggested that the media, for the most part, had the effect of reinforcing existing attitudes. The subject still suffers from the 'hypodermic" approach of early theorists who postulated an inert audience responding to injections of information from the media. This has led to dangerous over-simplifications. Until quite recently analysts of election Press coverage would add up the circulations of papers supporting each contestant and conclude that the recipient of the largest favourable Press was the beneficiary!

An extensive reassessment of the effect of the Press, radio and television has taken place in the 1970s.[8] Not only is the possibility of their power and influence being re-admitted but effects are now being sought and identified in a wide range of directions. In a resumé of this length only three can be noted, being of particular value.

1. Effects on institutions and elite groups.
2. Effects on other media.
3. Effects on individuals' political behaviour.

The first two will be touched on only briefly.

Institutions and Elites

The Press, radio and television and certain prestige sources in particular are used by other groups and elites to monitor opinion in contexts where their first-hand knowledge is inadequate. This was the case over Scottish devolution where many British politicians, party workers, journalists, civil servants and other opinion leaders had to come to a conclusion on the strength of Scottish demands for devolution, making up their minds in a relatively short period. The prestige Scottish Press available in London consists of *The Scotsman* and the *Glasgow Herald*. *The Scotsman* has always favoured some form of devolution and appears to give more space to the subject than wider-circulating rivals. This impression has been borne out by the present study.

In the mid-1970s when Government policy formulation was at a critical stage, anyone consulting the four Scottish nationally-circulating papers would have found a concerted demand for devolution.[9] (The *Express* subsequently recanted: The anti-devolutionist *Dundee Courier* is not readily available in London and anyhow has a reputation for eccentric views. In as much as the Press of an area influence decision-makers by providing a surrogate version of public opinion, the better known Scottish Press, right up to the referendum itself, would have been providing an over-estimate of Scottish enthusiasm for devolution.

Effects on Other Media

The environment surveyed by any member of the media includes all other media and their activities. The claims of rival papers made news for each other, so too did their polls. The difficulties of the broadcasters balancing the debate made news. Any action by one newspaper or broadcasting organisation is liable to affect others. Journalists lack audience feedback or the opportunity to test their image of their audience.[10] Instead they write to a large extent for the approval of other journalists and judge their own work by the performance of others. Thus it is very difficult for any newspaper to ignore persistently a topic given extensive coverage by rivals. The *Daily Record* failed to report the launching of the small but controversial "Labour Vote No" organisation but once it received coverage from other papers, assisted by the publicising flair of its leaders, the *Record* quickly gave it mention. Conversely if a paper raises an issue it tends to find its way onto the agenda of other papers or of radio and television by direct report, or because they attack it, or, under pressure for fresh news, develop a new angle.[11] In Britain the requirement on broadcasters to display balance enables viewpoints which might be excluded by a partisan Press to get onto the agenda nevertheless.

Moreover, once a new topic is linked to people or institutions already on the media agenda its coverage is assured. Thus whenever the referendum campaign was taken up by well-known politicians, Parliament, the courts, the Church of Scotland and the established parties, it was assured of coverage.

This process enabled one paper, or a group with access to one paper, to feed an item onto the agenda of the rest of the Press. The arguments for and against were thus carried (if only to be attacked) by papers of all persuasions. This process should serve as a salutory warning to those bemused by the simplistic image of papers for and against a topic, or by the fact that the average reader has access to only one newspaper. Thus although the homogeneity of the Scottish Press has been questioned in this paper, the tendency towards a homogeneous agenda should be emphasised.

Effects on Individuals' Political Behaviour

"Media effects" are regularly taken, in colloquial usage, to mean effects on the audience. The impact of mass communications on their recipients has, traditionally, been the area of the subject which has generated most interest. In the absence of any comprehensive model relating mass media to political behaviour there is no justification for asserting that the Scottish Press "caused" any particular development in Scottish political behaviour.[12] However, much work is underway exploring the link between Press and politics and two developments in particular shed useful light on the referendum coverage. They concern the concepts of "agenda-setting" and the "spiral of silence".

The study of agenda-setting is concerned with the consequences of a media system which, from an infinite range of available data, extracts and disseminates a very particular selection of information and news.[13] It has been said that the mass media are not very good at telling people what to think but very successful at telling them what to think about. Research on agenda-setting has sought to demonstrate that people exposed to the media's agenda will, over time, modify their personal agenda of important issues to conform to the media's agenda. This has been found to occur in certain limited circumstances. However, implicit in the concept of agenda-setting is that of 'arena-setting". The notion of arena-setting but not the term is alluded to by McLeod et al when they say: "To the extent that the agenda, as set by the media, forces political campaign 'games' to be played in a 'court' more favourable to one candidate than another, the effect may be to change not only the 'action' but also the outcome of the contest."[14]

Whether or not the audience internalises the media's agenda, the items on the agenda constitute the arena in which political debate is conducted. Contestants certainly behave as though this was the case and political campaigners make great efforts to push favourable issues onto the agenda and keep unfavourable issues off it. If the referendum agenda presented by the Scottish Press is viewed as an arena it is possible to postulate which side succeeded in establishing favourable issues on the agenda, or, to put it another way, which side could show itself to most advantage in the arena set up by the Scottish Press.

The main items on the agenda were described above. The

issues covered by the Press fell into three distinct categories: the campaign itself, the details of the devolution proposal, and the consequences. These will be considered in reverse order. When it came to forecasting the consequences of devolution the "No" campaigners set the pace. The "Yes" campaigners spent much time and energy disputing charges of increased costs, more bureaucracy and the break-up of Britain, thus competing in the arena set up by their opponents. In contrast the "Yes" campaigners were singularly unsuccessful in using the Press to sustain a positive debate on post-devolution Scotland — despite the sporadic efforts of *The Scotsman.*

The "Yes" campaigners turned instead to the familiar motive power of tartanry and much of the pro-devolution Press took up the theme. One of the "Yes" campaigns launched its final push with a pub Press conference at which pressmen were supplied with haggis and whisky as well as Press releases. Had there been an Edinburgh pub called the 'Kailyard" the "Yes" campaigners would doubtless have used it. The *Daily Record* and *Sunday Mail* resuscitated their own versions of Scottish history and in Whig style presented a "Yes" vote as the logical redress to the 1707 Act of Union or consequence of the 1314 Battle of Bannockburn. On the eve of poll the *Record* readers were reminded: "Now's the day, and now's the hour" (a quotation from "Bruce's Address to his Army at Bannockburn" by Robert Burns). Thus were three of nationalism's more potent symbols invoked in one familiar line. *The Scotsman* found time to ponder the voting intentions of Sir Walter Scott and sparked some lively correspondence from readers undeterred by the fact that he had been dead some 150 years.

Lasswell, writing on nationalism, has observed: —

> "The rationalism of capitalism has rendered it peculiarly dependent for positive values, ethical imperatives and unifying goal symbols upon legacies from previous cultures."[15]

His observation was certainly supported by the Scottish Press content in 1979. Of the trim, modern, self-sufficient Scandinavian-style Scotland which once inspired Home Rulers nothing was heard during the referendum campaign above the skirl of nostalgia and the jeremiads of old-style unionism. In terms of arena-setting, two themes for debate were laid down: one extrapolated from past experience of rising costs and growing bureaucracy and exploited the ingrained antipathy of the majority to total independence and the break-up of Britain: the other made a yearning appeal to the deep-rooted sense of Scottish consciousness.

No data exists to determine which side benefited from these arena issues: in future and more sophisticated studies of media effects, methods will have to be devised to evaluate the scale and direction of any benefit derived from the composition of the agenda. However, at the level of informed interpretation, it can be said that prophecies of more government generating more bureaucracy and a higher tax-burden would, given the audience's experience, appear to have a certain credibility. The forecast of the break-up of Britain would, on the continuing evidence of opinion polls, alienate more voters than it would attract. And the stressing of Scottish consciousness and traditions would in no way guarantee a distinctively Scottish form of political behaviour. Research has suggested that there is no lack of Scottish awareness or pride in the cultural heritage, but it has also been shown that there has been no consistent link between this Scottish awareness and political behaviour.[16]

The detail of the Scotland Act also featured on the agenda. The only evidence of possible effect is derived from an ORC/ *Scotsman* poll which reported the awareness of voters on the devolution proposals.[17] Each devolved topic was only recognised as being devolved by roughly half the sample and even among "Yes" voters 34% believed police powers were to be devolved and 18%, taxation, although neither was to have been an Assembly function.

All the Press in the sample took the trouble to provide factual information on devolution but it accounted for a very small fraction of the total coverage and could obviously be overlooked. Much attention was given to the hall prepared for the Assembly in Edinburgh and this attracted speculation on its use if the Assembly failed to materialise. The preparation of the hall also implied the Government's pre-emption of the voters' decision. This point, however, was raised only occasionally in anti-devolution letters.

The campaign itself was prominent on the agenda. It included the controversy over the 40% rule, the role of the political big names, the activities of the various campaign groups, and the shifts in public opinion.

The 40% rule served as a focal issue in two ways. For

the "Yes" campaigners it was a symbol of grievance and West-minster trickery. *The Scotsman* referred to the "rigged election". Secondly, in the speculation on the outcome, the 40% require-ment was a novel point of discussion. In this respect it posed a trap for the "Yes" side. On the evidence of their own claims and of opinion polls up to the autumn of 1978, support for devolution was overwhelming and 40% represented no threat. But as a grievance issue it was irresistible — there were points to be scored off the ethics of the requirement, off injustices in the register, and the effects of abstentions. Attention thus settled on the 40% requirement, on the outcome of the poll and on signs of changing fortunes on either side. The "yes" side's claims that the 40% rule could wreck devolution could be in-terpreted by "No" voters as an indication that they might succeed.

At this point the concept of the "spiral of silence" can usefully be introduced. The concept postulates that public opinion is based on a "quasi-statistical sense" whereby individuals seek to keep themselves integrated in society by monitoring the climate of opinion and giving voice to those of their predisposi-tions they believe to be in the ascendant.[18] The idea is more sophisticated than the notion of band-wagonning. People do not embrace a new idea because it is seen to be popular, rather they assert a hitherto dormant predisposition because they believe it is now acceptable to do so. By the reverse process less currency is given to opinions deemed to be in decline. The spiral theory allows the existence of committed elements at both extremes of an opinion who will not be moved and are immune to changes in the climate of opinion: the spiral effect is dis-played by the middle ground whose range of predispositions is such that they are potential supporters of either side.

In the period of the study the climate of opinion as presen-ted by the morning Press showed the anti-devolution tendency to be on the advance. Through most of 1978 the level of support for the Assembly remained, according to the opinion polls, relatively constant, enjoying the endorsement of two-thirds of those offering an opinion.[19] As the campaign developed the gap narrowed until by polling day it was virtually a dead heat.[20]

The development of the campaign is worth noting. The "No" campaigners were slower to organise and later in the field. So too were those papers opposed to devolution or neutral on the subject. Although most people read only one paper the point has already been made that papers influence each other. This slow build-up was pointed out by several anti-devolutionists early in the campaign who noted that their case was still to be put. Given that, it was predictable that once criticism of the devolution plan was finally made, there was likely to be some slippage of the "Yes" support. If the spiral concept was operating then it could be expected that this slippage would accelerate. In such circumstances the opinion polls were likely to reflect the changes and, in as much as they are one indication of the climate of opinion, were liable to feed the process. Other aspects of the agenda may have been relevant to the spiral process. Much attention was given to the big names, particularly the Government Ministers who campaigned. The Labour Yes Campaign linked its publicity directly with the Prime Minister. But in the process it may have forged a link with another spiral — the declining fortunes being experienced by the Government over the winter period of serious industrial disputes.[21] The coverage, frequently alarmist, given to these disputes during the devolution campaign is a further possible media effect to be noted. It cannot be expanded upon in this study but it emphasises the danger of analysing the Press coverage of the one item in isolation.

There was also much emphasis on other names. Both sides capitalised on well-known supporters though latterly the "No" campaign made most use of the device. The *Daily Record* grumbled about impressionable voters hitching themselves to a star. This complaint missed the point. Committed devolutionists were not going to forsake their allegiance to follow a pop-star, football hero or captain of industry. But for the less certain these public declarations demonstrated that other people had doubts and, while Scottish, could oppose the Assembly. The publicity legitimated a point of view and gave substance to a current of opinion. In the early part of the period the anti-Assembly reader of most papers might have believed he was on his own. By the end of the campaign this impression would have been dispelled.

One final paragraph must be devoted to the question of editorial comment or leader columns — popularly regarded as the voice of a paper. The impact of editorial opinion on other institutions and elites has been noted, but there is no evidence to suggest that such columns themselves influence readers. A major contribution to the study of media effects has been the recognition that audience members use the Press, radio and television for many different reasons — entertainment, information, social status among them. Some people do seek reinforcement of their own views but others, who may buy the paper rather for sports news or car adverts or local gossip, may use the paper's political position much as a navigator may be acquainted with a landmark but will never visit it. Papers are associated with a cluster of views and their position on a new topic will be interpreted in the context of their existing views. In Dundee for example, the Labour movement, in backing devolution, made the connection that the Dundee *Courier*, anti-trade union and anti-socialist, was also anti-devolution.

Conclusion

It is worth repeating that, given the present understanding of the subject, there is no ready means of assessing the effect of the Scottish morning Press on the referendum campaign. There is, however, a growing awareness that the Press performs a central role in the political process and is potentially of great influence.

The role of the Scottish Press in presenting to outsiders an image of Scotland more passionately devolutionist than the popular vote indicated, has already been noted. It has also maintained devolution on the agenda of political issues and provided a forum for the development of the subject. These are both considerable effects.

As for effects on the electorate, the agenda-setting function and the spiral of silence have both been found to operate in certain circumstances with certain people. If they were operating in the referendum campaign it can be argued that the more likely beneficiary in each case was the "No" campaign. This observation contrasts with the pro-devolution stance of the majority of the Scottish Press and serves as a warning against confusing media effects with media intentions. A study of the Scottish Press on any future political occasion could usefully develop the concepts of agenda-setting and the spiral of silence. There is no reason to suppose that these and other explanations of behaviour need be mutually exclusive. There may well be a complex of effects in operation on such occasions with different aspects of media activity affecting different groups of audience members. The very limited assessment possible on this occasion should, however, serve notice that the traditional approach of cataloguing the Press and its declared positions contributes little to understanding the effects on political behaviour.

REFERENCES

1. McLean, I. "The Politics of Nationalism and Devolution". *Political Studies* 25:3, September 1977. p. 427.
2. Royal Commission on the Press. Chairman McGregor O. R. HMSO Cmnd 6810, 1977 pp. 15ff.
3. Ibid. pp. 77-78.
4. MacKay, D. I. (Ed.) *Framework for Change.* Edinburgh: Paul Harris, 1979.
5. See, for example, the successive Nuffield General Election studies.
6. McQuail, D. *Towards a Sociology of Mass Communications.* London: Collier, 1969, p. 63. His comments on the Third World are equally applicable to the Western world.
   Fagen, R. *Politics & Communication.* Boston: Little, Brown & Co., 1966, p. 42.
7. Murdock, G. & Golding, P. "Capitalism, Communications and Class Relations". *Mass Communications & Society* (Ed. by J. Curran, M. Gurevitch & J. Wooleacott). London: Arnold, 1977.
   Wilson, B. "Devolution is appeasement that is doomed to fail". *Journalism Studies Review* 1:1, 1976.
8. Blumler, J. "The intervention of television in British Politics". Appendix E to the Report of the Committee on the Future of Broadcasting. Chairman Lord Annan HMSO Cmnd, 6753-1 1977. pp 3-13.
9. Dalyell, T. *Devolution: the End of Britain.* London: Jonathan Cape, 1977, pp. 196-99.
10. Pool, I. de S. & Shulman, I. "Newsmen's fantasies, audiences, and newswriting." *People, Society & Mass Communications* (Ed. by L. Dexter & D. White). New York: Free Press, 1964, pp. 14ff.
11. White, T. *The Making of the President.* New York: Atheneum, 1973, p. 259. This provides an illustration of one medium acting as "bulletin board" for the rest.
12. Blumler, J. op. cit. p.1.
13. Kraus, S. & Davis D. *The Effects of Mass Communications on Political Behaviour.* Pennsylvania: Pennsylvania State University Press, 1976, p. 213.
14. McLeod, J., Becker, L. & Byrnes, J. "Another look at the agenda-setting function of the Press." *Communications Research* 1:2, April 1979.
15. Lasswell, H. "Nations and classes, the symbols of identification". *Public Opinion and Communication* (Ed. by B. Berelson & M. Janowitch). New York: Free Press, 1966, p. 39.

84   SCOTTISH GOVERNMENT YEARBOOK 1980

16. Budge, I. & Urwin, D. *Scottish Political Behaviour*. London: Longman, 1966, p. 136.
17. *The Scotsman* 20/2/79.
18. Noelle-Neumann, E. "Turbulences in the climate of opinion: methodological applications of the spiral of silence theory". *Public Opinion Quarterly* 41, 1977, pp. 144-45.
19. *Glasgow Herald* 9/10/78.
20. *Scottish Daily Express* 1/3/79.
21. Gallup Opinion Polls, passim 1978-79.

6

A TIME TO LAY DOWN REFERENDUM RULES*

CHRIS BAUR
The Scotsman

There must be a sore temptation in some sulking Government quarters to regard the so-called "indecisive" Scottish referendum as an event which seriously discredits this particular method of popular consultation. The reason is that, unlike the 1975 Common Market referendum, this one committed the unforgiveable sin of giving the Government the answer they didn't want. Far from getting them off an awkward political hook, it has impaled Labour even more firmly than before.

This has been a severe caution to politicians about the unexpected perils of "asking the people". And, as a matter of fact, that warning applies just as much to future Conservative governments, however loudly the Tories may now be crowing about the way they imagine this particular poll has vindicated their trust in the permanence of the Union and the wisdom of the electors.

For, whether it is about complex constitutional matters like this, or about more sharply-focused issues like trade union rights, individual liberties or even penal reform (all of which have been suggested, from time to time, as subjects for consultative polls), the fact is that at the end of the day only governments can order referendums. What this one has shown is that governments can sometimes get it wrong.

Of course, it is perfectly possible to represent this poll as some kind of mystical vehicle of divine justice. Didn't Labour, after all, get exactly what they deserved? They were unable to agree about the Scottish Assembly proposals in Parliament. So they passed the parcel to the people. The people shook it, squeezed it, listened to it and promptly passed it back again.

---

* This article is reprinted from *The Scotsman* of 16 March 1979 with the kind permission of the editor.

"I don't know what's in it either, mate. Here, you take it. Anyway, Tam says it's ticking."

In any case, should we necessarily be surprised that the people, having taken a bewildered lead from their confused elected representatives, should have produced such an appropriately ambivalent result? The debate in Parliament and the campaign itself had both been confusing enough, in all conscience, so why shouldn't the result reflect this?

On the "Yes" side, the crucial ambiguity, which continues to disfigure the parliamentary debate about what to do next, is how on earth Labour could seriously propose that a Scottish Assembly would strengthen the UK, when their main campaign allies, the Nationalists, said it was the first step to independence.

On the "No" side, the principal contradiction, which will contort discussion for just as long, is how on earth the Tories could seriously hint at a richer pot of gold at the end of another devolution rainbow, when most of them are quite clearly prepared to regard a "No" vote (even this minority one) as the absolute end of the matter.

The referendum was quite unable to resolve these inconsistencies. Indeed, it reinforced them. It did so because of its central defect: the fact that, whatever the original intention, the poll was very soon transformed from being a straightforward test of the popular acceptability of the Scotland Act, into an additional subterranean battle about the popular acceptability of the Government.

This shaped the tactics on both sides. It enabled the Tories to unite solidly behind the expectation that a "No" vote would cripple the government in its most vulnerable year. Labour managers encouraged this by assuming at the outset that the poll would be a convenient and final celebration of their party's regained ascendancy in Scotland, just before a General Election. In this, the referendum was simply an extension of the Scotland Act itself, which the Government had insisted on treating as a purely Labour party matter.

The message was clear enough. If Labour were going to be obliged to have this confounded Assembly, then by heavens they would make sure they shared with no one the credit for having delivered it. They proceeded in a manner which effectively excluded from any working relationship all those Conservatives, Liberals and Nationalists whose personality or machinery could have helped them deliver the full potential "Yes" vote.

For the politicians the main lesson in all this is surely the clear demonstration of three dangers: the first is the danger of putting the Government's authority on the line through a referendum called on a specifically sectional issue; the second is the danger of doing so when the Government's own party has such internal doubts as to be incapable of providing enough troops on the day; and the final danger is in chosing a time for the poll when the result itself is put in hazard by the unpopular management of totally unrelated issues like — in this instance — pay policy and industrial relations.

For the rest of us — the two-thirds who voted both this time and last — the main lesson is surely the way the Scottish exercise has now confirmed what we may only have suspected in 1975: that we were not after all, as we may have fondly imagined, engaged in a solemn and historic consultation with our parliamentarians.

Only now is it possible to see the reality . . . that the device of the referendum is in fact little more than a shabby plaything of party politicians whose most spectacular facility throughout has been the perfectly dazzling display of fancy skating around some of the accepted conventions of British democracy.

It is this, much more than the Government's insufferable hand-wringing about the "inconclusive" result, which goes furthest towards discrediting the still-popular idea of the referendum as a useful and lasting part of the constitutional machinery of this country. Its validity will only be restored properly if we draw on the experience of this unsavoury Scottish poll to establish now some clear rules and firm understandings about the conduct of referendums in the future.

There are five quite specific respects in which Parliament badly needs to do itself and the rest of us a favour by thinking again about the non-existence of referendum rules, and about the propriety of those which have already been established through the "case law" of the two polls we have had so far. These are:

1. Timing

The Common Market poll established that the Government would dictate the timing of the poll, in much the same way as they have prerogative to decide the date of a General Election at the most favourable moment in a five-year term. The Scottish exercise significantly modified that freedom.

A legislative amendment and a verbal promise extracted by the Assembly opponents ensured that this particular poll could not be held during the month immediately before or the three months immediately after a General Election. This helped to guarantee that the referendum became a secondary pawn in the primary manoeuvrings about the timing of an Election.

With almost eighteen months of Labour's term still to run, the opponents' amendment nevertheless made it impossible for the Government to make an immediate announcement about the timing of the referendum without also closing some of the early options for the all-important Election. For a critical period last summer, therefore, the date of the referendum had to be as uncertain and secret as that of the Election.

The way in which the referendum became inextricably bound up with the fate of the Government was a massive initial distraction from the debate about the issue of devolution itself. For future referendums the Government should announce the timing of the poll as part of the legislative package — much as was done, in fact, with the Common Market referendum.

2. Threshold

Both the Common Market and the Scottish referendums were "advisory". In theory Parliament retained the right to say that it would not consider itself bound by the result, however clear the majority. In practice, MPs did accept the straight 67-33% UK "Yes" majority on a 65% poll in 1975.

They broke new ground, however, with the Scottish poll by setting a voting threshold below which the Scottish Assembly scheme could not be considered entirely secure. If the "Yes" votes represented less than 40% of all those entitled to vote, then MPs would be given a chance to reject this year's straight 52-48% "Yes" majority on a 64% poll, and repeal the whole legislation.

This tricky little notion established two things. First, no matter how much MPs may protest the opposite, it did in fact breach the theory of the referendum as a purely advisory device. It not only instructed the Government on a specific course of action following a sub-40% "Yes" vote. In doing so it also tacitly defined the mandate for implementation — for a "Yes" vote of more than 40% would clearly have had the moral force to bind Parliament, without the sour argument we are now having.

Secondly, it introduced an entirely new concept into British politics by ensuring that the final judgement of the result would take account of those who did not vote. On 1 March there were just as many abstainers as in 1975. But this time they have effectively been laid against the "Yes" total in a way which permits the Assembly opponents to proclaim, quite predictably, that 67% of the eligible voters did not want devolution. How many of them claim, by the same token, that 56% of eligible voters did not want the UK to stay in the Common Market?

There is a perfectly respectable case for inventing a yardstick to measure popular enthusiasm for a constitutional change of this sort — let us say two-thirds of those voting. There is absolutely no respectable argument for doing it in this way. It quite needlessly convulsed and embittered the campaign and damaged the prospect of reconciliation in the aftermath. Moreover, it set our electoral registration system a task for which it was never designed and for which it proved to be no match.

If MPs are ever tempted to play with this toy again, they will prevent it being regarded as a tawdry manipulation only by making two gestures: first, by ordering beforehand a comprehensive overhaul of our creaking and, in parts, rotten annual survey of eligible voters; and second, by insisting beforehand on a substantial increase in the scope and effectiveness of the postal franchise for the many thousands of voters whose disablement, illness and removal enforced their abstention when it really mattered.

3. Information

The Government made a serious error of judgement in not issuing a simple explanatory leaflet to all voters about the proposed change. This was done during the Common Market referendum. But on this occasion, the opponents of devolution threatened behind the scenes to withhold financial authority for the publication on the quite spurious grounds that it would be impossible to produce an unbiased description of the scheme.

The Government believed these threats and caved in. As

G

a result we are now being treated to febrile claims from the very people who were instrumental in preventing the distribution of such a leaflet, that voters did not understand the issues. In any future referendum, finance should be allowed for such a leaflet. Its "neutrality" could quite easily be guaranteed by an all-party committee.

4. Broadcasting

The Scottish campaign has left the normal understandings about Party Political Broadcasting (PPBS) in a total confusion. Tam Dalyell will not easily be forgiven for putting an elegant Etonian knee into the groin of Keir Hardie House, by persuading the Court of Session to ban the projected PPBs because they would have favoured the "Yes" side in a ratio of three-to-one.

Yet he had no alternative. Labour were determined to deny their influential "No" rebels the airtime which common fairness suggested they were entitled to have. The Court of Session ruling seems to have established that sponsored broadcasting during referendums should be sanctioned only on a strict "Yes-No" division, and not according to party interests.

That seems fair enough, but only if the ruling is now used to work out some clear new understandings about equality of access to sponsored broadcasting for future referendums.

5. Money

It is a simple fact that neither of the two British referendums have been regulated by any rules regarding finance. In normal elections, there are quite strict limitations on the amount of money that constituency organisations are permitted to spend to solicit votes. An election agent's accounts are open to legal challenge.

These requirements have not applied to the referendums. Even if it was impossible (which it is not) to ensure an upper limit of expenditure by both sides, it should certainly not be impossible to insist on the publication of campaign accounts.

It is, finally, a fair bet that not one single political finger will be raised in a serious effort to achieve any of these five reforms, as a means of rekindling the notion of fairness in the public's perception of the referendum device. By the time the next one comes round, the political circumstances will have changed — and so, you can be absolutely certain, will the rules.

7

THE 1979 GENERAL ELECTION CAMPAIGN IN SCOTLAND

PETER HETHERINGTON
The *Guardian*

The days of the Labour Government were numbered from the moment the referendum result was declared in the counting centre at New St Andrews House, headquarters of the Government's devolved administrative machine in Scotland, in the late afternoon of March 2. Mr Bruce Millan, the Secretary of State for Scotland, looking tired and dejected, promised at a hastily arranged news conference that the Cabinet would closely study the outcome before reaching a decision. But in his heart he must have known that the Government's battle for short-term survival, since the ending of the Lib-Lab pact, had been lost; that there was little chance of whipping Labour backbenchers into line, even if the Government favoured such precipitate action.

The Scottish National Party, for a change, was relatively united on the tactics to adopt in Parliament the following week: a firm commitment from the Government to act speedily on the close-run "Yes" result, by imposing a three-line Whip on Labour MPs . . . or else. When, almost three weeks later, Mr Callaghan rose to make his long-delayed announcement on the future of the Scotland Act, followed by a special television broadcast to explain the Government's motives — surely one of his least impressive, and unconvincing performances? — there were those both in the parliamentary Labour Party and outside who thought the eleven SNP MPs were bluffing. In some quarters there were rumours that the group was sufficiently split to guarantee the Government's survival in any confidence vote. But, in the words of one moderate Nationalist member who has often differed with his colleagues over tactics and ideology: "Everyone by then was bloody weary — they had a couldn't-t-care-less attitude and didn't want to prolong the agony any longer."

Mr Callaghan's offer of bilateral talks, to determine "whether a measure of agreement might not be found to provide for the better government of Scotland", cut little ice. Mr Donald Stewart accused him of treating the Scots with contempt and promptly slapped down a no confidence motion, although some leading members of his party back home — notably Mrs Margo MacDonald and Professor Neil MacCormick — did appear to express doubts about the parliamentary's group's tactics. The Tories then jumped in behind the SNP to table the official opposition motion.

At the end of the crucial debate, six day later on March 28, the SNP MPs proudly proclaimed that, for the first time, a Government had been brought down on a Scottish issue by a group of Scottish MPs who were not prepared to see their country betrayed by Westminster yet again. Nevertheless, several SNP members — notably Mr George Reid and Mr Hamish Watt, who had recently rebelled twice against the group — did apparently have some reservations about the timing of the exercise.

The MPs, while bracing themselves for a setback, still expected to remain a reasonably influential force after the Election. They were genuinely undismayed by recent opinion poll findings, which put Nationalist support at less than 20% and falling, pointing out that in the two elections of 1974 SNP standing was consistently underestimated by around 10%. The predictions of Labour's Mr Willie Hamilton during the no confidence debate that "the SNP will soon be able to get their MPs into a single taxi, if not on a bike", were laughed out of the Palace of Westminster. As it turned out, a tandem would have been quite handy.

Although the campaign proper was still two weeks away, the gloves came off only hours after the Government defeat — by one vote — in a heated Radio Scotland discussion. Mr Millan, annoyed and somewhat puzzled by the Nationalist tactics, labelled the SNP — rather appropriately — the "suicide squad". Mr Donald Stewart, then leader of the parliamentary party, calmly puffed his pipe and maintained that the Scots were seething with indignation over Labour's "refusal" to honour its manifesto commitment. The SNP slogan, repeated time and again during the campaign — "we wuz robbed" — was already wearing thin. After all, how could the Nats expect to convince voters that Labour was not to be trusted when they, not the Government, had effectively killed the Act by rejecting Mr Callaghan's offer of talks on the future of the legislation. Not surprisingly, there are now those in the SNP who think the party could have salvaged rather more from the Election, displayed a more credible image, had the MPs given the Government the benefit of the doubt — "a longer rope to hang themselves on", as Mrs MacDonald might have put it.

Of course, the great mass of the party, instinctively lukewarm towards devolution anyway, was quite pleased to see the back of the Scotland Act. At a rally on Edinburgh's Calton Hill, high above the splendid Royal High School that had been renovated to provide a home for the Assembly, only two-hundred activists turned up for what was billed as a major pre-campaign rally, the weekend after the Commons vote, under the slogan "Scotland Said Yes on March 1". A couple of years ago several thousand could have been expected. After a short time, it broke up in disarray as a more belligerent faction chanting "independence — nothing less" paraded down Princes Street, against police advice, to the embarrassment of more moderate elements. There was the odd scuffle and a couple of arrests.

Right at the start of campaigning it seemed that the subject which had topped the political agenda in Scotland for the last twelve years or so was destined to become the great non-issue in the Election, relegated to the bottom of the priority league by the overriding all-British issues — prices, jobs, the economy — which were to dominate the campaign. Perhaps there was some faint home-rule passion lingering in the subconscious, but as the *Glasgow Herald* reported in one of its regular System Three polls shortly before the Election, only 3% of those questioned put devolution as a key issue. It fell behind the power of the unions (4%) while law and order — to the amazement of Teddy Taylor — attracted only 8%. Right at the top were jobs and employment (28%) and the cost of living — predictably — with 47%.

Nevertheless, from the outset all the main British parties, for the first time, were determined to inject a noticeable Scottish dimension into the campaign with separate manifestos — differing in varying degrees from the main documents — and separate policies in certain areas. Until 1974, when the SNP shook the British Constitution to its foundations, the two main parties did not see the need to campaign on a Scottish manifesto (although the Scottish Liberals, devolved from their London machine under a quaintly Liberal federal structure, have invariably gone their own way to some extent).

Labour experimented with a modest document in February 1974, then with a much bolder manifesto the following October, positively radical in tone compared with its successor last April. No mention, this time, of an irreversible shift in the balance of power in favour of working people and their families. The Tories, on the other hand, published a short, typewritten "Charter for Scotland" in October 1974. It was unimpressive in design, but near heretical in content by today's Tory standards: separate Scottish budget, oil fund, legislative Assembly, and generally much stronger on the Home-Rule front than Labour's commitment for an Assembly with substantial powers over the "crucial areas of decision-making".

This time both main parties were noticeably cooler on the subject. Labour naturally retained its commitment to devolution, although several prominent members of the Scottish party had been urging the Scottish executive to ditch its support for the Scotland Act at Labour's Scottish conference the previous month in Perth. But there was no mention this time of "crucial areas of decision-making", although Mr Millan claimed at a news conference to launch the manifesto that such a commitment still stood.

The Tories, after successfully mobilising much of the "No" lobby in the referendum campaign — and converting others with a little help from Lord Home ("vote no for a better act") — could afford to be vague. No wild talk about an Assembly this time, only a pledge to repeal the much-maligned Scotland Act because "fewer than one in three people" supported the Government's proposals. Perhaps so, but still a considerably higher level of support than the Conservatives achieved in Scotland on May 3.

Then there was, predictably, more waffle about the need for an all-party conference — the classic get-out from them — to see if improvements could be reached in the system of government: "We aim to bring government closer to the people and allow more decisions affecting Scotland to be made in Scotland." No one, least of all the party hierarchy, seemed quite sure what this meant although Mr Teddy Taylor, as the

Tories' chief Scottish spokesman, had privately canvassed the idea of bringing the Scottish Grand Committee from Westminster to Edinburgh (presumably with a suitable weighting of English MPs to reflect the party balance at Westminster) and televising its sittings.

Labour, like the Conservatives, did not rate devolution as a top priority: the former placed much emphasis this time not on creating "more and better jobs in Scotland", but on saving existing jobs; the latter, as in England, was largely pre-occupied with cutting income tax, law and order — that is, setting up anti-vandal squads, reviewing the working of children's panels, etc. — selling council houses and reforming trade unions.

Yet, unlike the party south of the border, Labour effectively managed to set the tone of the campaign from day one, to drive the Tories into a corner from which they found it difficult to escape. The only way out for them, it seemed, was compromise, and by the end of the campaign the seemingly aggressive Tory industrial policy had been considerably tempered north of the border. "Forget what Sir Keith Joseph and his allies are saying — we'll be much different in power up here", they were implying at the end of Press conferences.

Mr Callaghan began the assault in his opening speech to 3,000 supporters in Glasgow's Apollo Centre on 9 April. (He warned that Scotland could become an industrial desert — more and more jobs at risk — if the Tories practised what they were preaching. Mr Millan, two days later, elaborated. "We take the very simple view that we shall save jobs wherever we can," he said. "The Tories, as I understand it, are fighting this election on the basis that where jobs are uneconomic and profits are not being made the Government should stand back . . .".

The following week Mr Millan drove the message home further as the Tories desperately searched for a new initiative to counter this onslaught: there was not a single industrial project in Scotland, he said, that did not depend on Government support of one form or another. As if to underline this point, he then persuaded the Secretary of State for Industry, Mr Eric Varley, to keep open two plants run by Prestcold Refrigeration (a subsidiary of British Leyland employing almost 1,000 on the doorstep of his Glasgow constituency) which the parent company wanted to close, pending an investigation by the National Enterprise Board. The Government, he said, would foot the bill to keep the factories open in the meantime. Mr Teddy Taylor, fighting for his political life in a predominantly working-class seat, naturally found it extremely difficult to condemn the exercise, although Sir Keith Joseph was more forthright; "a shabby political manoeuvre", he thought.

Labour had more ammunition in its armoury. What was the Tory attitude towards the Scottish Development Agency, created by the Wilson Government with the awesome task of regenerating the Scottish economy? Mr Denis Healey, visiting East Dumbartonshire — then Britain's most marginal seat with a majority of twenty-two — claimed the Tories would cripple the agency, then litter Scotland with bankrupt firms. In fact Conservatives, although hostile to the concept of the Agency, had only promised to issue it with new guidelines to ensure that investment was channelled towards assisting industries with a "viable" long-term future — exactly what the Agency had been trying to do anyway. No doubt aware that she had to counter the Labour onslaught before it got out of hand, Mrs Thatcher, at a subsequent news conference in Glasgow, was rather more explicit: the Agency, she said, had a tremendous advantage over its big brother — the National Enterprise Board — because it had to open its books to the House of Commons Public Accounts Committee. Then in her first speech since assuming office, the week after the election at a truncated Scottish Tory conference in Perth, the new Prime Minister actually accepted that investment through the SDA was necessary — in the short term at least — to plug an equity gap for venture capital which private institutions were unable to fill. With some justification, Labour claimed afterwards that its vigorous campaign had at least educated Mrs Thatcher in the economic facts of life in Scotland.

Meanwhile the Scottish National Party, which had become used to forcing both main British parties onto the defensive over the previous five years, found that it was actually being pushed onto the periphery of the campaign — squeezed out, as frustrated party leaders finally conceded — as Labour and the Tories slogged it out on the economic front. Ruefully they remembered Callaghan's jibe on 28 March that if the SNP voted for the no confidence motion "it would be the first time turkeys had voted for an early Christmas". Indeed, there were times when the SNP almost seemed an irrelevance, which just goes to prove that when the tide is running against a party no amount of publicity can put it back on course. Party election funds had been swelled by two sizeable bequests. Tens of thousands of pounds were spent on a series of advertising hoardings, SNP election broadcasts were snappy, even impressive on occasions. But the advertising was often long-winded, indigestible and certainly not eye-catching. And, of course, there was little or no mention of independence. The message, simply, was that the SNP had put Scotland at the centre of the Westminster stage — and wouldn't the electors be foolish to throw all that away by reinforcing the tired, discredited, two-party system. Well, they did.

SNP election addresses were often uncharacteristically defensive, pointing out that the party was pro-NATO, pro-Queen and pro-Commonwealth, in favour of an association of British states, for a mixed economy and the *status quo* and certainly against customs posts at Gretna Green and Berwick upon Tweed. Mr Douglas Crawford, defending Perth and East Perthshire, even managed to dig out a photograph of himself shaking hands with the Queen during her jubilee visit to the constituency.

The Nationalist campaign really got off to a disastrous start. Mr Willy Wolfe, the retiring chairman, was forced to take the opening Press conference in Glasgow single-handed. Party officials, at times, found it difficult to hide their embarrassment at the absence of some of the former MPs. Suddenly, rather pathetically, the SNP was portrayed as a crankish party, on the fringe of politics, which was not to be taken too seriously. "If I was watching them for the first time I would dismiss them as a bit of a joke," remarked one seasoned observer despairingly afterwards.

Valuable television time had been wasted by the party leader's uninspiring performance. In the final week of the campaign the SNP attempted to repair the damage by persuading Mr Donald Stewart to venture into the Glasgow conurbation for a brief visit from his Western Isles outpost. He reckoned the pundits had it all wrong, and that the party would do considerably better than the opinion polls suggested. Few took him seriously, although the scale of the party's collapse exceeded the most pessimistic forecasts.

By the end of the campaign, both main parties could afford virtually to ignore the Nationalists although Mrs Thatcher made a token visit around North-east Scotland to rally the Tory troops in the region where the SNP made its most significant break-through in 1974. At a preceding rally in Edinburgh, she re-peated that the Tories would never lumber the Scots with what she called "fresh and costly layers of bureaucracy". As for constitutional change: "The devolution in which we believe above all is the devolution of power from politicians and the state to the people themselves." When Mrs Thatcher glanced at *The Scotsman* that same day, she no doubt noticed the findings of an Opinion Research Centre poll. It showed that since the referendum, support for scrapping the Assembly had declined; two-thirds of those questioned said they would back moves to either improve the Scotland Act, or find an alternative for it. Ah well.

Then, six days before the Election, the Tories produced what they hoped would be their trump card: a Labour convert — well, he actually hadn't been a party member for some time — in the shape of Lord Wilson of Langside, one time Solicitor General for Scotland, who had been sitting in the Lords as a crossbencher. He had been joint chairman of the wealthy Scot-land Says No group during the referendum campaign. Mr Teddy Taylor could not hide his excitement, on a Press conference platform, when he introduced Lord Wilson as the latest in a long line of Labour Ministers who had been forced out of the party by the Left. In fact, when questioned, Lord Wilson stressed that he would not be joining the Tories, only working for them for the first time. He admitted at one stage that he had no real objection to the Labour manifesto. Indeed, he conceded that the 1945 manifesto, on which he originally cam-paigned, was a far more radical document. But, said Lord Wilson, times had changed since then.

However, this ingenious little public relations exercise did not seem to benefit the Tories greatly. As expected, they picked up seven seats from the Nationalists, by slender majorities, but failed to make any great impact in the areas that mattered: the industrial heartlands of West Central Scotland, where the Tories were so (relatively) strong in the mid-50s. Their share of the vote rose from 24.7% to 31.3%, almost entirely at the expense of the SNP. Writing in *The Daily Telegraph* the fol-lowing week, Mr Teddy Taylor — who lost Cathcart because Labour, for the first time, managed to pull out their vote in the hugh Castlemilk scheme, and put against him John Maxton, nephew of the legendary Jimmy Maxton, leader of the ILP in Scotland — said the Tories would only become acceptable again in the West when they were judged by their deeds, not their words:

> "The inherent suspicion of Conservative policy . . . can in my view, only be overturned by a Conservative Government in action showing that its policies of enterprise and incentives can help to create the new secure enterprises and jobs which Labour policies have so singularly failed to bring about."

Liberals, who were surprisingly the only party to campaign on an ecological theme — they called for restrictions on nuclear power and on private cars in cities — increased their vote slightly from 8.3% to 8.5%. Like the SNP (down from 30.4% to 17.2%) they found it impossible to convert thousands of newcomers in North-east Scotland — where they had high hopes of taking West Aberdeenshire from the Tories — to their cause.

Labour (up from 36.2% to 41.8%) was naturally pleased, but certainly not overjoyed with its performance. It gained three seats — two from the SNP — to give the party exactly double the Tory number of twenty-two. But party officials are convinced they could have done even better had Mr Callaghan gone to the country the previous autumn, when Labour did particularly well in the Berwick and East Lothian by-election.

The tiny, breakaway Scottish Labour Party, as expected, was all but obliterated although Mr Jim Sillars, its founder, while losing his seat, polled more than 12,000 votes in South Ayrshire. Afterwards, he came close to conceding, in a Scottish Television interview, that the whole exercise, in retrospect, might be considered questionable. "An historical mistake?" asked the interviewer, Colin Mackay. "Oh, that's possible," replied a surprisingly cheery Mr Sillars, who said he was now finished with politics. "Time alone will tell." Mr George Reid, the ex-television journalist who masterminded the SNP's election broadcasts, was also reflective. Sad, he thought, that Scotland would not now be getting a fair share of her resources. Then, in apparent disillusionment, he called for a new political initiative by supporters of Home Rule. Time, perhaps, for a new "third force" in Scottish politics?

The problem for the Conservatives was how to govern

Scotland when they were so far behind Labour, although the Tories would undoubtedly have been seen in a more favourable light under a system of proportional representation. Even then, however, they would probably still have been eight seats behind Labour, whose representation could have been cut from forty-four to thirty. Mr George Younger, the new Secretary of State for Scotland, was undismayed, although mildly conciliatory on the social and economic front. There had been several times in the past, he recalled, when Labour had come to power nationally solely on the basis of its strength in Scotland — and the English hadn't complained then.

But, as the normally moderate Mr Donald Dewar implied in an untypically hard-line speech in his Glasgow Garscadden constituency a couple of weeks afterwards, there would be a limit to the patience of a Labour-dominated Scotland over the next year or so as a Thatcher Government pursued policies against the wishes of a large number of voters. The clamour for some form of self-government was still strong, indeed would get stronger during the lifetime of the present Government, he thought. "It may be that many who did vote No, or who abstained, may come to regret the indecisive result of the referendum as Mrs Thatcher's shock troops ride rough-shod . . . over Scotland," he predicted.

Perhaps Home Rule, once again, will become increasingly popular inside a Labour Party which, ironically, strongly resisted pressure from Transport House to accept devolution in the first place six years ago. Sadly, this time, Labour will be in no position to deliver. It has had its chance.

THE SCOTTISH OFFICE 1954 - 79*

MARY MACDONALD
Retired Assistant Secretary, Scottish Office

ADAM REDPATH
Research Assistant

List of abbreviations

DAS = Department of Agriculture for Scotland (till 1960)
DAFS = Department of Agriculture and Fisheries for Scotland (from 1960)
DHS = Department of Health for Scotland (till 1962)
PUS of S = The Permanent Under-Secretary of State
SDD = Scottish Development Department (from 1962)
SED = Scottish Education Department
SEPD = Scottish Economic Planning Department (from 1973)
SHD = Scottish Home Department (till 1962)
SHHD = Scottish Home and Health Department (from 1962)

"The Secretary of State", unless otherwise indicated, means the Secretary of State for Scotland.

Twenty-five years have passed since the functions of the Scottish Office were described in evidence to the Royal Commission on Scottish Affairs 1952-54. What were they at the outset of 1979? Diverse enough to begin with, they had been further diversified, and increased in scale. The staff (excluding prison officers and State Hospital staff) had increased in number from about 5,000 to 8,000. This article attempts to describe some of the main areas of change, and how the structure of the Office has been modified in response to changes.

At the time of writing, our end-point is in the recent past; we have no knowledge of — nor do we intend to discuss — the outcome of devolution or any other possible new arrangements. Hence our use of the historic past tense, although the Scottish Office is alive and well and living in Edinburgh.

* © The Scottish Office. See introduction.

1. Industrial Development

The Gilmour Report 1936, which led to the creation in 1939 of the four Scottish departments, recognised that the Secretary of State had a general function of promoting Scotland's interests. They described this function as "penumbral"' and thought that the most senior Civil Servant in the Scottish Office, the Permanent Under-Secretary of State, (who was otherwise mainly a co-ordinator) should advise him on it rather than any of the departments. One of the most interesting stories is how this penumbra became the area in which Secretaries of State took perhaps the greatest interest, and wielded the most influence — winning some notable encounters with their Cabinet colleagues — until eventually it developed into a department with executive functions.

Scotland's interests were, in fact, closely identified with the promotion of industrial growth. This had been of concern to Secretaries of State since the Special Areas Act 1936. During the war, under Tom Johnston, an industry division was created in SHD. It was in close touch with the Scottish Council (Development and Industry) and with the Scottish Tourist Board; and it maintained continuous discussion in the Scottish interest with the departments directly responsible (particularly the Board of Trade) whom it also met at the Scottish Board for Industry and the Scottish Distribution of Industry Panel. The division prepared an annual White Paper which served as the text for a debate on Scotland's economy.

In 1961 the Toothill Report by the Scottish Council (Development and Industry) put forward ideas which were influential in the next decade. It recommended that the industrial and planning functions of the Scottish departments should be brought together in a new department which should have an economic unit. It also referred to the need for regional economic planning.

In 1962 came the reorganisation of departments under which the former SHD and DHS became the Scottish Home and Health Department and the Scottish Development Department. Industrial development was thus combined in SDD with local authority administration, land-use planning and New Town development, housing, electricity, water, sewerage, clean air and tourism. Planning was seen as giving coherence to all these functions. An interdepartmental group of officials, the Scottish

Development Group, was set up in 1963 "to stimulate and co-ordinate action designed to re-invigorate the Scottish economy".

Giving evidence in 1969 to the Select Committee on Scottish Affairs, Sir Douglas Haddow (then Permanent Under-Secretary of State) said "Scottish thought and Scottish practice pioneered in this country regional development policies". The first evidence of this was the White Paper, "Central Scotland: a Programme for Development and Growth", published in November 1963, which gave prominence to the concept of growth areas. A paper on north-east England was published at the same time.

With the advent of a Labour government in October 1964 a Department of Economic Affairs was set up to co-ordinate the Government's strategy for economic development in Great Britain. The Secretary of State was to take the lead in framing the plan for Scotland and in co-ordinating its execution. A Regional Development Division was set up, separate from the four Scottish departments and reporting to the Secretary of State through the Permanent Under-Secretary of State. This was in effect the counterpart of DEA in so far as the Scottish regional plan was concerned, DEA being responsible for the plans of other regions; but DEA was "the key department in evolving top policy". The machinery also included the Scottish Economic Planning Council chaired by the Secretary of State (1965); the Scottish Economic Planning Board of officials chaired by a member of RDD (1965); local consultative groups, each chaired by a member of the SEPC; a group of five economic consultants chaired by the Permanent Under-Secretary of State (1963).

In September 1965 the Government issued "The National Plan" which stated a growth target — a 25% increase in national output between 1964 and 1970. This was followed in January 1966 by "The Scottish Economy 1965-1970; A Plan for Expansion" which embodied the results of sub-regional studies. Transportation studies were also carried out. These papers marked the high point of large-scale economic planning; later the concept came under attack because the growth rates were not achieved, but much valuable information had been assembled, particularly in the sub-regional studies.

In 1965 the Highlands and Islands Development Board, of which more will be said in section 10, was set up.

In 1970 an economic and statistics unit, headed by a senior economic adviser, was set up in RDD. This strengthening was well timed, because the 70s were to set a new scene. Planning took second place to the task of coping with new events, notably the development of North Sea oil from 1973 onwards; the rise in fuel prices following the Middle East war of October 1973; and Britain's entry into EEC. In the same year the word "planning" was dropped from the title of the Scottish Economic Council.

In May 1973 special responsibility was conferred by the Government on Lord Polwarth, as Minister of State Scottish Office, for all aspects of oil development which affected Scotland. Shortly thereafter the Scottish Economic Planning Department was set up, on the same model as the other four Scottish departments — with a Secretary reporting to Ministers. In addition to the Regional Development Division functions it took over from the Scottish Development Department electricity supply, New Towns, Highland development, and the sponsorship of the Small Industries Council for Rural Areas of Scotland (SICRAS).

North Sea oil developments concerned all the Scottish Office departments: infrastructure, education and health services were needed, and fisheries were affected. Arrangements were set up within SDD to co-ordinate the provision of infrastructure. Great Britain departments were also concerned, notably the Department of Energy, set up in January 1974, which had a general remit on oil; and there were numerous other interested parties. Co-ordinating bodies were therefore required, and these included an Oil Development Council chaired by the Minister of State; a Standing Conference on North Sea Oil; and a Task Force of senior officials. When oil developments had got under way the pressure eased somewhat and these bodies were discontinued, with the Scottish Economic Council taking on the oversight of oil-related problems. A Fisheries and Offshore Oil Consultative Group continued to meet.

Meantime the rise in oil prices called for an energy policy which would include conservation. SEPD, being responsible for electricity, was given the task of co-ordinating this policy for Scotland.

Throughout the period of our study, government assistance in one or other form had been available to industry — either throughout the country, or preferentially in certain areas, which generally included the whole or part of Scotland. This was administered by the Departments of Trade and Industry or their predecessors. The Industry Act 1972 provided for regional development grants for capital projects in development areas, and for selective financial assistance.

In 1975 the function of providing selective assistance (and responsibility for export services) was transferred to the Secretary of State, acting through SEPD, which thus became an executive department with statutory functions and a sizeable block of casework. In the same year the Scottish Development Agency was set up with Government funds to provide investment facilities for firms in Scotland (the Agency also absorbed the functions of SICRAS; and it had functions in land reclamation, which are referred to in section 8). Meanwhile Britain had entered Europe, so that Scottish industry became eligible for aid from European funds, while at the same time it was necessary to ensure that aid from British Government sources complied with EEC directives. This entailed regular visits to Brussels.

"Economic planning" was now out and "industrial strategy" was in. This involved analysing the performance of individual industries, a process in which SEPD assisted.

The new department was faced almost immediately with the news that Chrysler (Detroit) was proposing to wind up its UK operation. This was high politics and it is not for us to conjecture what part the Secretary of State played either in the rescue operation as a whole, or the inclusion in it of Chrysler's Scottish factory at Linwood. But it is certainly typical of the personal attention which successive Secretaries of State have had to pay to Scotland's industrial interests.

One important ingredient had still to be added: responsibility for manpower. In 1977 the Secretary of State acquired joint sponsorship with the Secretaries of State for Employment and Wales of the Manpower Services Commission. A Director of Manpower Services was established in Scotland and a Manpower Services Committee for Scotland was set up.

2. Relations with Local Authorities

In 1954 there were 230 local authorities with populations ranging from over 1 million to under 400. Their powers varied, for example thirty-five were education authorities but all of them were housing authorities. It was difficult to obtain a con-

H

certed view from the three main negotiating bodies. The formula-based Exchequer Equalisation Grant was paid to equalise their rating resources, but their main source of central finance was specific grants towards some fifteen or more services, of which education was by far the largest. Departmental controls were exercised over the spending of these grants. Numerous detailed controls were also embodied in the enactments under which the authorities operated. There was a stated intention to give them more freedom of action, but this was difficult because many were too small and too weak in resources to carry out their functions effectively.

The first step was taken in 1959, when the specific grants for education and some other services were replaced by a general grant. The total for Scotland was negotiated annually and was related to the total estimated expenditure of all authorities on the relevant services, but the distribution between authorities was based on demographic factors. They were thus free to determine their priorities in spending this revenue resource. Capital expenditure was controlled through the Secretary of State's consent to borrowing. But there were still some important subsidies and specific grants which remained (e.g. police). In 1967 the Rate Support Grant was introduced which combined the main features of the general grant and the Exchequer Equalisation Grant, together with an element to finance pre-scribed reductions in domestic rates.

Proposals for local government reorganisation were made by the Wheatley Commission and were enacted, with some variations, in 1973 to take effect in May 1975. There were then nine regional authorities with major functions, fifty-three district councils whose functions included housing and local planning, and three general purpose island authorities. The Strathclyde Region covered about half the total population and was widely held to be unwieldy for many purposes, though well fitted for major planning. Many detailed controls were abolished. Consent was now required to capital expenditure instead of to borrowing. The new authorities formed themselves into a single negotiating body, the Convention of Scottish Local Authorities (COSLA).

This reorganisation enabled the departments to negotiate with the local authorities new methods of controlling capital expenditure. In 1977 a financial planning system, devised by a joint Scottish Office/COSLA working party, was introduced

for capital expenditure. Local authorities put forward their proposals for a five-year period, and formal consents were given for
the first year together with guideline figures for the ensuing
two years. Block allocations for services were issued, leaving
authorities to determine priorities of individual projects.

Professional staff in departments became more concerned
with design guidance to authorities than with project control.
Some staff reductions in departments were effected.

In educational building each authority was given a block
allocation covering all school and further education college
building; and project control by SED was relaxed. In water
supply and sewerage, in cases where specific grants applied, there
was still a degree of project control, but procedures were simpli-
fied. For roads and public transport, an annual statement of
transport policies and programmes was prepared by each council
and submitted as the basis for consent to capital expenditure.
The system for housing, which was on similar lines, is described
in more detail in section 3.

The concept of "disengagement" applied in other spheres
besides finance. Some of these are described in sections 4 and
8.

3. Housing

In the early years, the need was to keep up a big building
programme of houses for general purposes, subsidies being payable at a fixed rate per house. To qualify for subsidy, houses
had to conform with the department's standards. In 1957 the
department had "housing inspectors, each of whom pays regular
visits to the local authority schemes in his area where building
work is in progress, and examines in particular the standards
of workmanship".

As time went on there was more emphasis on housing for
particular needs (overspill, incoming industry, redevelopment of
town centres), on housing for older people, and on the improvement of existing houses. The subsidy was differentiated to take
account of varying factors, and was revised several times, but
always within this general concept. But there was still emphasis
on expansion. The White Paper "The Scottish Economy 1965-70
— A Plan for Expansion" was matched by "The Scottish
Housing Programme 1965-70" which announced a programme of
50,000 houses a year to be reached by 1970. It was not until

1976 that expenditure on new house building, which had for many years been open-ended, in so far as no limit was placed on the number of houses started in any year, became subject to annual expenditure limits.

Following on local government reorganisation, a joint SDD/ COSLA Working Party recommended in 1977 a revised system which would enable local authorities to plan according to their own concept of need, subject to the Secretary of State's consent to capital expenditure. Authorities were accordingly asked to submit for approval their first five-year housing plan for 1978-83. Each plan was to incorporate an analysis of housing provision and housing needs; a statement of the authority's objectives; and a costed capital programme. Project control was largely replaced by the issue of design guidance. These plans were to be reviewed and rolled forward annually; at the time of writing a second round was in progress.

To match this system a new form of government subvention, the Housing Support Grant, was enacted in 1978 to take effect on 1 April 1979. The total amount was to be fixed annually in consultation with COSLA and was to be related to estimated expenditure and estimated reasonable contributions from rents and rate funds. The distribution to each authority was to be based on that authority's need for expenditure in excess of a basic amount to be met from local resources.

The development of the new housing plans and the introduction of the Housing Support Grant were fundamental to the Green Paper "Scottish Housing — A Consultative Document" published in 1977; but that document also reviewed progress generally and invited consideration of a number of options.

Scotland pioneered the control of standards in housing as well as other types of building with the passing of national legislation to replace the former local authority by-laws. By 1963 the Building Standards (Scotland) Regulations had come into effect. Their review, updating and administrative oversight became the responsibility of a division in SDD reporting to the Chief Architect.

4. Education

The Scottish Education Department in 1954 was a small, tightly-knit department, much occupied with approving detailed schemes of educational provision and administering the education grant to local authorities, and through HM Inspectorate with the formal inspection of schools. The Inspectorate conducted the school-leaving examination and hence controlled the curriculum for many pupils. The department also exercised control over the grant-aided central institutions for higher education (other than the agricultural colleges which were the concern of DAS). Such institutions were mainly concerned with technical and vocational training. From 1955 the department administered the school milk scheme. The history since then has been one of diversifying functions — partly as education itself has extended and diversified — a lessening of detailed control, and greater involvement of other parts of the educational system in framing policy guidance.

Functions were added to the department in 1960. The administration of grants to students in higher education entailed a large block of routine work. Child-care functions came over from SHD, foreshadowing later developments in social work; also certain functions relating to the four older universities. The main Government involvement with universities remained however on a Great Britain basis, with SED providing an assessor to the University Grants Committee.

Some relaxations of financial control were made in 1959 when the former specific grant for education was merged in the general grant to local authorities. HM Inspectors were relaxing their regular detailed inspection and reporting of individual schools, and were devoting more time to development work. In 1965 the Scottish Certificate of Education was taken over by the SCE Examination Board. The Consultative Committee on the Curriculum was set up under SED chairmanship; by 1978 there was a network of working parties and sub-committees dealing both with individual school subjects and also with broader aspects of education. In this way the teaching profession, local authorities and others were brought in. HM Inspectors were still involved both in helping to frame the guidance produced by the committees and in bringing it to the notice of the education authorities mainly through their territorial organisation. They continued to produce reports of their own on general themes.

In 1965 the General Teaching Council was set up to maintain a register of qualified teachers — and thus to take over responsibility for the recognition of teachers from the Secretary of State — and to carry out functions, mainly advisory, relating to standards of entry to the teaching profession and to the training and supply of teachers.

Among the main growth points in education during this time were further education and vocational training; informal further education; and the provision of recreational and cultural opportunities for young people. These entailed the appointment of more specialists within the department as well as the setting up of bodies such as SCOTEC (The Scottish Technical Education Council) and SCOTBEC (The Scottish Business Education Council). The central institutions, reduced in number when Heriot-Watt and Strathclyde Universities were established, continued to be grant-aided by the department although subject to less detailed control. Another growth point was the teaching of the mentally handicapped, extended in 1974 to all mentally handicapped children some of whom had earlier been labelled "ineducable".

The Education (Scotland) Act 1969 relaxed a number of detailed controls. But some important controls were maintained, notably the requirement of the Secretary of State's consent to school closures. The Secretary of State's duty to inspect schools became a power. Inspection is now conducted with less formality and on a less comprehensive scale, but it remains the SED view that there is value to the teaching profession in a regular programme of inspections.

5. Social Work

The Kilbrandon Report on Children and Young Persons (Scotland) (1964) made two recommendations: a system of children's panels to replace juvenile courts; and a social education department in local authorities to cater for children with special needs. Comments on the report indicated a need for a more widely based department catering for families. A group was set up to study this concept and the result was a White Paper, "Social Work and the Community" (1966), which announced the Government's proposals to set up integrated social work departments. The decision to set up children's panels had already been announced.

These concepts were pioneered in Scotland. In 1968 the Seebohm Committee reported for England and Wales with broadly similar proposals for the setting up of social services departments: it did not deal with juvenile justice. There were exchanges of ideas among departments leading up to the enactment of the Social Work (Scotland) Act 1968 and the Local Authority Social Services Act 1970. The former Act took effect partly in 1969 and partly in 1971; and the latter in 1970.

An interdepartmental unit was set up to prepare for legislation and in 1968 this became the Social Work Services Group attached to SED. Social work advisers, working closely with the administrators, were organised as a Central Advisory Service.

The new local authority departments were to be built up from a number of elements, including probation which in England and Wales remained a separate service. Kilbrandon had recommended that the equivalent of probation supervision of children should be provided within the new departments; and a separate service for the adult offender would have been too small to be viable. This was among the most controversial aspects of the legislation. The Scottish service had been criticised in a 1962 report as not sufficiently linked with the court service, and its disappearance as a separate entity raised further criticism. Over subsequent years a better relationship with the courts was achieved but the service was still under stress in some areas.

Aftercare of offenders, which till 1963 had been carried out by SHD officers working to the Scottish After Care Council, had since then been a function of the probation authorities and was transferred to the new departments. Some of this work was still done by SHHD prison welfare officers who in 1973 transferred to local authority employment.

Other elements included the welfare and aftercare services which had been provided by local authorities for old people, for the ill, and for the mentally or physically handicapped; child care; and the care of homeless families — later to be transferred to housing authorities by an Act of 1977. All these functions were subsumed under a general duty on local authorities to promote social welfare in their areas: this function was more broadly expressed than in the English Act, and there were wider powers to give financial assistance. The approved schools, henceforth called "List D Schools", continued to receive Exchequer Grant and remained under direct control by SED in accordance with transitional provisions of the 1968 Act.

The Social Work Services Group had a heavy task, together with the local authorities, in laying the groundwork for the new system. The legislation, which was controversial, had to be prepared and carried through. Panels of volunteers to conduct the children's hearings had to be set up, the volunteers had to be trained and full-time reporters appointed. There were negotiations with training institutions to set up courses for social workers. Although Scotland had been ahead in ideas, the physical and other provision which existed at the time was poorer in some respects than in England and Wales; and it took several years to begin to build up towards a more acceptable level.

6. Roads and Transport

The transfer of "roads, bridges and ferries" from the Ministry of Transport to SHD in 1956 followed a recommendation by the Royal Commission on Scottish Affairs. It included the department's direct responsibility for the construction and improvement of trunk roads, together with the payment of grant to local authorities in respect of their expenditure on other roads. The timing was fortunate; Government expenditure on roads was increasing, and an Act had been passed to authorise a Forth Road Bridge. Work was started on the bridge in 1958 and it was opened in 1964. Subsequent major schemes included the Tay Road Bridge which opened in 1966. A good start was also made on the construction of a motorway network in Central Scotland and on the improvement of road links with England.

In 1967, with the object of giving local authorities more freedom in planning and programming the improvement of local roads, the financial support which they received through specific grants was incorporated in the general support to local authority revenues through the newly introduced Rate Support Grant. A specific grant continued to be payable for building or improving "principal roads". Central government expenditure on roads increased from £6m in 1957 to £42m (excluding Rate Support Grant) in 1970.

In the Highlands some limited assistance had been given since 1897 to rural roads and steamer services, and for some years past there had been further Government underpinning of MacBraynes. Wider powers to assist Highlands and Islands shipping services were conferred by an Act of 1960. The DAFS went into this with a will, taking part in the design of ships which were built to their order and chartered to MacBraynes and to the Orkney Islands Shipping Company Limited. A revenue subsidy was also paid.

The Transport Act 1968 created the Scottish Transport Group which took over the entire shareholding in the Scottish Bus Group and the half-share in MacBraynes which had been owned by the former Transport Holding Company. The assets of the Caledonian Steam Packet Company were also taken over, and later the Group acquired full control of MacBraynes. Responsibility for the Transport Group was placed on the Secretary of State who thus for the first time acquired functions on road passenger transport. A new division was formed within SDD to deal with the Secretary of State's responsibilities, which included grants to the Group for facilities in urban areas and to improve transport in rural areas. Other forms of transport such as railways and air services were not included in the Group's remit, nor were they among the Secretary of State's statutory functions, but throughout the period he had intervened in discussions on these matters when Scotland's interests were at stake.

In 1973 the Group's major ferry services were transferred to a new subsidiary, Caledonian MacBrayne, for operation on an unsubsidised basis. However, in 1975, owing to increased oil prices, the company could no longer pay its way without an unacceptable increase in charges and the Secretary of State introduced a revenue grant.

With the reorganisation of local government in 1975 a new financial and administrative framework was introduced for local authority activities on roads and public transport. An annual statement of transport policies and programmes was prepared by each regional and island council and submitted as a basis for consideration for consent to capital expenditure and for Rate Support Grant.

7. Water and Sewerage

The Secretary of State was responsible for national policy on water and sewerage services and for the quality of the aquatic environment. Local authorities and river purification authorities shared the management and operational activities for these functions.

Over the years SDD guidance influenced the planning of

major developments such as the Loch Lomond scheme to supply water in bulk to authorities in the populous central belt of the country. Through management of local authorities' programmes, control was exercised over their expenditure on the provision of services.

The growing concern of the public with the quality of the environment and the need for legislation to improve the appropriate services was recognised. The success of government policy in this field was monitored by surveys carried out and published on a national basis.

8. Land Use

The central department for statutory land-use planning was the Scottish Development Department. We have described in section 1 how this function, linked with others in the department, broadened out into the concept of regional planning in the 60s. Studies were made of sub-regions, and joint activities by local planning authorities were promoted.

A major concern at this time was the development of New Towns to take overspill population from the overcrowded areas of Glasgow and to provide growth areas for new industry. Development corporations were set up for five New Towns over the period 1947 to 1966. Other measures were taken to improve the environment and to promote its enjoyment. Reclamation of derelict land was carried out by local authorities and attracted a high rate of specific grant. The Countryside (Scotland) Act 1967 established the Countryside Commission for Scotland to develop facilities for the enjoyment of the Scottish countryside and for the conservation and enhancement of its natural beauty and amenity. The Act also provided for grants payable by the Commission on behalf of the Secretary of State for countryside purposes. The transfer to the Secretary of State of policy on ancient monuments, in 1969, recognised his concern with Scotland's heritage. The Secretary of State's responsibility for ancient monuments was made complete by his assumption, in 1978, of their care and custody.

The statutory machinery for land-use planning involved preparation of development plans by the local authorities and consideration by the Secretary of State of appeals against refusal of planning permission, as well as applications for permission which he had "called in" because of their importance. The small size of some planning authorities posed problems, especially in West Central Scotland. In 1972 a reporters' unit was set up as part of the Scottish Office Central Services (of which more will be said in section 16) mainly to secure greater speed in reporting of planning inquiries. The Planning (Scotland) Act 1969 divided the development plans into two tiers of which only the structure plans, in narrative form setting out the authority's policy and general proposals, were to be submitted for the Secretary of State's approval. There could then be a public examination in front of the reporter which would be confined to important issues previously announced, together with any other issues raised in representations. The system came into force with local government reorganisation and the new authorities were also required on this first occasion to prepare regional reports covering their economic and social plans as well as land use.

Agricultural and forestry uses of land were not subject to planning permission. Here DAFS had the main interest. The Forestry Commission, responsible for most tree planting in Scotland, agreed its proposals with DAFS. The department itself owned and managed a landed estate comprising mainly small holdings of land acquired for settling people on small plots, together with land acquired by the Secretary of State under the Forestry Acts but used meantime for agriculture. Including certain other properties the total extent of this estate in 1954 was 780,907 acres. But the department also had a more general interest in the effective use for food production of Scotland's sixteen million acres of agricultural land.

Agricultural executive committees, on which local interests were represented, had been appointed under an Act of 1948 (they were a revised form of a war-time organisation) to assist in promoting this interest. Up to 1958 they had powers of enforcement to ensure good husbandry and good estate management. Thereafter their function was confined to commenting on planning proposals which involved the diversion of agricultural land to other purposes. They also concerned themselves with pest control. In 1972 the committees were abolished and the functions reverted to the department.

Crofting was a special problem, because of the small and poor units and the type of tenure, which gave security but was not always helpful to the crofter in developing his holding. In 1955 the Crofters Commission was appointed; it had powers which were extended in 1961 relating to the tenure of the crofts, and also acted as the Secretary of State's agent in administering grants for agricultural development on crofts. The Commission recommended, and it was enacted in 1976, the crofters should have power to buy their holdings.

Numerous other public bodies also had an interest in land use — and the lack of any mechanism for "binding together separate policy strands" was criticised by the Select Committee on Scottish Affairs, "Land Resource Use in Scotland" 1972. A standing committee on land-use resources was thereafter appointed, representing three Scottish Office departments (DAFS, SDD and SEPD) together with the Countryside Commission for Scotland, Forestry Commission and Nature Conservancy. This proved a useful forum.

Meanwhile, in the 70s, the situation continued to change. North Sea oil developed, and this gave SDD the opportunity to issue national planning guidelines on coastal development — to be followed later by guidelines on the location of industry. Concern with overspill was replaced by concern for the decay of inner city areas. An urban renewal unit was set up in SDD in 1975. Shortly thereafter the development of Stonehouse, recently designated as Scotland's sixth New Town, was discontinued; and a number of initiatives followed to reverse the decline of Glasgow and its conurbation. The most notable of these was the Glasgow Eastern Area Renewal (GEAR) Project, led by the Scottish Development Agency but with close continuing departmental involvement. This project set the pattern for a number of inner city "partnership" schemes subsequently established south of the border. Also in 1975 the Scottish Development Agency (as one of its functions — the others are mentioned in section 1) took over from local authorities the grant-aided programme of land reclamation.

Forestry policy was reviewed by the Government in 1972; the planting programme was restricted and more stringent conditions were placed on grant aid to private forestry, though grants were increased in 1977. Following criticism by the Public Accounts Committee of the net cost of maintaining the small-holdings estate, DAFS began encouraging sitting tenants to buy their holdings. As a result of this and other measures, in 1975 the total extent of the estate managed by DAFS was reduced to 599,983 acres.

9. *Assistance to Agriculture and Fisheries*

The development of the Department of Agriculture and Fisheries for Scotland's role in supporting agriculture and fisheries during the period might be described as "from war time to Europe".

In 1954 there was still much concern with such matters as the control of scarce materials, the organisation of extra workers for the harvests, a machinery service to provide farmers with the use of tractors. Fixed prices for the staple agricultural products were decided in collaboration with the Ministry of Food, after an annual review in which producers were consulted. There was a ploughing-up grant to bring as much land as possible under cultivation.

Other subsidies were also payable, for example hill cattle and hill sheep, calf rearing and marginal agricultural production. Three Scottish milk-marketing schemes were in operation. Schemes were administered for livestock improvement. Pest control was actively pursued by the agricultural executive committee and grants were payable. The department was responsible for seven agricultural research institutes (later increased to eight), and was associated with three agricultural colleges which also provided an advisory service. Crop inspection and certification was provided as a service to the industry; there was provision for grants to capital works such as arterial drainage; minimum agricultural wages were enforced, and measures taken for the safety of workers.

By 1979 there had been many changes. Animal health responsibilities had been acquired, and with the dissolution in 1955 of the Ministry of Food, the annual price review had been conducted along with the Minister of Agriculture, Fisheries and Food on the basis of guaranteed minimum prices. Other added responsibilities included meat hygiene, milk and dairies hygiene, and administration of the Royal Botanic Gardens. Inspection duties under the fat stock guarantee scheme had been shed to the Meat and Livestock Commission, and safety of workers to the Health and Safety Executive. Pest control was still a concern, and was the subject of research, but the department was no longer taking the initiative in promoting co-operative schemes. The Red Deer Commission, set up in 1959 to deal with marauding deer, had gradually taken on a wider interest in the conservation and management of the national stock of deer. Marketing co-operation schemes had been set up under an Act of 1967. Relations with the agricultural colleges were concerned more with commissioning of research, in accordance with the Government statement "Government Research and Development" 1973, and less with the details of administration.

Accession to the European Community made a big impact on many of the department's functions. Up to 1973 the annual review had been a self-contained affair involving only the agricultural departments and the producers. But from 1973 its purpose changed to assisting in the formulation of UK policy in relation to the common agricultural policy of EEC. And since the UK was concerned to give due weight to consumer and manufacturing (including food-processing) interests, it was necessary to bring these interests into consideration. The Secretary of State, as a multi-purpose Minister, was well placed to take a broad view in the discussions at Ministerial level. For DAFS officials, it meant participation in the UK team engaged in formulating the policy which was generally presented at Brussels by MAFF.

The Secretary of State was one of the four Ministers responsible for the Intervention Board, set up under EEC policy to buy surplus stocks if the support price was not reached. DAFS officials were employed to check the quality of dairy products before purchase by the Board.

Application of the Community's common agricultural policy entailed changes in the system of grant and subsidy support. EEC directives were concerned with farm modernisation; income levels of those engaged in agriculture; and (of particular importance to Scotland) special aids for farming in less-favoured areas. Capital assistance for the development of farms and horticulture, along with the hill-farming subsidies, had to be adapted to Community requirements. Assistance was given from EEC funds for individual projects in Scotland. Other grants continued under UK or Scottish enactments.

In 1960 the department had acquired on transfer from SHD fisheries functions which included subsidy, capital assistance to the industry, responsibility for fishery harbours, research, fisheries protection, and participation in international negotiations. In the 70s there were crucial events. North Sea oil was developed; overfishing caused a decline in stocks; nations sought to extend their fishery limits; Britain entered the EEC. The English industry, which had depended more on distant-water fishing, declined relatively in importance so that Scotland came to have at least an equal voice in the affairs of the industry.

North Sea oil problems were met by the formation of a consultative group (also mentioned in section 1) which helped to foster better relations between the industries. Fishery limits and conservation presented a more intractable problem. In 1977 the UK and other EEC member states extended their limits to 200 miles, thus bringing the main fishing grounds under the jurisdiction of coastal states, but there was no agreement on a common fisheries policy covering quotas, access, conservation structure and control of enforcement. Interim arrangements were maintained. In all these discussions Scotland played an important part at Ministerial and official level.

The extension of limits increased the task of fishery protection. This was met by co-operation between the Royal Navy and the department's protection fleet with air surveillance by RAF Nimrods. Fish producer organisations, covering most of the fleet, were set up to operate the EEC marketing and support price system. Applications were submitted for aid from EEC funds towards capital schemes to improve fish marketing and processing.

10. The Highland Problem

The small minority of Scotland's population who live in the Highlands and Islands, and the large empty spaces around them, took up a good deal of departmental thinking. Some of this has been mentioned already: assistance to crofters and assistance to shipping services. The shipping services later became part of the Scottish Transport Group; and earlier there had been other Highland projects which paved the way for wider developments. The North of Scotland Hydro-Electric Board preceded the nationalised electricity industry; the Highlands and Islands (Medical Services) Scheme was a forerunner of the NHS.

In 1954 SHD, which had inherited from the old Scottish Office the responsibility of aiding MacBraynes, claimed also to have Highland responsibilities "of a more general kind". Jointly with DAS it serviced the Advisory Panel on the Highlands and Islands and it also chaired an interdepartmental committee which "keeps the whole Highland problem under review". This problem had been defined, in a programme presented to Parliament in 1950, as one of furthering economic development rather than preserving the existing population in their traditional pursuits. There was also a Highland division in DAS dealing with assistance to crofters, transport piers and township roads, and DAS had relationships with bodies such as the Scottish Country Industries Development Trust. In 1960 DAFS took over the general Highland responsibility along with fisheries and steamer services, while surrendering their township roads to SHD roads division. There followed a period of activity on shipping services as described in section 6.

The Royal Commission on Scottish Affairs had rejected the idea of a Highland Development Authority, with comprehensive powers and displacing the existing bodies with particular responsibilities for the Highlands. In the 1960s, however, there was growing recognition that special measures were needed to tackle the long-standing and intractable problems of the area; and there was continuing pressure from the Highland Panel for the introduction of executive machinery with powers to initiate and sustain economic development. This led to the establishment in 1965 of the Highlands and Islands Development Board, charged by statute to improve the economic and social conditions of the Highlands and Islands and to enable the area to contribute effectively to the national economy. The Board had executive powers to initiate developments and enterprises at its own hand, to make investments and to assist and support private sector undertakings across the whole range of the economy of its area. It did not however replace such existing bodies as the Crofters Commission, or the Forestry Commission, nor did it take over the discharge of the functions of individual Scottish Office departments in the area. A representative body, the Highlands and Islands Development Consultative Council, was set up to advise the Board on the exercise and performance of its functions.

The Board promoted developments in agriculture and fisheries but its main interest was in industry, for which it identified three growth areas. In 1968 it was given power to acquire equity in new or existing companies, in supplement of its previous powers to assist by grants and loans. In the same year it announced a major industrial development — the decision to locate a new aluminium reduction plant at Invergordon.

In the same year departmental functions were rationalised by the transfer from DAFS to SDD of responsibilities for Highland development. This included not only sponsorship of the Highlands and Islands Development Board, but shipping services, marine works, and relationships with bodies such as the Scottish Country Industries Development Trust. The transfer took account of the increasing emphasis on industry, including large-scale projects, and also brought together all transport functions in the department which was to deal with the newly formed Scottish Transport Group. When SEPD was set up in 1973 it took over Highland development together with tourism; transport matters, however, reverted to SDD in 1977.

In 1966 the population of the Highlands and Islands became stable, after a long period of continuous decline, and from then to 1977 it rose from 299,789 to 330,823. This, and marked improvements in employment rates and *per capita* earnings relative to Scottish and GB levels, can surely be regarded as consequences of the efforts made to deal with "the Highland problem". Then in the 70s came the development of North Sea oil which benefited some parts of the area. But the problems of the area as a whole were certainly not solved. And the Highlands had no monopoly of problems: even before the Highland clearances were forgotten the clearances of central Glasgow (to which so many Highlanders had emigrated) were beginning to cause anxiety.

11. Health Services

In 1954 the DHS was well established in its role of central department for the NHS which had been set up in 1948. The three arms of the service were administered by regional hospital boards, executive councils (for general practitioner services) — both directly responsible to the Secretary of State — and local authorities (mainly for preventive and aftercare services).

Health care changed and developed. Tuberculosis waned, geriatric problems increased. New medical discoveries created new demands. Long-stay care fell behind public expectations. As the services (and particularly the hospital service) became more complex there was a need for more tasks to be carried out on an all-Scotland basis. Some of these — for example the provision of legal advice to hospitals — were carried out by boards acting jointly, while in others — such as running the

I

Hospital Centre with its library and exhibition facilities — the boards and department participated. But many tasks fell on the department, which at one time was even running practical courses for hospital domestic workers.

Operational research, work study and collection of statistics were combined in 1965 to form a health service research and intelligence unit. In 1958 the Health Education Unit was set up. Central contracts for supplies were placed by the department. When the hospital long-term building programme was inaugurated in 1962, the department became heavily involved in the preparation of planning guidance. It was also involved in an actual building job: health centres could be provided either by local authorities or by the department, but it was the department which took the major part till 1974. In 1970 the Hospital Advisory Service was set up to monitor and advise on care in long-stay hospitals.

The reorganisation in 1974 of the Scottish and English health services was the outcome of a lengthy debate, in which Scotland — prompted by the disadvantages of a tripartite service, particularly as seen by general practitioners — was the first to raise the questions and to suggest some of the answers. Once the need for change had been accepted, the main point at issue was whether the local authority services should be brought into the new combined service. A difference on this between the two countries would not have been tolerated by the local authorities, so doubtless the point had to be argued out. But on other points there was agreement to differ; for example England had an extra tier of authorities and a more complex management structure.

In Scotland there were now fifteen health boards, each responsible for all health services in its area; and a Common Services Agency to carry out all-Scotland services under joint departmental and health service management. This agency took over from the department the Health Education Unit, the Research and Intelligence Unit (renamed Information Services) and the Supplies Division (except procurement policy). It also had diverse other functions, ranging from ambulance services to prescription pricing. It must have seemed a tidy idea: the department would be left free to concentrate on its policy functions, while various other *ad hoc* management devices (such as the provision of ambulance services by contract with the St Andrews Ambulance Association) would be rendered un-

THE SCOTTISH OFFICE 1954-79

necessary by bringing all these units within one agency. But the result was an unwieldy body which soon developed management problems.

One of the basic aims of the reorganisation was that long-term planning should be carried out in consultation with the professions working in the service. This involved the creation of the Scottish Health Service Planning Council, with several programme groups and advisory groups, a network of professional consultative committees, and a planning group within the department. So the department's professional staffs found their roles changing. In earlier years while maintaining contact with members of their professions, they had had a mainly advisory role within the department. Now they became increasingly involved with programme and advisory groups as well as in long-term planning. To make way for these new tasks there was a need to disengage themselves from other work; but this was not easy in a situation where fifteen new boards, faced with new responsibilities at a time of financial stringency, were finding the going hard.

12. Law and Order

From 1954 to 1978 the prison population more than doubled; figures for crime increased even more. Legal aid was extended by stages, covering criminal legal aid and advice and assistance. Capital punishment was abolished, and with it a painful area of decisions by the Secretary of State on the Royal Prerogative of Mercy, but difficult decisions still had to be made in this field and were sometimes the subject of public controversy. There was growing dissatisfaction about the prevention of crime and in various areas of law such as liquor licensing and divorce. There was the threat of nuclear war and the need to provide against civil emergencies, whether produced by storm, flood, fire or industrial action.

The department was heavily involved in the problem of crime, though needless to say no magic remedy was found. A Criminal Justice (Scotland) Act of 1963 incorporated recommendations of an advisory committee, mainly on custodial measures and compulsory aftercare for young adult offenders under twenty-one. Other measures substantially increased the courts' powers to impose monetary penalties. Accommodation in prisons and other penal establishments was increased, but not at the same rate as the prison population, so there was over-crowding. The Scottish Council on Crime in 1975 directed attention to preventive measures and gave support to developments in urban renewal. Community service orders, as an alternative disposal for offenders, were introduced experimentally in 1976 and were made generally available by an Act of 1978.

The main effort went into the strengthening of the police, whose numbers increased from 7,654 in 1954 to 12,399 in 1978. This increase was accompanied by a reduction, in stages, in the number of police forces; in a series of amalgamations these were reduced from thirty-three at the start of the period to twenty by 1970 and after the reorganisaion of local government to eight. The larger forces that resulted were better equipped to combat crime. During the same period the number of civilians employed in support of the police more than trebled.

Police training was developed. Centralised training for inspectors and sergeants began at the Scottish Police College in 1954. They were joined there by probationers in training in 1960. By 1978 the College provided training for all ranks from constable to superintendent. As part of the greatly increased emphasis on crime prevention, encouragement was given to police initiatives to involve themselves more positively with young people and the community at large in order to obtain their co-operation.

The licensing law was revised in 1962. By an Act of 1970 the State Management Districts in Easter Ross and Dumfries-shire (where all licensed premises had been owned and managed by the Secretary of State — there was a similar district in England) were abolished. The system had been set up to deal with problems of the First World War and may have become something of an anachronism — of a state-owned kind which was particularly unacceptable to the Government of the day.

Law Commissions for England and Wales and for Scotland were set up in 1965 to make proposals for systematic law reform. The programme of the Scottish Commission was approved by the Secretary of State, who also appointed the Commissioners jointly with the Lord Advocate. In 1972 these functions all passed to the Lord Advocate, but SHHD was still involved in consideration of the Commission's proposals. Legislation was passed on divorce, land tenure, damages and other civil law matters.

A new body, the Scottish Courts Administration, was set up in 1971 under a Director to take over from SHHD the administration of the sheriff courts. As well as reporting to the Secretary of State on court administration the Director reported to the Lord Advocate on certain subjects transferred from SHHD in 1972.

In 1975 the burgh and JP courts were replaced by district courts, where the judges were JPs and the staff were provided by district and island councils. Departmental interest in these courts was shared by SHHD and the Secretary of Commissions.

On home defence (formerly civil defence) the departmental effort was greatly reduced in 1968 when the local Civil Defence Corps and Auxiliary Fire Services were disbanded. Thereafter the main function was contingency planning and maintenance of a central warning system and other reserve facilities. Co-ordination of effort in civil emergencies however produced was at times a strenuous task. Departmental control over the fire service was mainly financial and varied little over the period, changes stemming mainly from alterations in the grant arrangements. In recent years a growing proportion of fire service resources was directed to fire prevention.

13. Administrative Devolution

A number of functions were transferred during the period from Great Britain to Scottish departments. These are detailed in Appendix 4: among the most important were electricity in the South of Scotland (1954), roads (1956), selective assistance to industry (1975). In the main these were political moves arising from the continuing pressure for "more Scottish say in Scottish affairs" though some minor moves (e.g. Botanic Gardens 1969) may have been dictated by administrative convenience. At least one (formation of Scottish Transport Group 1968) appeared from Press reports to have been a personal victory by the Secretary of State of the time. The moves were paralleled by the appointment of a Secretary of State for Wales in 1964 and his assumption, in 1971 and 1978, of full responsibility for health and education.

But was the Scottish Office going its own way in all these fields or was it merely copying English policies? In many contexts there was no question of copying, because it was doing something different. It was assisting a different kind of fishing industry, attending to the reform of a different body of civil and criminal law, confronting a different set of housing problems, relating to different educational institutions and to a different system of local government. Or it was devising uniquely Scottish solutions, such as the Highlands and Islands Development Board, for uniquely Scottish problems. But there were also government policies which applied over the whole country, because of their wide repercussions (raising of the school leaving age) or because they embodied the Government's political thinking (phasing out of pay beds from hospitals). Any Scottish considerations bearing on such policies were a matter for the Secretary of State to raise in Cabinet. Apart from this, there was a good deal of common thinking and mutual influence between departments; this is well known, but it is not so generally appreciated that the Scottish Office often took the lead in such thinking. Examples are: the integration of social work departments; the reorganisation of health services; regional economic planning; control of building standards.

Another point, which is perhaps not fully appreciated, is the extent to which customer expectation of parallel facilities was often the deciding factor. An interesting case study is afforded by the inception in 1970 of the Scottish Hospital Advisory Service. An inquiry report having revealed bad conditions in a mental handicap hospital in Wales, Richard Crossman decided to set up an advisory service which would visit long-stay hospitals and report. It then became inevitable to set up a Scottish counterpart, not because of any pressure from Government or DHSS, but because the Secretary of State would otherwise have been criticised for his inaction if any Scottish hospital had been found wanting. But the Scottish service was organised on somewhat different lines, which have proved acceptable in the Scottish situation.

14. Professional Staffs

Even to define this term is not easy, since administration is itself a profession, and since persons qualified in other professions may be employed wholly or partly on administration. We include in the term those civil servants in the Scottish Office who were qualified in some profession other than administration and whose main role entailed making use of their professional expertise.

From the outset departments had need of such people.

Indeed one professional group — HM Inspectorate of Schools — having been founded in 1840, antedated by some thirty years the department itself. Throughout the whole period which we are considering the professions employed were diverse and their tasks even more so. But during the period there was certainly an increase both in numbers of staff and diversity of professions; new ways of organising their services emerged, and their roles in many ways changed.

Some groups increased in relative importance: for example the nurses, whose increased role in the central department matched the recognition, throughout the Health Service, that this large and important group of staff should have more say in policy decisions. In 1954 the DHS nursing adviser was a solo post; by 1979 the chief nursing officer had a staff of nine nursing officers.

Agricultural economists had been employed in DAS from the outset, but the role of economists became more extensive with the growing emphasis on industrial development, and in 1970 an economics and statistics unit under a chief economic adviser was set up which in 1973 became part of SEPD. A chief statistician in Central Services headed the statistical organisation for all departments.

During the period HM Inspectorate of Constabulary was also strengthened and its role was altered to exercise a greater influence on development of policing methods; from about 1970 onwards the former system of formal inspections was replaced by informal discussions in depth at which all ranks had the opportunity to express their views.

Social work was represented, at the beginning of the period, by case workers in SHD and in the prison service who dealt with welfare and after-care. By 1979 there was a strong team of social work advisers in SED, and all casework functions had been handed over to local authorities.

Following the Government statement "Government Research and Development" in 1973, departments were required to control, as customers, the research which they commissioned. This called for more extended scientific advice within the departments. A Chief Scientist Office was set up in SHHD, taking over from the previous Advisory Committee on Medical Research which had more limited functions; and a Scientific Adviser's Unit was set up in DAFS. The Central Research Unit had been formed earlier to handle social science research for all Scottish departments. Arrangements for the commissioning of research were also made in the other departments.

A trend which applied to several groups was that of disengagement from the detailed inspection or control of particular situations, with greater emphasis on the issue of general guidance. This arose largely from the policy towards local authorities, although in the case of HM Inspectorate of Schools it was the teaching profession, just as much as the authorities, whose work was the object of inspection and detailed comment. It seems to have been the Inspectors themselves from the late 50s onwards who felt the need to take a more positive role in assisting change and development rather than commenting on what existed, and to bring in the teaching profession and others to collaborate in this process.

The trend was influenced in some cases by a change in the statutory framework — for example the 1969 Planning Act, under which the Secretary of State's approval was required only to structure plans — or by changed administrative arrangements, as in the case of housing, roads, educational building.

One group whose role did not change was the solicitors. What did greatly increase was the number of GB or UK departments operating in Scotland and other bodies for whom they acted and, in consequence, the range of subjects over which they exercised their traditional roles. From 1974 the Solicitor who headed the group was one of two professionals holding the rank of Deputy Secretary — the other one being the Chief Medical Officer.

The role of the doctors and other health care professionals in servicing the consultative machinery of the reorganised health service has already been mentioned.

Where a substantial number in one profession or related professions were employed, they tended to be grouped in one department or in Central Services, giving service to other departments. When SDD was formed in 1962 most of the building professionals were brought into it, and provided services to SHHD and SED. DAFS continued to have their own staff of surveyors and engineers until 1972 when DAFS and SDD engineers were amalgamated to form one division within SDD with the responsibility of advising the two departments on all civil engineering matters other than roads. In 1978 a building directorate was formed in SDD comprising architects, surveyors, and mechanical and electrical engineers. Similarly, advice on health care was obtained from SHHD, and on social work from SED, at the many points where these two services were inter-related.

The Fulton Report on the Civil Service, 1968, recommended that professional staff should have a greater role in management and should in some cases be employed in administrative divisions within the line management. This happened to a limited extent in the Scottish Office. Within SDD the head of the building standards division reported to the Chief Architect and the urban renewal unit to the Chief Planning Officer. The engineering division, headed by a professional, in addition to advising all departments took over in 1974 the administrative management of the water and sewerage programme, which included consent to capital expenditure and the approval of some projects for specific grant. Coast protection and flood prevention were added in 1977. In SHHD the Chief Scientist Office, Planning Unit and Hospital Advisory Service were headed by doctors.

In DAFS there were several large groups of professional staff, many of them out-stationed in offices throughout Scotland. This was a natural consequence of the department's close and direct contact with its client industries. The largest group was the agricultural staff, comprising surveyors, land officers and "inspectors": the last being a somewhat misnamed group of officers whose duties ranged from crop certification to the assessment of farms for capital grants. Some administrative functions were assigned to these professional staff.

The profesionals did not appear on the whole to regret the fact that Fulton had not been applied more widely. They appeared to value highly the independence of their professional advice, which did not derogate from their close involvement in policy formation; and they were concerned to organise themselves in ways which facilitated their links with administrative staff.

15. Fringe Bodies

Like other government departments, the Scottish Office was far from being a self-contained structure. A large number of bodies — over sixty at the last count — related to it in ways too numerous to mention and too diverse to summarise. The somewhat inadequate title "fringe bodies", officially applied to them, reflects the difficulty of describing them collectively. They included for example the fifteen health boards (replacing over 100 pre-1974 bodies) wholly financed from the NHS Vote and administering services for which the Secretary of State was responsible in detail to Parliament; the two electricity boards and the Scottish Transport Group, administering nationalised industries subject only to limited Ministerial control; the New Town Development Corporations; research associations; boards and commissions connected with agriculture and industry and with environment. Not included in the count were the numerous purely advisory committees and bodies representing consumer interests or professions which were regularly consulted.

The tendency — with the notable exception of NHS bodies — was towards an increase in number. In some instances departmental functions were transferred to Boards — for example, the Scottish Certificate of Education from SED to the SCE Examination Board; but more usually the bodies were given new functions. Towards the end of the period there was criticism, particularly directed to the extensive patronage represented by the Secretary of State's appointment to these bodies and to the feeling that they exercised some measure of power without accountability. This latter feeling was reflected in the acronym "QUANGOS" (quasi-autonomous non-government organisations).

An analogous though smaller scale development took place in the nineteenth century, and for similar reasons: a rapid expansion in the range of matters in which it was felt that some public control should be exercised. The reorganisation of offices in 1939 was the last of several stages in an attempt to tidy up the situation for Scotland by bringing more Government activities under the Secretary of State's direct control, exercised through career civil servants. The last of the nineteenth-century boards and commissions, the General Board of Control for Scotland, survived this reorganisation because of the respect felt for its quasi-judicial functions in relation to mental patients. It soldiered on till 1962, when the management of the State Hospital at Carstairs passed to the Secretary of State and the Board's quasi-judicial functions were vested in a new body, the Mental Welfare Commission.

By this time the functions of government had once more

proliferated, and any future tidy-up would have to be on a scale too daunting to contemplate. Indeed, a tidy-up which involved bringing all these matters within the direct control of Government and civil servants would no longer have been in line with public opinion; delegation to elected bodies was more the type of solution that was being suggested. Meanwhile the problem of co-ordinating all these bodies — in relation to appointments, scales of pay where applicable, etc — was formidable, and was not completely solved.

16. Structure of The Scottish Office

Till 1939 there were various boards and departments and a Scottish Office, reporting direct to the Secretary of State, which had its own functions and also acted as his link with the other bodies. From 1939 there were four departments whose heads (called Secretaries, but holding the Civil Service rank of Deputy Secretary) reported direct to Ministers. The SHD looked after some common services. The Permanent Under-Secretary of State had a somewhat shadowy role, co-ordinating the departments and commenting if he thought fit on their submissions to Ministers, but with no direct power to give them instructions. He advised the Secretary of State on his functions as "Scotland's Minister", but a major part of this function soon fell to SHD — as described in section 1.

From time to time there were transfers of work from one department to another. These are detailed in Appendix 4. The main changes were in 1962, when SHD/DHS became SHHD/ SDD; in 1968 when the Social Work Services Group was set up and (probably for reasons of size) attached to SED; and in 1973 when SEPD was set up.

In early years the departments were somewhat isolated and self-contained. Interchange of staff, starting at senior levels, helped to remedy this.

As the work became more complex there was need for more common services, which had to be attached for management purposes to one or other department. In 1966 the four departments combined their training units to form the Scottish Office Training Unit which was attached to SED. The DAFS library was made available to all departments and was expanded to cover their interests. So also was the computer service, set up by DAFS to deal with subsidies; from the middle 60s there was a move to computerise all clerical work, including statistical work, and by 1979 the Scottish Office Computer Service with 400 staff was carrying out over 150 different tasks for the Scottish Office and some other departments. From 1962 an architectural and building service was provided by SDD. The Scottish Information Office was attached to SHD. So also was the Solicitor's Office, formed in 1946 to provide a solicitor service for the four departments and HM Treasury in Scotland, together with legal advisory work for DAS and DHS. From 1963 it provided almost a full range of legal services to all Scottish Office departments, as well as being solicitor, or solicitor and legal adviser, to numerous other Great Britain or UK departments and bodies functioning in Scotland.

Meanwhile the Permanent Under-Secretary of State was emerging from the penumbra. The setting up of the Regional Development Division in 1964, reporting direct to him (see section 1) was partly a response to the situation but it also met the wishes of the Under-Secretary of the time for some more definite task. And the co-ordinating task itself was becoming more onerous, starting with the Plowden Report of 1961 which recommended a system of financial forward estimates by programme. By the late 1960s the public expenditure survey system was in full operation. Forward estimates over a rolling five-year period were submitted for discussion in Cabinet. The Secretary of State was being presented by his departments with several programmes, whose English equivalents — each presented by a different Minister — could well be in competition with each other; so clearly some co-ordination was required, and this fell to the Permanent Under-Secretary. Then in 1968 came the Fulton Report with its emphasis on personnel management and organisation — and the Secretary of State had four departments, each with different management policies and office procedures. It was a timely coincidence, perhaps, that the next Permanent Under-Secretary had a special interest in management; but the build up of Central Services to meet these needs had already begun to take place.

In 1970 an under-secretary for finance was appointed, reporting both to the Permanent Under-Secretary and to heads of departments on financial planning. By 1972 he headed a finance division, taking over all functions from the previous departmental divisions. From 1970 to 1972 a common establishments division was built up, and was then divided into two — management and organisation, and personnel — each operating on a functional as distinct from departmental basis. A common payroll and common seniority lists for all staff had been introduced in 1971. The various common services, and RDD, became attached to Central Services as detailed in Appendix 4. In 1972 the departmental votes were combined in a Scottish Office Vote for which the Permanent Under-Secretary was the accounting officer. This vote covered the staffing and related expenditure of the departments; the services which they operated — e.g. NHS, assistance to agriculture — were carried on separate votes for which the department heads were accountable. In 1973 the informal meetings, which the Permanent Under-Secretary had held every week for many years with heads of departments, were formalised as a management group with a permanent support staff. Co-ordinating units were set up from time to time to deal with specific problems, for example the urban policy group and the group on local authority statutory planning.

In 1975 a deputy secretary was placed at the head of Central Services. This was partly to meet the growing pressure of work on legislative devolution. The deputy secretary was also given responsibility for local authority finance and was made accounting officer for Rate Support Grant. These finance responsibilities — hitherto exercised by SDD — had assumed growing importance with the increased proportion of local authority expenditure met by central government support; with the interest aroused by the Layfield Committee on local authority finance (which reported in 1976); and with the current constraints on public expenditure. There was also, on local government reorganisation, a better basis for negotiation with the authorities collectively. An additional under-secretary for local authority finance was appointed in 1976.

Thus from the simple concept of 1939 — four departments with a one-man co-ordinator and a few common services — there had emerged a federal organisation unique among government departments. The whole complex, with its 8,000 staff, was not large by comparison with some Whitehall departments which had a much simpler pyramidal structure; and it might have seemed a tidier solution to create such a structure, with the Permanent Under-Secretary at its keystone. Whether this was ever seriously contemplated we do not know, but in any case

134   SCOTTISH GOVERNMENT YEARBOOK 1980

the federal structure — even if it just grew — was in many ways well suited to the unique diversity of the Scottish Office functions. All staff were assigned to the Scottish Office and had extended chances of experience and promotion, which was helpful not only to the staff themselves but in the process of co-ordination and exchange of views between departments; while at the same time the customers were still dealing with individual departments, to which their functions gave a distinct character. But the key issue was accountability: did this create problems, with the Permanent Under-Secretary accountable for staff, while the department heads were accountable for the services on which the staff were engaged? If it did, they appear to have been resolved through the management group which co-ordinated staff policies and expenditure programmes. In a pyramidal structure there could still have been more than one accounting officer, but seven, in a relatively small department, would have made the structure somewhat unreal; while the alternative — that a smaller number of officers should each account for two or more widely diverse programmes — would hardly have made for convincing reports to the Public Accounts Committee. The point should also be made that the federal structure stopped at official level: the Secretary of State, although delegating much of his work to his team of Ministers, had the final Ministerial responsibility.

Note — Two appendices to this chapter are included in the Reference Section at the end of the book:—
    Appendix 4: Scottish Office — Transfer of Functions 1954-1979.
    Appendix 5: Scottish Office — Summary of Responsibilities in 1979.

9

POLICY-MAKING FOR THE SCOTTISH HEALTH SERVICES AT NATIONAL LEVEL*

COLIN WISEMAN, M.Sc.

Research Consultant, Scottish Institute for Operational Research

Introduction

For many years, Scotland has enjoyed considerable *administrative* devolution on health matters. This has not been fully appreciated by the ordinary "man in the street" and indeed it has not been unknown for a Scottish MP to make the mistake of posing a parliamentary question on the health service to the Minister responsible for the DHSS rather than to the Secretary of State for Scotland.

The involvement of central government in the health service through the Scottish Home and Health Department (SHHD) can be contrasted with the nature of its involvement with many other services through its departments both in Scotland and the rest of the UK. Firstly, central government is responsible for financing virtually all aspects of the NHS. And secondly, the Secretary of State is ultimately responsible for the administration of the National Health Service via SHHD — the fifteen health boards are his agents. So, in effect, SHHD acts as the headquarters administration of the NHS as well as a central government department concerned with Ministerial policies. Another important feature of SHHD which distinguishes it from many other departments is its interdependence with the professional providers of health services. This is reflected in the employment of considerable numbers of professional advisers, mainly doctors and nurses, within SHHD itself and in the external professional advisory bodies set up by statute.

* This paper was given during a seminar on health at the University of Edinburgh on 15th December, 1978. The seminar was one of a series organised by the Scottish Council for Social Service on the theme of "Social Policies in Scotland and Devolution". The research discussed in the paper was sponsored by the Chief Scientist of the Scottish Home and Health Department. © Tavistock Institute of Human Relations 1979.

Reorganisation of the NHS in 1974, while primarily aimed at the integration of health services, offered the opportunity to reform policy-making and planning at national level. At local level, fifteen health boards were created and, in addition to the professional advisory committees, such as the National Medical Consultative Committee and the National Pharmaceutical Consultative Committee, local health councils (LHCs) were introduced to provide for some public involvement in health board affairs. Some of the key agencies created at the national level were:

1. A small Planning Unit within the SHHD was to introduce a new planning system to facilitate planning activities generally — the staff being drawn from the Civil Service.

2. A planning Council which was to involve health boards in national policy-making and act as a source of advice to the Secretary of State. In the event, the Council has provided a framework within which a wide range of interests can be drawn together to study major planning issues through the use of working parties and programme planning groups.

3. A number of National Consultative Committees (NCCs) for each of the main health service professions. Each of these was established as a source of specialist advice to the Planning Council and also to SHHD.

4. A Planning Council secretariat, staffed from within the NHS and SHHD which services the Planning Council, its various sub-committees and most of the NCCs.

In addition, in 1978, an Association of Local Health Councils was formed to provide a central focus for the many LHCs.

It is against this background that this paper reviews policy-making within SHHD in the past, and considers the effects of changes in the organisational and procedural arrangements for the development of policies. A recent programme of research undertaken for SHHD by a team from the Scottish Institute for Operational Research (SIOR), in which the writer was intimately involved, provides the basis for this discussion. The paper draws on this research to discuss what we, the research team, learnt about collaboration between government departments in the framing of policy, about some of the opportunities for and impediments to a more participative and democratic approach to policy development, and about the complexities involved in the identification of health service priorities. An understanding of these issues is essential if the way policies are developed in the future is to be improved and will be of direct concern to a Scottish Assembly, should one be created, or indeed to any other political forum which might be established.

Policy-making in the Past

Various studies of central government (for example, Griffiths 1966) have recorded that policy-making has been more a matter of advocacy than of reliance on systematic research evidence. In a recent lecture Professor Lewis Gunn (1978) noted one or two examples of a more planned approach to the development of policies, but he indicated that for the most part central government took a "reactive" stance on matters of policy, that is it reacted to pressures for change in an *ad hoc* and unplanned fashion. In the NHS, the various crises that arose in the 1960s concerning the poor conditions and treatment of elderly and mentally ill patients in many institutions, provoked central government to introduce a number of policy changes (Klein 1974); these incidents provide somewhat extreme examples of this "reactive" approach. Another study (Maddox 1972) of the DHSS in the late 1960s suggested that decision-making was incremental, with only minor adjustments in policy occurring in response to various partisan pressures; policy-making was seen to be a process of "muddling through" (Lindblom 1965).

In one of SIORs recent studies within SHHD — undertaken at around the time of the NHS reorganisation — we discovered a similar situation (Wiseman 1979). The department's activities were very much geared to the administration and management of existing services; new policies were developed mainly in response to external advocacy pressures and stimuli. Thus, the issues that found their way onto SHHDs "agenda" for attention tended to arise in an *ad hoc* fashion and few resulted from a systematic evaluation of the existing situation. Figure 1 shows that the advocacy for change came from four main groupings. As one might expect the *government* could itself bring pressure to bear through Ministers, but more often pressures for change were created by the actions of other departments; the DHSS

K

Figure 1

advocacy of policy change

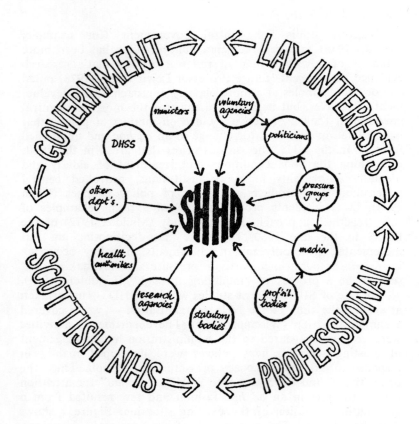

played a particularly important role by producing its own reports and guidelines since this often stimulated SHHD to review its policy statements too. Also by requesting advice from the department or raising difficulties concerning existing guidelines, the NHS field authorities often stimulated a change in policy. The health *professions,* particularly doctors, exerted a very significant influence on which issues were regarded as important both directly through the professional advisory committees which met regularly with SHHD officials and through the publication of reports by the Royal Colleges. Finally, *lay* interests were able to exert some pressure through selected voluntary agencies, through pressure groups and also indirectly through the media and the asking of parliamentary questions by MPs.

SHHD reacted to such pressures in a variety of ways — sometimes internal departmental discussions would be held or working parties formed. Sometimes an external professional committee might be formed with members from the statutory advisory bodies to advise on future policy. The topics on which studies were to be mounted in order to develop new policies tended to be chosen in an *ad hoc* way and the studies were often undertaken by uni-professional groups without the benefit of systematic methods or analyses. The reports that emerged from these external committees were usually circulated to the professions and field authorities for comment which allowed a further period of advocacy to take place. These comments then formed the basis of internal discussions within the department before the Minister was advised about future policy; new policies were for the most part promulgated by the issuing of a circular to Regional hospital boards, local health authorities and other agencies involved in the provision of health services at that time. Sometimes statements would be made in Parliament or even new legislation introduced. Of course for some issues SHHD might decide that no action or change was required.

While this description provides a general indication of how policy-making was undertaken within SHHD, there were exceptions where attempts had been made to introduce a more planned approach to various problems (see for example the SHHD reports on nurse manpower planning 1974-77).

Some might argue that the process described is not a bad way to go about policy-making and that a responsive approach to problems is what is required of a government department. While we believed that such responsiveness was desirable and indeed essential since unpredictable pressures for change would always arise, we had a number of worries about the processes we had observed.

In the first place, the opportunity or power to bring pressure on SHHD was not necessarily equally distributed among all groups with a legitimate interest in health service matters. It seemed to us that 'decibel" planning could occur with those who were in a position to shout loudest influencing which issues got onto the "agenda" and that "urgent" issues might push out "important" ones.

Secondly, the basis for the selection of problems for attention was far from clear, yet often the decision to undertake a study seemed to give the particular problem the "inside track" for a more favourable reallocation of resources in the future.

Thirdly, the policy development activity or study was for the most part undertaken by professional groups and committees which could not be regarded as representative. Finally, there was no strategy for the development of services and to a great extent the future shape of the NHS was being determined by the tide of events.

However, reorganisation provided an opportunity to overcome some of these problems and did bring some changes in the process of policy-making; there seemed to be an increased interest in comprehensive planning systems, an apparent desire for more participation in policy-making — although the participation under discussion at this time was of health boards and professionals rather than of the general public — and a recognition of the need for more integration and co-ordination of health service activities with those of social work and other local authority departments. A singularly important innovation in Scotland was the setting up of Programme Planning Groups (PPGs) within the framework of the Planning Council to study and advise on new policies for major problems within the health service such as care of the elderly and child health; while the membership of these groups has been predominantly professional they have brought together representatives from a wide range of interests including voluntary agencies, health boards, local authorities and government departments.

It is now over four years since the NHS was reorganised.

During this time, we have worked closely with SHHD on the programme of research studies which were intended to help the department in developing planning processes for the Scottish NHS — as researchers we have enjoyed a privileged position and have been able to examine how certain aspects of policy-making have developed over this period and to reflect on experience with the changes.

In the course of this research, we put forward proposals for a systematic yet participative planning system (Wiseman 1979) which SHHD have drawn on in their development of planning within the new organisational structure at national level. Suffice it to say here that these original proposals were based on a mixed-scanning approach to planning (Etzioni 1967) and involved three components:

1. *A periodic review process* in which the pattern of health service activities would be considered across the board though not in great detail; by this means major problems would be identified or their likelihood anticipated. This general overview of the NHS would, it was hoped, encourage discussions about future developments in the services.

2. *A selection procedure* to identify important planning issues which would justify detailed planning attention, given the limited planning resources and skills likely to be available (Wiseman 1978).

3. The use of *systematic yet participative approaches* in the detailed planning on issues of major planning importance.

The proposals were designed to allow a wide range of interests to contribute to planning at appropriate stages. While we believed these proposals would overcome some of the deficiencies of policy-making in the past, we also recognised that our understanding of some aspects of policy-making was still somewhat limited. Viz:

1. We had so far viewed planning and policy-making very much in an SHHD context (although some need to build in information exchange with other non-health agencies at the time of a periodic review had been recognised in the

proposals). Yet many major problems, such as care of the elderly, mental disorder and alcoholism clearly involved other non-health agencies. What were the implications of such links for health service planning and could the existing proposals be adapted to cater for them?

2. The use of advisory groups in policy-making had only been outlined in our proposals and little practical experience was available, Programme Planning Groups were beginning to operate and learning from their experience might help to develop more detailed proposals. How were these innovations in participative planning working out? How should such groups be set up and operated to aid the development of new policies? Were there alternative ways of proceeding?

3. Proposals for a periodic review within SHHD would produce information which it was thought could be useful in the setting of priorities within the NHS. Yet priorities had never been set across the board before and had emerged largely by the piecemeal development of policies for particular sectors of the NHS. What did we mean by priorities? How would the setting of priorities differ from policy-making anyway? What kind of information would be relevant to the setting of priorities and would this be met by the existing proposals? Who should participate in the setting of priorities and how might such participation be organised?

Thus, we set in hand further research studies on each of these themes.

Research Studies Concerning Policy-making

(i)   Collaboration between SHHD and Social Work Services Group in National Policy-making

In many of the official documents prepared at the time of reorganisation both in Scotland and in the south, considerable stress was placed on co-ordination and collaboration between social work and health services. It is interesting to note that words such as "conflict" and "competition" were rarely used in these documents, yet it is inevitable, and in some cases desirable, that differences of interest occur. We undertook a number of case studies which were designed to explore the relationship of the respective central government departments concerned with social work and health viz. — the Social Work Services Group (which is in fact a section within the Scottish Education Department) and SHHD. These studies investigated how particular problems or activities in which there was an obvious joint interest were handled.

All the case studies pointed to some conflicts of view or of expectations between SWSG and SHHD officials. This was not an unexpected result since it ties in with other research findings and experience on the general problems of working across administrative boundaries.

However, we discovered that officials experienced difficulty in finding a constructive approach to handling these conflicts and in collaborating effectively. There seemed to be a number of reasons for this:

1. The organisational structure of the Scottish Office; this was departmental and the usual method of handling issues was for one department to take a "lead" — in other words "departmentalism" was a strong factor and mechanism for making a more "corporate response" to difficult issues seemed poorly developed.

2. The tendency for a "lead" department to consult with others rather than to participate jointly in exploring issues in which there was an obvious conflict. There was also a tendency to internalise the matter and try to resolve any problem before seeking views elsewhere — in particular there seemed to be a reluctance to involve any higher corporate level within the Scottish Office, or to consult with Ministers or indeed to seek views from amongst the wider range of interests outwith the Scottish Office.

3. The relationship with Ministers. Civil Servants were usually reluctant to consult Ministers in the early stages of policy development. They seemed to assume that any difference of views had to be resolved before making contact with Ministers and liked to put forward clear-cut recommendations rather than a set of options for consideration.

4. The many goals and objectives being pursued by SWSG and SHHD. Some of these concerned services to patients and clients and some the internal functioning and operation of the departments themselves. Therefore, even where potential changes might seem to be in the wider public interest conflicts could arise and prevent progress because of these "internal" objectives.

5. The importance of particular individuals in shaping a department's response on specific issues. Generally, the training and education of Civil Servants with its emphasis on avoiding risks and any possibility of political embarrass- ment could inhibit the generation of proposals with wide- ranging effects and hence the resolution of conflict at an official level. More specifically, individuals in key positions could exert a major impact on the way issues were handled and in providing (or not providing) the necessary motivation to resolve differences of view.

6. The different organisational and political contexts in which the departments were operating. There was a tendency on the part of one side to forget that life on the other side of the administrative boundary was quite different. This resulted in unreal expectations about what others could do. For example, the health service operates in accordance with an apolitical model in which the involvement of prac- titioners and professionals is of major significance whereas local authorities are democratically elected political bodies. Furthermore the degree of influence or control that can be exerted by SHHD and SWSG differs.

7. The reluctance to challenge previously agreed policy posi- tions, for example SHHDs policy of not earmarking funds to health boards and the reluctance of SWSG to put out guidance to local authorities which could be construed as having financial implications.

Some of these practices have been developed for quite understandable and rational reasons. For instance, the fact that the Scottish Office has only a small number of Ministers covering a vast range of topics and that these Ministers must spend most of their time in Whitehall restricts the contribution they can make and the range of matters Civil Servants can bring to them for discussion. However, while the development of these practices may be understandable, they have certain disadvantages particularly for collaboration across government departments, and in our view warrant further consideration.

The nature of the impediments to collaboration listed above indicates that bringing together SWSG and SHHD within one department of the Scottish Office would not be the panacea that many seem to believe. It seems to us that the handling of issues on which there is a potential conflict between departments, such as SWSG and SHHD, could be improved:

1. If relevant departments, and, where appropriate, external bodies, could be involved in *joint explorations* through the medium of working parties or planning groups;

2. If more attention were to be given to the nature of the problem and the range of possible solutions by adopting a *more systematic approach to problem-solving;*

3. If there could be *more direct political input* at the formative stage of defining the problem and in considering the possible solutions or policies that emerge.

However, we are not suggesting that all the problems uncovered would be solved in this way nor that these proposals could be adopted in isolation — they have implications for the relationships between Civil Servants, Ministers and the Secretary of State and the corporate machinery of the Scottish Office. Also, the proposals raise questions about how such issues which cut across administrative boundaries can be identified and processed within the Scottish Office and how any *joint* study group would be set up and operated. The study of the use of groups in policy-making provided some insights into the latter question and is discussed next.

(ii)   The Use of Groups to Aid Policy-making

Groups and working parties are often used by central government departments to aid in the development of new policies. Some groups are set up to operate within a department while others — usually acting in an advisory capacity — operate externally. Reorganisation led to the setting up of Programme Planning Groups (PPGs) under Planning Council auspices — these were intended to be an improvement on previous advisory groups because they could have a more balanced and representative membership and use more systematic methods of working. Among the PPGs set up were groups concerned with care of the elderly, with mental disorder, with child health, and with cardiac surgery.

However, experience with such groups within SHHD was extremely limited and systematic planning approaches had been used only occasionally by small, mainly internal officer teams (see, for example, SHHD 1974). So PPGs lacked a well-defined basis on which they could be set up and operated with confidence. As they were essentially experimental, we undertook research to learn from their early experience, in the hope of improving the use of such groups for policy-making in future.

In the course of our studies, we found that expectations about what PPGs would achieve were many and various. Most prominent amongst these were that PPGs would develop policies for the provision of services both within the NHS, and where appropriate within social work services; that they would gain the commitment to any proposed changes of the various interests who were participating in the groups' activities and that they would enable inter-agency and inter-professional conflicts to be worked through.

One of our studies concerned a PPG in which there was a social work and health interest and indicated that the important implications of the *organisational and political* context for the eventual influence of the group had not been fully appreciated. This PPG had been set up at the behest of the Planning Council, but because its subject was as much a social as a health problem, it eventually came under the joint parentage of the Planning Council and the Advisory Council on Social Work (ACSW). The research, based on interviews with departmental officials and analysis of file material, suggested that PPGs being essentially a health service creation were by nature apolitical and professional in orientation and that this conflicted with the political nature of local authorities; that making ACSW a joint parent posed problems because in contrast to the Planning Council it was a professional advisory body which did not possess a policy or planning orientation and did not allow for the participation

of field authorities; and that differences in the political relationship between SHHD and health boards, and SWSG and local
authorities created varying expectations about what a national
PPG could do effectively. The research also indicated that these
difficulties had been compounded by the 1975 reorganisation of
local government (which occurred after the setting-up of this
PPG) which had created the new more self-sufficient regional
councils and a new national body, the Convention of Scottish
Local Authorities (COSLA). This meant that the way the PPG
had been set up, the joint parentage arrangement with ACSW
and the lack of direct links with local authorities became even
more questionable and reduced the likely influence of the group,
particularly as far as social work services were concerned. This
again reinforces the point made earlier, that there is great danger
in assuming that local authorities or indeed other bodies operate
on a similar basis to the health service.

Yet other studies considered the internal *operation* of PPGs
and these indicated:

1. That PPGs operated in a free-flowing and relatively
    unstructured way. The groups seemed to be effective in
    enabling participants to share insights and understanding
    and in providing good group motivation, but were also open
    to domination by members with high status or strong person-
    alities, and were relatively low in creativity;

2. That the tasks given to PPGs were of considerable com-
    plexity and in many ways were beyond the resources and
    skills available to participants. Consequently, the emphasis
    was often placed on looking for solutions with only limited
    consideration being given to the underlying problems of the
    client groups under study;

3. The dominant method of working was along the lines of
    a business committee with a formal agenda and minutes.
    This did not seem to be appropriate to the complexity of
    the task being faced nor did it help participants to keep
    track of the pattern of group discussions. Value conflicts
    and philosophical differences were for the most part not
    discussed, and arriving at a group view on specific issues
    proved difficult.

As indicated earlier in the paper, previous attempts at using advisory bodies for the purposes of policy development had been found wanting and so the aim of our work was to use these criticisms constructively so that future PPGs could learn from this experience and avoid some of the pitfalls discovered. While these findings were reinforced by a survey of participants which we undertook, the survey also indicated widespread support for the concepts underlying the PPGs creation. In particular, their multi-disciplinarity, the participation of different interests in national planning, the bringing together of field and central government perspectives — along with the opportunities they provided to influence developments — were highly valued by participants. Even so, to varying degrees and for various reasons, participants felt that PPGs were not yet realising their potential or exploiting the opportunities as fully as they might. The implication of these studies was that the likely contribution of a PPG to effective policy-making was largely determined by:

1. The choices made in *setting up* the PPG, for example in deciding its remit, timescale, membership and the role of members;

2. The choices made concerning the *operation* of the PPG itself, for example the methods of working or approach adopted, the procedural arrangements for meetings, the approach to reporting and consulting with other groups, the skilled support provided;

3. The expectations that existed about the *product* of the group, for example about the content of group discussions, the performance of participants, the report of the group, the influence the group would exert on individual participants or outside interests and agencies;

4. The organisational and political *context* in which the PPG worked, for example the relationships with other agencies and groups, and the external influences of the environment on the group or its members.

This framework is illustrated in Figure 2. On the basis of the studies undertaken, *we concluded that for a PPG to operate effectively then the way it is set up, the way it is to operate,*

Figure 2:

A BASIS FOR DECIDING HOW TO SET UP AND OPERATE A PPG

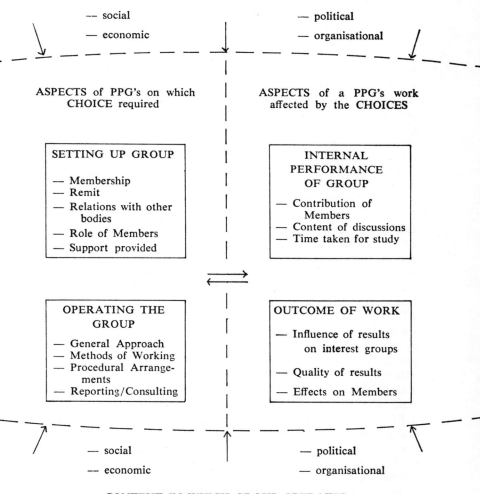

CONTEXT IN WHICH GROUP OPERATES

— social   — political

— economic   — organisational

ASPECTS of PPG's on which CHOICE required

ASPECTS of a PPG's work affected by the CHOICES

SETTING UP GROUP

— Membership
— Remit
— Relations with other bodies
— Role of Members
— Support provided

INTERNAL PERFORMANCE OF GROUP

— Contribution of Members
— Content of discussions
— Time taken for study

OPERATING THE GROUP

— General Approach
— Methods of Working
— Procedural Arrangements
— Reporting/Consulting

OUTCOME OF WORK

— Influence of results on interest groups
— Quality of results
— Effects on Members

— social   — political

— economic   — organisational

CONTEXT IN WHICH GROUP OPERATES

*the expectations about what it can achieve and the organisational
and political context within which it is to work have all to be
in harmony one with another.* We also concluded that the initial
PPGs did not meet these necessary conditions.

The consequence of this work is that future PPGs should
not automatically be set up on a uniform or consistent basis —
the characteristics of the group should be selected to vary
according to the particular circumstances. For instance, we
would expect a group which is given a short-term and highly
constrained remit and for which acceptability of the eventual
proposals is of paramount concern to require a different membership, a different approach, a different level of creativity and
a different relationship with interested bodies from, say, a group
looking at the long-term future in a relatively unconstrained way
with the primary aim of producing ideas to influence the climate
of debate about the future NHS. Also when the organisations
represented in a PPG enjoy considerable local autonomy in
decision-making then expectations about the role that their
representatives can play in the group as well as about the
group's eventual influence on the local level must be tempered
accordingly. For instance, where the task of a PPG is of particular importance to local authorities, then their central body,
COSLA, could be asked to nominate representatives to the
group. However, since the constitution of COSLA means it
cannot take decisions which are binding on individual local
authorities, it would be inappropriate and unrealistic to expect
these representatives, in the course of the PPGs work, to enter
into commitments on behalf of these authorities. Similarly,
where a particular PPGs activities are of direct concern to the
medical profession, the National Medical Consultative Committee could be approached to nominate representatives to the
group, but in spite of their participation, here again the PPGs
proposals could not bind individual medical practitioners at local
level without infringing their clinical freedom. In these circumstances, the most that can be expected of the participants in
a PPG is that they act as a channel of communication between
the group and the national bodies they represent. In this way,
the eventual proposals made by a PPG should stand a better
chance of proving acceptable to the various national bodies
represented on the group. Furthermore it would seem reasonable
to hope that these bodies would be prepared to exert influence on

the individuals or agencies at the local level that they themselves represented.

These studies suggest that before introducing any new PPGs, or indeed similar groups, we need to consider carefully the requirements for a group. However, this is not a simple exercise and will involve considering the nature of the problem or task in hand, identifying the interests to be taken into account and deciding which of the interest groups it is hoped to influence through the activities of the group. The research also suggests that there are many ways in which groups can be set up and operated, and that therefore the possibilities which might meet the specified requirements will need to be explored and their respective pros and cons considered before deciding what kind of group will be most appropriate.

(iii)   The Setting of Priorities

Use of the term "the setting of priorities" implies consideration of the possible candidates for priority before decisions are made about what to do. Until very recently though, no attempt had been made to issue statements of priorities for the NHS. Indeed as we discussed earlier in the paper, in the past national policies were usually developed in response to *ad hoc* pressures — this led to piecemeal changes in services and so the priority for resources accorded to different client groups was reached more by default than by design. This reaction to pressures is an inevitable part of any NHS planning process and thus will be a continuing influence on what services or groups do actually receive priority treatment. Nevertheless, we believed that our planning proposals which entailed an across the board review of what was happening and what the future might hold for the NHS would enable views to be formed about the directions along which specific sectors of the NHS might best develop, and about the overall priorities for resource allocation. In this way, some degree of control might be exerted over the future development of the NHS.

However, there were considerable uncertainties about these proposals to be explored. Firstly, the word priority was in common usage and seemed, like planning itself, to mean different things to different people. Secondly, there was uncertainty about the kind of information required to make judgements about the directions in which the NHS should develop. Finally, there were questions about who should be involved and what part they should play in reaching such judgements. In seeking to research further into these questions, one of our main difficulties was that no statements of priorities across the board had ever been made for the NHS. Thus we were fortunate that DHSS, having developed its own comprehensive planning system, used this in 1976 to produce a consultative document "Priorities for Health and Personal Social Services in England" (DHSS 1976). This initiative coupled with the White Paper on Public Expenditure that year led SHHD to produce its own strategic document "The Way Ahead" (SHHD 1976) soon after.

These initiatives provided at least some empirical evidence on which we could draw and we were fortunate in being able to investigate how "The Way Ahead" was produced. What emerged from our analysis was that the decision to draft "The Way Ahead" was in part prompted by the DHHS producing its strategic document but also in part by the felt need to give some sense of direction to health boards at a time when public expenditure cuts were being made. We also found that, because time was short, outside interests (for example, the National Consultative Councils, the Planning Council) had not been actively involved in the development of priorities and consultation with these bodies had been curtailed; that the work had been undertaken and influenced by a small number of individuals within SHHD; that relatively little time had been given to deciding priorities and these were based mainly on the work of DHHS and on the previous SHHD policy statement about such groups as the elderly and mentally disordered. In short, this research told us more about the process of central government in dealing with pressing issues than about the kinds of information that might have helped in forming judgements about priorities. More importantly, it provided only limited insight into how such activity might be organised in the future if a more systematic and a more participative approach was desired.

As a result, we decided to look at the experience of priority-setting on a wider front and undertook a major review of the research literature on the topic covering the health field generally but also looking at a selection of other fields too (Lind and Wiseman 1978). The review was not restricted to experience in Scotland.

What the review revealed was that decisions about priorities at a strategic level tend to be discussed along a number of distinct dimensions. Arguments have been put forward in an attempt to influence priorities between different geographical areas, between different groups of the population, between different disease/dependency groups, between different forms of intervention and between different agencies. These dimensions are clearly interdependent. For instance, an argument which suggests that more resources should go to the elderly implies a change in the pattern of service provision and similarly a move towards more preventive forms of intervention would affect people with certain kinds of disease or dependency conditions more than others. However, many of the studies identified in the course of the review focused on only one of these dimensions at a time. In general, the principal criteria used in arguing the case for shifting resources from one group or activity to another concerned the needs of the population, the quantity and quality of services, their effectiveness and their efficiency. Only a few studies were found which attempted to make direct comparisons between one disease/dependency group and another. Also it appeared there were major gaps in the quantitative information and research base available for making comparisons.

The research also considered the role of different agencies and interests in the priority-setting process. This again indicated the importance of pressure groups and interest groups in shaping the agenda of issues for consideration at the national level and the predominant "muddling through" approach adopted by decision-makers in responding to these pressures. More recently though, there has been a general trend towards the introduction of planning systems and also of organisational changes which allow for more participation and more consumer involvement in policy-making. How far these changes would produce a balanced set of pressures on central government departments and how far a more participative involvement in priority-setting would result it was too early to say. What was clear, though, was that priority-setting was a process requiring that political judgements be made.

On the basis of the review, we concluded that no consistent or coherent basis for setting priorities existed. In looking to the future, it would be possible to allow priorities to be set very much as before by a process of "muddling through" in which pressures from different interests would largely shape policies in

L

different sectors of the NHS and hence indirectly affect priorities. On the other hand, it would also be possible to take a more selective and controlled approach in which systematic consideration was given to the development of new policies (and hence priorities) in *selected* sectors of the service — the development of national standards and norms for specific services offers a good example of this sort of activity. But given the interest in a more comprehensive approach to planning, there remains the question of whether or not it would be possible to find a way of looking across the board at priorities. The review indicated two main possibilities — largely theoretical — which could be considered for this purpose. One of these is based on the development of a health status index which would enable an individual's state of health to be measured and allocated a score on a single scale running between normal health and death: this approach is heavily dependent on the gathering and technical analysis of qualitative and quantitative information. Methods for the aggregation and weighting of such data are still needed. The other approach, to which we referred as a "criteria model", covered a range of possible approaches — the common features of these being the explicit specification of a list of criteria which are relevant to the case for priority attention and the reliance on "political" processes to consider information on these particular criteria and to arrive at decisions about priorities. The evidence assessed in the review suggested that an approach based on health status indices would not be politically realistic even if other problems of measurement were surmountable — which they are unlikely to be. Whether or not a "criteria approach" is possible remains a moot point but one which we felt to be worth further investigation. The research has also highlighted a number of the practical problems of attempting to develop such an approach. Information about certain aspects of health service activity is lacking and there are problems in defining a comprehensive set of patient or disease categories for comparison and in enabling a wide range of interests to participate in the decision-making. If such problems cannot be overcome or if the effort required to do so is too great, then the alternative will be to abandon attempts at a systematic and comprehensive approach to the setting of priorities and to rely on "muddling through" or other more piecemeal ways of changing policies.

How Can We Improve Policy-making in the Future?

At the beginning of the paper we discussed policy-making processes in the past and identified various deficiencies. After this we put forward proposals for a planning system which we believed would result in improvements. However, as we have seen, the more recent research studies discussed above indicated to us that there were still aspects which were not satisfactory. We felt the most pressing needs to be:

1. To devise systematic approaches to the development of policies (and the setting of priorities) which would cater for the participation of a wide range of interests; this participation might require the formation of multi-disciplinary and multi-agency groups such as PPGs.

2. To provide for more direct political inputs into policy-making and administration — both at an early formative stage in these activities and also at a later stage when decisions about new policies are to be made.

3. To improve the way issues which cut across departmental boundaries are handled within the Scottish Office; this would require the introduction of mechanisms to facilitate a more corporate response from central government and to encourage *joint* studies on problems which are common to a number of departments and regarded as sufficiently important.

In response to 1. above, we have refined and developed further our original proposals for a planning system. We have suggested a framework for the setting of health service priorities and we have devised procedures to help decide how PPGs or similar groups tackling specific problems can be set up and operated most effectively. While these proposals are theoretical in that they have not been tested in practice, they are grounded in practical case experience and offer a possible way of improving policy-making still further. In introducing such approaches (or any planning system for that matter) many practical problems will need to be overcome, but they are likely to be surmountable. If such proposals are not introduced then the only alternative will be to retreat to past methods of policy-making which have been found wanting. In recent years, SHHD has discussed with health boards and the Planning Council, the introduction of a strategic planning system which has taken on board some of the ideas contained in our proposals for a periodic review process within the department. However, so far progress in putting health planning into practice within Scotland has been very slow. This can be contrasted with the position in England. Although one can argue about the appropriateness of the English planning system, there is no doubting the progress that has been made, since reorganisation, in implementing the system. However, the introduction of a planning system and new approaches will not cure all the problems of policy-making that we have discussed above — changes in the organisational structure and in the relationship between politicians and government departments are also required.

At the time of writing, it looks as if the Scotland Act will soon be repealed. However, other reforms are under discussion and it seems to be fairly widely accepted that the present political arrangements for Scotland will have to be revised. Assuming then that some new Assembly of elected politicians is created, whatever form this takes and whether or not it is given legislative powers, how could it help to improve policy-making? The remainder of the paper draws on our research findings to make some suggestions on this question and to speculate on some of the implications of an Assembly.

The changeover to a new Assembly would in itself provide an opportunity to challenge and review the appropriateness of past policy-making practices. The Assembly would be in a good position to capitalise on the knowledge that now exists about the deficiencies and difficulties of policy-making and also about what would be involved in introducing the proposed planning system and associated procedures. So an Assembly could, if it chose, provide the necessary commitment and motivation to introduce a more planned approach to policy-making. An Assembly could also provide the stimulus to improve policy-making through the introduction of linked structural changes too. Clearly, the introduction of an Assembly would raise many questions about who was to be involved in policy-making and how that involvement was to be organised. Indeed, it is a moot point whether the complex national advisory structure that now exists should continue in the new situation that would be created. However, too many organisational changes too quickly could lead to the baby being thrown out with the bathwater.

In fact, since the 1974 NHS reorganisation there have been a number of innovations which are worth retaining and developing. The introduction of PPGs and the wide participation in policy-making they make possible has been an important and exciting development. While the initial experience with these groups has thrown up difficulties and criticisms and while there has been a bias towards professional involvement, PPGs are valued by those involved in their activities and offer considerable scope for the worthwhile involvement of many disciplines and agencies in the shaping of national policy. An Assembly could build on this innovation to allow professionals, health board officials, trade unions, voluntary agencies and other consumer groups to advise on policies for specific problems. In some ways then, although the NHS is not under democratic control and the rationale behind its administrative structure is difficult to discern (Stewart 1977), the trend towards a more pluralistic and participative involvement in policy-making may hold lessons for any new political Assembly, and indeed for local government too. For groups like the PPGs, if operated in the right spirit could provide a possible alternative to the rigid committee structures that are generally to be found in local authorities in which usually only councillors can play a part.

The creation of an Assembly might also mean changes in the organisation of existing Scottish Office departments and in the nature of the relationship between Civil Servants and politicians. Ideally, an Assembly should arrange its own internal structures and stimulate organisational changes within departments in such a way that political inputs can be provided into policy-making at appropriate times and so that cross-departmental problem-solving will be encouraged.

If we look first at possible changes to the organisation of the departments within the Scottish Office then there are numerous possibilities to be considered. For example, departments could be organised on a functional basis (that is according to the service to be provided, such as health or education) or in relation to specific population or client groups. Whatever the basis decided upon, many issues that arise for consideration will cross such artificial administrative boundaries. Therefore, it would seem sensible to encourage flexibility in the internal organisational structure of these departments so that they can respond jointly to these issues. An Assembly could also facilitate this more corporate capability by the way it established its own committees and this is discussed next.

The creation of an Assembly would mean that there were Ministers and other politicians with a direct interest in health matters in Edinburgh virtually all the time and this would in itself provide more time and more resources for political involvement in the consideration of health problems and in policy-making activities. If it were to be decided that the Ministers alone could not provide sufficient political input into the affairs of the relevant government departments then the introduction of a Health Committee drawn from within the Assembly, possibly with investigative powers, might be worth considering. However, there would be some dangers in an Assembly adopting a committee structure too closely aligned with government departments since many of the important problems would cut across departmental boundaries. Furthermore such committees can take on a somewhat negative watchdog role *vis-à-vis* Civil Servants and Ministers at the expense of a more forward-looking approach. Thus, an argument can be made that within the Assembly *ad hoc* committees should be formed from time to time with forward-looking remits to focus on key issues, such as the elderly, the multiply-deprived population, and alcohol-related problems, which cut across departmental lines. These committees could provide the necessary parentage and legitimacy for joint work by departments. However, what kind of groups should be set up in support of such committees, how active the committee members would be in any study and what would be required in the way of support services obviously requires further consideration — one possibility would be for the committee to steer the activities of a planning group, similar to a PPG. If the Assembly created did lead to the setting up of such committees, then these would need to be serviced and supported. There could be advantage in having a skilled secretariat which was independent of the Civil Service and Ministers — this would be particularly so, if it was intended to encourage the participation of a wide range of national bodies in policy development activities.

The creation of a new political Assembly would also change

the relationship of SHHD or its successor department with the UK Parliament and with UK government departments. In the past, as we have seen, DHHS has exerted considerable influence on the agenda of issues to which SHHD has given attention. Furthermore on many politically sensitive issues, SHHD has been able to adopt a low profile precisely because there was a DHHS. So while the presence of DHSS may on occasion have diverted effort and attention towards UK rather than Scottish health problems, SHHD has also benefited from time to time by being able to draw on the work of DHSS — certainly, DHSSs size allows much greater and more specialised resources to be brought to bear on certain issues. The one thing of which we can be certain is that the nature of this relationship would have to change if an Assembly were to be created.

The overall conclusion of this paper is that there is ample scope to reform and improve the way health service policies are developed in Scotland and that sufficient information and knowledge are now available to help guide the search for improvement. This search should take place whether or not an Assembly for Scotland is eventually created. If such an Assembly is created though, we should capitalise on the opportunity it provides for reviewing existing organisational arrangements and policy-making practices, and for introducing improvements. In any event, the opportunity exists for Scotland to be at the forefront in the development of a systematic yet politically realistic health planning process and in so doing to make sure the policies that are developed are sensitive to Scotland's future health needs and problems.

REFERENCES

Department of Health and Social Security. *Priorities for Health and Personal Social Services in England: A Consultative Document.* London, HMSO, 1976.
Etzioni, A., "Mixed-Scanning. A 'Third' Approach to Decision-Making". *Public Administration Review,* Dec. 1967.
Griffiths, J. A. G., *Central Departments and Local Authorities.* London: George Allen and Unwin, 1966.
Gunn, L., "Identifying Scotland's Problems". Paper given on 28th Oct. 1978, in seminar on "Social Policies in Scotland and Devolution", organised by Scottish Council of Social Service.
Klein, R., "Policy Problems and Policy Perceptions in the National Health Service". *Political Quarterly* 42:4, Oct./Dec. 1974.

Lind, G., and Wiseman, C., "Setting Health Priorities: A Review of Concepts and Approaches". *Journal of Social Policy* 7:4, Oct. 1978.

Lindblom, C. E., *The Intelligence of Democracy: Decision-Making Through Mutual Adjustment*. London: Collier-MacMillan, 1965.

Maddox, G. L., "Muddling Through: Planning for Health Care in England". *Medical Care* 9:5, Sept./Oct. 1971.

Scottish Home and Health Department, "The Child Health Service. A Systematic Planning Approach". Edinburgh: SHHD, 1974.

Scottish Home and Health Department, "Nursing Manpower Planning Reports". Nos. 1-8. Edinburgh: SHHD, 1974-77.

Scottish Home and Health Department, "The Way Ahead". Edinburgh: HMSO, 1976.

Stewart, J., "The National Health Service — The Structural Problem". *Hospital and Health Service Review* 73:9, Sept. 1977.

Wiseman, C., "Strategic Planning in the Scottish NHS — A Mixed-Scanning Approach". *Long Range Planning*. April 1979.

Wiseman, C., "Selection of Major Planning Issues". *Policy Sciences* 9, 1978.

10

MORE AND LESS COERCIVE WAYS OF
SETTLING DEBTS*

MICHAEL ADLER

and

EDWARD WOZNIAK

Department of Social Administration
University of Edinburgh

Debt is the corollary of credit and, without the latter, the former would largely cease to exist. However, in our consumer-oriented society, a number of factors have combined to encourage the growth of credit. Many people appear to obtain goods and pay for them on a regular instalment basis rather than save up enough to make an outright cash payment. In many cases, goods are priced at such a level, that, without availability of credit, the average consumer could simply not afford to buy them. Credit facilities have thus been developed in order to promote and sustain the high level of consumption which individuals appear to want and which our society appears to require. In other cases, bureaucratic convenience may encourage the provision of credit: this is the case with public utilities such as electricity and gas, where pre-payment meters are only allowed in exceptional cases. Most people willingly undertake to pay later — problems arise for some people when they find

* The authors would like to acknowledge the financial support of the Scottish Courts Administration for funding a two year research project on the Social Impact of Diligence which was carried out for the Scottish Law Commission. They would also like to thank Stewart Asquith, Gerry Maher, Bob McCreadie, David Nelken and Alan Paterson of the University of Edinburgh and Ann Connors, Barbara Doig and Ann Millar of the Scottish Office Central Research Unit for their helpful comments on an earlier draft of this paper. The views expressed in this paper are, however, those of the authors alone and no not represent those of the Scottish Courts Administration, the Scottish Law Commission or any of the individuals mentioned above.

that they cannot afford to pay, either because their resources will not stretch that far or because their circumstances have changed, possibly because the breadwinner loses his job, falls sick or leaves the household. All too often, the persons concerned cannot avail themselves of such useful income-stretching devices as the bank overdraft or the credit card.

When we think of individuals who are in debt we usually have in mind their failure to pay for goods bought on credit sale or hire purchase from private retailers. This may have been the case 100 years ago but this century has seen a very significant growth in "public" as distinct from "private" debt — i.e. in money owed to central government, local authorities and public utilities. However, although the nature of debt may have changed radically over the last 100 years, the law relating to the enforcement of default debts in Scotland has not been satisfactorily adapted to meet modern conditions.

The inappropriateness of the law and legal procedures to modern conditions should not imply that there have been no changes in the law over the last 100 years. The use of imprisonment as a general remedy to pay debts was restricted by the Debtors (Scotland) Act 1880 to failure to pay taxes, rates, aliment and fines. Since then, imprisonment for most tax debts has been abolished (under the Crown Proceedings Act 1947); imprisonment for failure to pay rates is now non-existent and it is quite uncommon for failure to pay aliment (in fact it is considerably less common than in England). Thus imprisonment is, in effect, only used for the non-payment of fines.[2] Earnings of up to £1 per week were protected from arrestment under the Wages Arrestment Limitation (Scotland) Act 1870. This level has, however, only been raised twice since then and the present position, following the Wages Arrestment Limitation (Amendment) Scotland Act 1960, is that a creditor may arrest half a person's earnings above £4 per week, except in respect of unpaid aliment, rates or taxes where the whole of a person's wages may be arrested. Finally, as a result of the passing of the Law Reform (Diligence) Scotland Act 1973 (a Private Member's Bill introduced by Gregor Mackenzie MP) an embargo was placed on the poinding (valuation) and sale of certain basic household necessities.[3]

In spite of these changes in the law, the statutory procedures for debt enforcement (which are collectively known as *diligence*) are still essentially those that were developed to deal with the problem of debt in the early nineteenth century. These procedures, which are graphically described in the 1854 Hill Burton Report[4] and are represented in bare outline in Figure 1, do

Fig. I

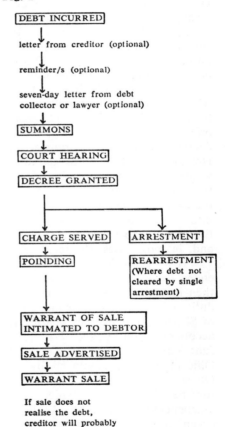

(i) PRE-JUDICIAL
DEBT COLLECTION
Debtor is requested to
pay but does not/ cannot
do so

DEBT INCURRED

letter from creditor (optional)

reminder/s (optional)

seven-day letter from debt
collector or lawyer (optional)

(ii) DETERMINATION OF
WHETHER OR NOT DEBT
IS LEGALLY OWING

Creditor resorts to legal
action and goes to court
to get a decree against
debtor

SUMMONS

COURT HEARING

DECREE GRANTED

(iii) POST-JUDICIAL DEBT
ENFORCEMENT
Creditor takes action to
enforce the decree

CHARGE SERVED

POINDING

ARRESTMENT

REARRESTMENT
(Where debt not
cleared by single
arrestment)

WARRANT OF SALE
INTIMATED TO DEBTOR

SALE ADVERTISED

WARRANT SALE

Creditor gets money
through arrestment of
wages or seizure of
debtor's property

If sale does not
realise the debt,
creditor will probably
give up, but he need
not do so

Figure 1. *Stages in the Process of pre-judicial Debt Collection Determination of Whether Debt is Legally Owing and post-judicial Debt Enforcement (Diligence)*

not take any account of the debtor's individual circumstances or the factors which give rise to the debt. Since September 1976, actions for debts of up to £500 have been dealt with under the new "summary cause" procedure in the Sheriff Court,[5] while actions for debts of more than £500 are known as "ordinary" actions and are dealt with somewhat differently.[6] In either case, the Sheriff has only to decide two issues: is the money legally owing and, if so, what kind of decree should be awarded to the creditor. In the great majority of summary cause actions, the debtor does not attend or put forward any defence or make an offer to repay the debt.[7] The Court therefore assumes (usually correctly) that a debt has been incurred and grants the creditor an open decree which allows him to decide how the amount which is owing (which will now include Court expenses) should be repaid. Less often, and usually only where the debtor has offered to repay in this way, the creditor is granted an instalment decree which fixes the rate at which the debt is to be repaid. However, if the debtor defaults on a single instalment, for whatever reason, the instalment decree may subsequently be treated as an open decree. Both decrees allow the creditor to use all lawful means of enforcement. The Court does not inquire into the debtor's financial or other circumstances and leaves the creditor to select the most effective means of enforcement and, in most cases, the terms of repayment.

If a decree is granted by the Sheriff, the Court has largely ended its part in the proceedings. The creditor or his agent will then instruct a Sheriff Officer to enforce the decree. The official duties of a Sheriff Officer mainly revolve around the enforcement of Sheriff Court decrees relating to debt or eviction from rented accommodation. Unlike Bailiffs who perform a similar set of functions in the County Courts in England and Wales, Sheriff Officers are not employed by the Court. Although a Sheriff Officer must have an appointment from the Sheriff Principal for the Sheriffdom in which he is to act, he functions as an independent contractor. While Sheriff Officers are usually organised into partnerships under a firm's name, many Sheriff Officers are also directly involved with firms of commercial debt collectors.[8] This arrangement has given rise to a good deal of criticism on the grounds that a Sheriff Officer, as an officer of court, should never have a personal interest in the decrees he enforces. However, from a strictly commercial point of view, a firm that is able to offer a combined debt collection and debt enforcement service must have obvious attractions for a large creditor. Where the firm can also offer the services of a lawyer to issue summonses and appear in Court the attractions are still greater.

The creditor or his agent has a choice between several modes of diligence but the two most common types of diligence are poinding and sale, and arrestment.[9] *Poinding and sale* is the appropriate procedure for property owned by the debtor and in his possession. It is the oldest form of diligence in Scotland and has been in use since the Middle Ages. It involves the valuation and, if necessary, the sale of certain of the debtor's possessions to satisy the debt. *Arrestment* is the appropriate procedure for property which is in the hands of a third party. The most important kind of property which is normally held by a third party is money. This can be in the form of wages held by an employer or money deposited with a bank or building society. Arrestment of wages is by far the most common form of arrestment, especially in the case of summary cause actions, and we shall therefore concentrate on it to the exclusion of other forms of arrestment. We should note that arrestment of wages can only be used against people who are in employment while poinding and sale are not restricted in this way. Other forms of arrestment, e.g. arrestment of a bank account, are not restricted in this way either but are rarely appropriate.

Once a decree is granted, the creditor or his agent may write to the debtor saying a decree has been awarded and asking for payment. If payment is not obtained, the creditor may then instruct a Sheriff Officer to enforce the decree. This cannot be done until fourteen days have elapsed, because an *"extract"* (or copy) of the decree, signed by the Sheriff Clerk will only be issued after fourteen days. An extract intimates that the Sheriff has granted decree and grants warrant to the creditor to use all lawful means of enforcement if the debtor fails to pay. In the case of poinding and sale, the first step is the serving of a *charge* on the debtor. This involves the delivery to the debtor of a letter ordering implementation of the decree. This is usually accompanied by a photocopy of the extract decree and is delivered by hand. If the charge does not result in payment within the allotted time (fourteen days) the creditor can proceed to select goods for sale. He can do this at any time within one year of the date of the charge. The Sheriff Officer, accompanied by one witness (who is almost always an employee from the Sheriff Officer's firm) visits the house and proceeds to value the debtor's personal effects. If no one is in the house, the Sheriff Officer is encouraged to make enquiries and to return at another time but if, after two or three visits, he is still unsuccessful, he will make a forced entry. As we have already mentioned, basic household necessities are now exempt from poinding and the kinds of items which are most likely to be poinded are washing machines, refrigerators, TV sets, radios, hi-fi sets, three-piece suites, sideboards, wardrobes, carpets etc. Goods being paid for on hire purchase, rented items or articles belonging to another member of the household are also exempt from poinding.

The Sheriff Officer will normally attempt to poind articles to the value of the outstanding debt, together with accumulated expenses. Once the goods have been selected, they are listed on a document called a poinding schedule which is left with the debtor or in the house and it becomes an offence to dispose of the items listed. The Sheriff Officer then has eight days to report the execution of the poinding to the Sheriff Court. If the poinding does not result in satisfactory arrangements for payment, the Sheriff Officer must present a *Warrant of Sale* to the Sheriff for his signature. Most Sheriff Officers would again inform the debtor that they had such a Warrant and that, if no satisfactory arrangements are made, they will advertise a sale in the local newspaper. The sale then must take place between eight and twenty-eight days after the *advertisement* has appeared. Most sales take place within the debtor's own home and must be attended by the Sheriff Officer (who supervises the sale in his capacity as Judge of the Roup) and a professional auctioneer. The price at which the goods are sold must not be less than their appraised value and if they are not sold they are adjudged to the creditor for this value. The Judge of the Roup then has a further eight days to report the Sale to the Sheriff.

The procedure for arrestment of wages is much simpler. The extract of the decree authorises immediate arrestment and arrestment can take place without a charge being served first. It is usual for a Sheriff Officer, accompanied by a witness, to call at the office of the debtor's employer and deliver the schedule of arrestment.[10] This document, which is signed by the Sheriff Officer, is directed at the employer and has the effect of freezing wages due but not yet paid over to the debtor to the extent permitted (normally half of wages less £4 but the entire weekly wage in the case of alimentary debts, rates and taxes).[11] The employee must sign a mandate authorising his employer to pay the arrested wage to the creditor. If the employee refused to do this, the creditor would have to raise a further court action, known as an action of *furthcoming*. However, this happens very rarely with arrestment of wages. If a single arrestment does not clear the debt and the debtor does not make satisfactory arrangements for paying what he still owes, the Sheriff Officer may serve one or more further arrestments.

The purpose behind both poinding and sale and arrestment is clearly to shock the debtor into settling the matter with his creditor. In the case of poinding and sale, each stage in the process (serving the charge, poinding, intimating a warrant, advertisement and the sale itself) involves an escalation of coercion and if the proceeds of the sale do not wipe out the debt, the creditor can still attempt to pursue the debtor for the outstanding sum. In many cases diligence must achieve its primary objective of bringing about a settlement between the creditor and the debtor. This is suggested by the reduction in the amount of diligence as diligence proceeds to later stages. However, part of the drop must also be due to creditors writing off the debt on the grounds that continued actions will not result in payment or that the expenses incurred relative to the amount of debt do not justify further pursuit.[12] The number of sales executed has fallen considerably in recent years to a total of 149 in 1977.[13]

If the amount of the more extreme forms of diligence is so limited and the number of repeated arrestments on the same debt is so small, what can be wrong with the procedures for debt enforcement in Scotland? The theory of diligence is very unsophisticated — it assumes that by hitting the debtor hard (where it hurts) and then threatening to hit him again (harder this time), he will be forced to make a satisfactory arrangement with the creditor to pay off his debt. However, the two parties can hardly be construed as equals and it is entirely up to the creditor to decide whether an offer from the debtor to pay by instalments is acceptable. Of course, as Paul Rock showed in his study of debt enforcement in England,[14] creditors have to balance intimidation with persuasion — if their conditions are too harsh they may get nothing out of the debtor at all and they may prefer to settle for something, however small, rather than nothing. However, the complete absence of control over the conditions of repayment by the Courts effectively grants licence to the strong creditor to exploit the position of a weak debtor if he wishes to do so. Under threat of further diligence, a debtor may agree to terms which are wholly outwith his capacity to meet and by doing so, create further problems for himself and his family. Thus the law serves to enforce a rather primitive commercial morality and to legitimate the power of the creditor over the debtor and the actions taken by the creditor to recover his debts. There is no equivalent in Scotland of the English procedure known as *attachment of earnings,* where the Court rather than the creditor decides, after an examination of the debtor's circumstances, whether and how much of the debtor's earnings should be attached.[15] And the Courts are clearly in no position to make the kinds of arrangements with creditors that the DHSS and local authority social work departments can make on behalf of social security claimants and social work clients who are in arrears with the Electricity and Gas Boards or with their rent.[16]

Poinding, advertisement and sale have been criticised for being degrading and unnecessarily stigmatising for the debtor. Sheriff Officers have been criticised for their heavy-handed methods of harassing debtors and for the low valuations[17] which they place on the debtor's poinded goods.[18] Poinding is likely to be most resented where it is accompanied by forced entry but advertising the items to be sold in the local newspapers is thought to be the most humiliating, and therefore the most resented, aspect of the whole process. The staging of the sale in the debtor's own home is thought to be particularly embarrassing and to yield lower prices than could be obtained if the sale took place in a public saleroom. All in all, the process is seen to hurt those most who can least afford it. Many of the Warrant Sales which are carried out yield pathetically small sums which frequently do not even cover the expenses of diligence, let alone the principal sum.[19] Thus, some debtors may be even more in debt after diligence has taken its full course than they were when they originally incurred the debt. It would seem that some people are required to suffer in order to serve as an example to others.

Arrestment has likewise been criticised on a number of

grounds. First, for imposing a quite unjustifiable degree of financial hardship on the debtor. This is especially so in the case of low-paid workers with large families. Thus, a man who, after paying tax and national insurance contributions, has net earnings of £50 per week could have half (£50 − £4) = £23 arrested and be left with £27. Fortunately for him, social security payments (e.g. child benefit and family income supplement) cannot be subject to arrestment. This can, of course, lead to the acquisition of further debts. Secondly, pressure may be put on the debtor to leave his employment,[20] but, even if it is not, the debtor may choose to leave voluntarily in order to escape a further arrestment. Finally, arrestment is quite inappropriate as a means of enforcing continuing financial obligations, such as aliment (maintenance), since it can only be used once arrears have been incurred.

A further criticism of both types of diligence is that they are unnecessarily expensive. Expenses are incurred at each stage of what may be a long and drawn-out process. Where decree is awarded against the debtor, he will have to pay Court fees, Sheriff Officer's expenses, the expenses of a solicitor (where the creditor has instructed a solicitor) and possibly the creditor's expenses in addition to the principal sum. As a result, particularly in the case of small debts, the expenses incurred often exceed the sum owed. It is often argued not only that the expenses are excessive but also that they could be avoided if a more effective system of debt enforcement could be devised. It is not even clear that the present system is particularly effective from the creditor's point of view. An analysis of all summary cause actions in the Sheriff Court in Edinburgh during November 1976, reveals that 41% of the actions that were brought were dismissed.[21] Dismissals mainly result from debts which were settled before the summons was issued and errors on the part of the creditor. Where a case is dismissed, the creditor has to meet the costs of his action. Where the debt is settled after receipt of the summons, a decree for expenses only is likely to be awarded. In this case the costs are passed on to the debtor. In addition, there is a good deal of attrition throughout the enforcement process and a substantial amount of debt gets written off when creditors and their agents decide that the costs of further attempts at enforcement cannot be justified in terms of the likely returns to the creditor.[22]

M

It would be wrong to assume from this discussion that debt, default debt, or procedures for statutory debt enforcement are matters about which people in Scotland know a great deal. As Paul Rock demonstrated in his survey of attitudes to debt collection, one of the main characteristics of debt enforcement is its "low visibility" — people supposedly don't know much about the processes of debt collection or debt enforcement or the officials who carry them out. Nevertheless, there has been a good deal of public criticism of the procedures of debt enforcement and the activities of enforcement officers. Because Scots law and procedure is, at least in this respect, so rigid and inflexible and because, to a greater extent than English law and procedure, it is still rooted in the strict commercial morality of a bygone era, it has been under considerably greater attack. MPs have asked questions in the House of Commons[23] and called for a total ban on Warrant Sales,[24] newspapers have run feature articles on debt enforcement[25] and on the involvement of Sheriff Officers with firms of debt collectors,[26] a Sheriff has issued a string of judgements against one particularly notorious firm of Sheriff Officers,[27] social workers have drawn attention to the social problems created for families by the insensitivity of debt enforcement procedures [28] and the Scottish Legal Action Group ran a very successful Conference on Debt[29] which was followed up by an excellent series of articles in the *Scottish Legal Action Group Bulletin*.[30]

In 1971, the Scottish Law Commission set up a Working Party, consisting of lawyers, Sheriff Officers and a Sheriff Clerk, to examine the then present law and practice of diligence in Scotland and to identify what changes, if any, in the law were required. The Working Party, in spite of being in existence for several years, never produced a report. This failure meant that, by 1976, there was considerable pressure on the Scottish Law Commission, not least from those quarters noted above, to do something about the procedures for statutory debt enforcement in Scotland. The Working Party was disbanded and, on the grounds that so little was known about the practice of diligence in Scotland, the Central Research Unit in the Scottish Office was asked to identify those areas in which research could broaden our knowledge of the present system of debt enforcement and contribute to the process of law reform. Eight areas of research were identified and an extensive programme of research in each of these areas is now in progress.[31] At the same time, the Scottish Law Commission has now begun to consider possible reforms to the law and practice of diligence and to produce a series of consultative memoranda on diligence in its widest sense. At some point in the future, the Scottish Law Commission will produce a report for Government based on the research results and the consultative memoranda mentioned above. In this paper, we have decided not to refer explicitly to the research we ourselves have undertaken but rather to speculate, in a general way, about possible models for reform.

Characteristically, there has been more concern among social reformers with the problems of debt enforcement than with the prevention of default debt. Perhaps this is not surprising since the existence of debt is so closely dependent on the availability of credit and since credit fulfils such an important role in stimulating consumption in our society.[32] Nevertheless, there are parallels between this concern with debt enforcement (rather than the prevention of default debt) and the dominant concerns of many other social reforms. Thus, to take two recent examples, the Supplementary Benefits Review attempts to strengthen the rights of people who are already poor without in any way concerning itself with preventing them from becoming poor while the Housing (Homeless Persons) Act 1977 likewise attempts to strengthen the rights of homeless families without in any way attacking the causes of homelessness.

What kinds of solutions can we expect from the Scottish Law Commission? Their latest Annual Report gives a number of important clues about their thinking [33] The Commission is to issue seven consultative memoranda dealing with various aspects of diligence. It is clear from the synopses that the proposals will attempt to "liberalise" the existing modes of diligence. There may well be an extension of those items that are currently exempt from poinding and an increase in the amount of money which is exempt from arrestment. The advertisement of Warrant Sales may be discontinued and their venue may be changed from the debtor's house to a public saleroom. An *extended arrestment order* and an *earnings transfer order* (similar to attachment of earnings and designed to deal with continuing financial obligations) may be introduced, as well as *debt arrangement schemes* (comparable to administration orders in England)

and designed to deal with wage earners in multiple debt situations. Debtors may be given more information about what is happening to them and more advice and the Courts may even assume some measure of control over Sheriff Officers at certain points, e.g. prior to a Warrant Sale. Nevertheless, the system for making and enforcing debt decrees is likely to remain largely unaltered — decisions will continue to be made in Court in the absence of the majority of debtors, creditors will retain the right to determine the mode of enforcement and the rate of repayment, while debtors will continue to be caught up in a system of enforcement which they do not properly understand, in which they are subjected to the authority of the law and a high degree of coercion by agents of the law. Sheriff Officers will continue to enforce decrees on behalf of creditors, with very little control by the Courts.

The reason for this is that the Scottish Law Commission by its very constitution, is almost bound to regard debt as a legal problem which is amenable to a legal solution. But should it be regarded in this way? Philip Lewis has written:

> "If certain problems are spoken of as legal ones and official support is given to legal methods of solving them, that is to take a particular attitude to problems of that kind, problems which may be capable of solution in some other way and which may be seen by those most closely concerned as best solved in that way".[34]

The vast majority of debtors against whom decree is granted admit to their debts.[35] What is more, nearly all of them accept that they are personally responsible for the debt and that they ought to repay the creditor.[36] The only real point at issue for them are the terms on which those debts should be repaid. A civil court may be the most appropriate forum for disputing debts — it is extensively used as a forum for asserting rights and disputing claims. However, it is not an appropriate forum for deciding how debts should be repaid — that ought to be a matter of good judgement and commonsense made in the light of the debtor's circumstances and should be decided elsewhere, perhaps through some new form of arbitration procedure. Before considering this possibility it is necessary to look at an alternative model for dealing with debtors, the *welfare model*.

In this model, people with debts are referred to welfare agencies who, after a thorough investigation of the debtor's needs and circumstances, decide whether to make a grant out of public funds to clear the debt or to intercede on behalf of the debtor by making arrangements (at least if the person is drawing social security) for bills to be paid directly (at source) to the creditor or for more convenient modes of payment in future. Examples of this model in action are the procedures which have recently been established whereby people who have fuel debts or are in arrears with their rent are referred to local authority social work departments or to the DHSS. We think there are several objections to this model. First, we ought not to require people to become social work clients before they can get help with their debt problems.[37] Secondly, it is hard to justify, however parsimoniously they are used, the existence of special facilities for social security claimants.[38] In any case, the system does not work very well and it is not at all clear that, unless there are special circumstances, people actually want cash handouts. Most of the debtors we interviewed in our study of default debtors were anxious to pay off their debts providing suitable arrangements for repayment were made.

We would like to propose for serious consideration procedures based on arbitration which, at least in the majority of cases, would neither resort to the institutions of law nor to the institutions of welfare. Under these arrangements, a creditor would seek to register debts owed to him with the new arbitration service. If the debtor admits the debt, his case would be considered by the arbitration service; if not his case would still go to Court for proof. Once proof of the debt has been established his case would, however, be referred back to the arbitration service. The arbitration service would first establish how the debt arose. The creditor would be asked to give a written account of how the debt arose and of his efforts to recover the sum owed. The debtor would likewise be asked to give a written account of how the debt arose and why he had been unable to repay it. The debtor would be required to furnish evidence of his income, outgoings (including any other debt repayments) and family commitments. Employers (in the case of people at work) or the DHSS (in the case of those who are dependent on social security) might be required to verify statements of income and the arbitration service could even check to see that debtors were in receipt of their full entitlement to social security and other related benefits. Where it is thought appropriate or where it is requested by the creditor or the debtor, either or both parties could be asked to attend a hearing. Whether or not there is a hearing, the task of the arbitrator would be to decide on an appropriate rate for repayment. Creditors would be asked what they would accept and debtors what they could afford. The appropriate rate of repayment would not necessarily reflect a compromise between the debtor's offer and the creditor's demands. It would, rather, reflect a decision which was thought to be appropriate in the light of all the circumstances. Although agreement between the parties would, of course, be desirable, it would neither be necessary nor sufficient.[39] A fixed level of income would have to be protected but we would not want to rule out paying small sums out of social security. After all, many claimants already do this and most of the debtors we interviewed were in favour of it. Where the creditor contravenes the Consumer Credit Act 1974 or, in the case of private creditors, fails to ascertain whether the customer is in a position to repay the debt, e.g. by ascertaining whether the customer is in employment or has any current repayment orders against him, the arbitration service would have the power to reduce or even waive the amount to be repaid. In most cases, the arbitrator would issue a *repayment order* which would be binding on employers or the social security authorities, for the agreed sum to be repaid from source. Where one or more repayment orders are already in force, the arbitrator would be empowered to alter these when imposing a further order. Multiple debts could be handled in this way and, for such people, advice on bankruptcy could be given. In appropriate cases, where debt was clearly a manifestation of deeper personal problems, the debtor could be referred to a social work agency which would still be empowered to pay off the debt out of public funds in appropriate circumstances. Debt counselling and advice with budgeting could be made available and the arbitration service could take the initiative in negotiating more convenient modes of payment, e.g. in relation to housing departments or fuel boards. Thus, some of the facilities which are currently offered only to recipients of social security would be extended to the much larger class of default debtors. Debtors subject to a repayment order whose circumstances changed could seek to have their repayment order adjusted accordingly and there might even be an obligation on employers and the social security authorities to report significant changes in circumstances. If a register of active orders was kept (possibly in a computerised data bank) the debtor's name could be removed as soon as the debt was repaid. Creditors might be enabled, or even required, to ascertain whether a potential customer has any active order against him before granting credit.[40] And, lest this be thought of as an invasion of privacy, we should point out that such an arrangement would be a considerable improvement over the blacklists which currently circulate in Scotland, which list all default debtors against whom a decree has been obtained.[41] Until recently it has been extremely difficult for anyone to get their name erased from the blacklists, even where the debt has been repaid.

The procedures adopted by the arbitration service would need to be kept simple and straightforward and it is important that they should not require an unrealistic level of "civil competence"[42] from the debtor.

Requests for information would be written in terms that people could understand. A debtor who wished to do so would be encouraged to appear and argue his case for himself, accompanied perhaps by his wife or by a friend. No legal or other expert representation would be allowed.

The description we have just given is no more than a sketch and many, if not most, of the details remain to be worked out. Although there is no reason in principle to restrict these procedures to debt of a certain size, it would probably be sensible to apply them in the first instance to debts that are recoverable under summary cause, i.e. to debts of less than £500. It is not clear who would most appropriately staff the new arbitration service or on what principles the level of repayment should be fixed. Both as a means of increasing community participation and a means of reducing costs, we are attracted to the idea of using lay arbitrators. However, even if this was possible (doubts have certainly been raised about whether people would volunteer for such a task) they would need quite a considerable back-up staff if the debt itself and the debtor's circumstances were to be fully investigated, contact maintained with employers, the DHSS and banks as well as debtors, creditors and the Courts, and the wide range of ancillary services outlined above were to be provided. We can, however, see no reason why the arbitrators, or the back-up staff, would need to be legally qualified and would prefer to see the arbitration service divorced from the Courts. For practical reasons, however, it may be sensible for the Sheriff Clerk's department to staff the services. Presumably it would be necessary to devise a set of rules which would relate the rate of repayment to family requirements and resources on the one hand and to the number and size of their debts on the other, and then to allow some discretion to depart from the rules on account of the circumstances in which the debt was contracted and the personal situation of the debtor. It is also not clear whether there should be some right of special appeal and if so on what grounds and to what body. If such a right of appeal was introduced, we hope that it would be used very sparingly. Although the arbitration service would have to be financed out of public funds, it is not clear that this should be through a direct grant from the Exchequer. It might well be more appropriate if it were financed through a special levy on those who grant credit in much the same way as redundancy payments are financed through a special levy on employers. Finally, it is unclear whether some, perhaps only symbolic, charge should be made for a repayment order as a means of encouraging voluntary repayments.

It would be dishonest not to acknowledge that a scheme of this kind would obviously encounter problems. Originally we thought that it would not be able to cater for the self-employed debtor but there is no reason in principle why the self-employed person should not be required to produce his annual profit and loss account, which he has to produce for the Inland Revenue, or why a repayment order should not be binding on a bank or a building society or on any third party which holds assets belonging to the self-employed debtor.[43] Likewise we thought that creditors might rush to use the new procedure without first attempting to secure voluntary repayments. If this were to happen, the number of applications to the arbitrator service could be greatly in excess of the 143,091 summary cause actions which were heard in 1977. However, this could be avoided by requiring the creditor to take certain steps before approaching the arbitration service and possibly also by requiring a certain amount of time to elapse between the date on which the debt is incurred and the date on which applica-

tion to the arbitration service can be made. Similarly, we thought that cost might be an obstacle until we thought of the special levy on the providers of credit. Since they would, no doubt, pass on these costs, this would put up the cost of credit but it would probably not be increased very much. Our proposal that a debtor's name should be removed from the register of active enforcement orders, which those who grant credit would be required to consult before doing so, as soon as his debt is repaid could prevent credit-granting agencies from properly establishing the credit-worthiness of potential customers. Whether or not this proposal is acceptable would seem to depend on the relative importance attached to the prevention of default debt (for which evidence of previous debts is highly relevant) and to the civil liberties of the debtor. We have concluded that the most difficult problem raised by our proposals will be to ensure participation in the new procedures. These require minimally that the debtor acknowledges the debt (or denies it and elects to go to Court), and provides details of his income, outgoings and family commitments. What if he does not do so? Attendance may not be necessary for the success of the new procedures but it could be encouraged if meetings of the arbitration service took place in the evening as well as during the day and/or if the expenses of attending the hearing were paid by the service. This would, however, raise many problems. On the other hand, it is absolutely essential that the debtor does acknowledge his debt and does provide the personal information mentioned above. Without some form of sanction, participation might well be very low and it would defeat our objective of removing debt enforcement from the ambit of the Courts if the new procedures were only voluntary, since those who did not participate could then be dragged through the Courts and sub-jected to diligence as at present. Under *attachment of earnings* proceedings in England, a debtor is required to provide evidence of his income and outgoings and to attend a Court hearing under threat of punishment. However, this is only possible because the debtor already has a Court order against him and can be held to be in contempt of court for failing to adhere to its terms. One sanction which could certainly be used would be to place the name of the non-respondent or the person who fails to supply the relevant information on a special register of unpaid debts but it will almost certainly be necessary to impose

stronger sanctions if the new system is to work. We have reluctantly concluded that the arbitration service will have to be able to demand a minimal level of participation under threat of punishment — a fine of £10 would probably be sufficient.

There are two obvious objections to this proposal. First, it might be thought rather bizarre to suggest that debtors should be fined for not participating in debt enforcement procedures, since that would only magnify their debts. However, it must be remembered that debts would no longer be compounded by the addition of Court and diligence expenses. Second, imposing a fine allows for the possibility that a debtor might be imprisoned for failing to pay the fine. Although we think this would happen very rarely, it can certainly be argued that this would be a very high price to pay for the abolition of diligence. However, to seek a wholly non-coercive mode of repaying debts is to seek the impossible. It should be clear though, the question of sanctions notwithstanding, that the procedures we have proposed will involve considerably less coercion for the vast majority of debtors than those currently in operation.

In spite of the problem just described there would seem to be considerable advantages to the new procedure. For the debtor it would be cheaper and more intelligible, it would have regard to his circumstances and would spare him the indignity and humiliation he undoubtedly suffers at present. It might well be more efficient for creditors than the present system and enable them to recoup a larger proportion of unpaid debts.[44] If this was the case, there would be much less incentive for creditors to sell their outstanding debts. How debts are repaid would become a question of public policy rather than private licence. There would be no need for diligence, since the repayment orders could all be served by post, and thus no need for Sheriff Officers. Poinding and sale, and lump sum arrestments would be abolished as the repayment order became the sole means of statutory debt enforcement. The DHSS and the local authority social work departments would be relieved of some of those responsibilities they have only taken on with great reluctance.

The proposals outlined here are in some ways modelled on the Children's Hearing system which replaced Juvenile Courts in Scotland in 1971. Just as the Children's Hearing system was designed to take the problem of dealing with child offenders, most of whom pleaded guilty, out of the ambit of the criminal courts, so the arbitration service is designed to take the problem of dealing with debtors, most of whom admit to their debts, out of the ambit of the civil courts. And just as the Children's Hearings are concerned to promote the welfare of the child but, at the same time, uphold conventional social norms and values, e.g. in relation to compulsory school attendance and respect of property, so the arbitration service would be concerned to protect the welfare of the debtor and his family while at the same time upholding the dominant contractual morality of the market place and ensuring that creditors are fully recompensed for money owing to them. How the debt should be repaid, rather than whether it should be, would be the dominant issue. The aim of the new procedure would be to come to a reasonable decision by balancing the well-being of the debtor against the right of the creditor to repayment. The shift away from a mode of debt enforcement in which the debtor is seen as a guilty person who is blamed for his debt and deserves whatever "punishment" he gets from an aggrieved creditor towards a mode of debt enforcement which is less concerned to attribute blame and more concerned to reach a solution which is in the interests of both parties also has analogies with the shift away from the concept of the "guilty party" in divorce and its replacement by the "irretrievable breakdown of marriage" and the shift in delict from the concept of fault towards "no-fault insurance".

The three models of debt enforcement outlined in this paper (the dominant *diligence model,* the alternative *welfare model* and the proposed *arbitration model*) are based on different "models of man" and different assumptions about the motives, attitudes and capabilities of debtors. Each of these sets of assumptions entails an explanation of why non-payment occurs and suggests a very different enforcement strategy.[45] Each is likewise associated with a set of enforcement difficulties.

The main characteristics of each model are set out in Figure 2.[46] The *diligence model* assumes that all debtors are "amoral calculators" who refuse to repay their debts because the advantages of non-payment exceed the costs (to them) of the sanctions that are applied. The model assumes that by gradually increasing sanctions, a point will be reached where the debtor will repay but problems arise where the person objects to the

	DILIGENCE MODEL	WELFARE MODEL	ARBITRATION MODEL
assumptions about debtor	"amoral calculator"	"inadequate" or unfortunate	unfortunate
assumed reason for non-payment	"benefits" of non-payment exceed costs (to debtor) of sanctions applied	debtors cannot repay debt without considerable costs to themselves or their families	debtor doesn't repay because terms are unrealistic or unacceptable
enforcement strategy	increase sanctions	pay debt out of public funds	agree terms of repayment
characteristics of enforcement agent	policeman	counsellor/social worker	arbitrator
associated problems	1. debtor may object to creditor's terms and refuse to pay for that reason 2. debtor may be unable to pay 3. enforcement is both inefficient and excessively harmful to debtor	1. costs if applied on large scale 2. inflation of client population 3. help may be seen as stigmatising	1. ensuring participation of some debtors ("amoral calculators") in the proceedings 2. cost of proceedings

Figure 2. *Main Characteristics of Three Alternative Models of Debt Enforcement.*

creditor's terms (and refuses to pay for this reason) or simply cannot afford to pay. Problems arise from the costs to such debtors of the sanctions which creditors are largely at liberty to apply. The *welfare model* assumes that all debtors are either "inadequate" or so unfortunate that they cannot repay the debt without considerable costs to themselves or their families. This model therefore assumes that their debts should be paid for them out of public funds and that they themselves should be given professional help to resolve their problems. Problems of cost would arise if this type of debt enforcement were applied to more than a small minority of debtors. Problems would also arise for the welfare agencies if being in debt transformed a large number of people into welfare clients, and problems do arise because this form of help can be seen as humiliating and may be strongly resented. The *arbitration model* assumes that debtors have simply been unfortunate, perhaps because their circumstances have changed in some way, but that they want to repay their debts and will repay them if suitable terms can be agreed. The model therefore assumes that some form of compromise should be sought either through mediation or, where this does not produce satisfactory results, through arbitration. The main problems here are that of ensuring the participation of those debtors who can perhaps best be described as "amoral calculators" and the likely cost of the new procedures.

As we argued earlier in this paper, public pressure forced the Scottish Law Commission to review the law practice of diligence. Public pressure must now attempt to get the Government to think about ways of preventing default debt as well as reforming procedures for dealing with it and to question some of the basic assumptions of diligence. It is clear that none of the models outlined above can apply to all default debtors but we hope we have made out a case for the arbitration model to become the dominant model of debt enforcement in Scotland. It most closely fits our understanding of the motives, attitudes and capabilities of the large majority of default debtors and we believe that its introduction would be welcomed by everyone, except perhaps by those who have a personal stake in our present antiquated procedures.

REFERENCES

2. In 1977, 5,631 people were imprisoned for non-payment of fines. They comprised 30% of receptions of prisoners under sentence — see *Prisons in Scotland Report for 1977*.
3. The Act provides that beds, bedding material, chairs, tables, equipment providing facilities for cooking, eating or storing food and for heating may not be poinded if they are *reasonably necessary* to enable the debtor and his family to live without undue hardship.
4. "Report on the Arrestment of Wages, the Effect of Abolishing Imprisonment for Small Debts and the Practice of Truck in Scotland." Parliamentary Papers 1854 LXIX.
5. The Sheriff Court is the principal local court of civil and criminal jurisdiction in Scotland — its civil jurisdiction is similar to but somewhat more extensive than the County Court in England and Wales.
6. In 1977, 143,091 "summary cause" actions and 21,000 "ordinary" actions were disposed of in the Sheriff Courts. The large majority of these were debt actions.
7. Of 117,592 summary cause decrees awarded in 1977, 113,988 were awarded in the absence of the debtor.
8. Examples of direct involvement are T. C. Gray Ltd. (debt collectors) and Gray and Donald (Sheriff Officers); Lawrence Jack Collections Ltd. (debt collectors) and Jack Lewis and Son (Sheriff Officers). Assured Collections Ltd. (debt collectors) and Arthur S. Kidd & Co. (Sheriff Officers).
9. Other modes of diligence are *ejection* (eviction) and *sequestration*. The former is used for the recovery of heritable property and the latter for arrears of rent.
10. Some Sheriff Officers post this document to the employer as a matter of routine. This is clearly advantageous for the debtor since it is cheaper, but its legality is questionable.
11. There is some confusion about whether arrestment should be made on gross or net wages. The legislation (Wages Arrestment Limitation (Scotland) Act 1870) refers only to earnings but that is not surprising since there was little difference between gross and net wages for the working man in 1870. Today it would appear that arrestments are usually but by no means always made on net wages.
12. There are no published statistics of diligence. The figures below were obtained through a special exercise carried out through the Society of Messengers at Arms and Sheriff Officers and refer to a six-month period, September 1974 - March 1975.

Charges	31,291	Arrestment of which	13,006
Poindings	17,900	Arrestment of wages	12,000
Sales Instructed	7,252	of which	
Sales Advertised	3,676	Repeated Arrestment	3,400
Sales Executed	386*	for same debt	

* This is now known to have been overstated.

13. Corrected official figures for the number of sales executed in recent years reported in *Civil Judicial Statistics (Scotland) 1977* are as follows:

1972	416 sales	1975	223 sales
1973	305 sales	1976	219 sales
1974	226 sales	1977	149 sales

14. Paul, Rock, *Making People Pay*. Routledge and Kegan Paul, 1973.

15. Under the Attachment of Earnings Act 1971, a creditor who is successful in a Court action for debt but who fails to obtain payment can make a further application to a County Court for an order of attachment. The Court fixes a date for the hearing, informs the debtor and orders him, under threat of punishment, to provide information about his income and outgoings. His employer is also required to provide information about his earnings. The Court is then empowered to fix a "protected earnings level" (related to supplementary benefit scale rates) below which earnings cannot be attached. A deduction rate (representing the amount which the Court decides the debtor should pay each week) is then fixed. This is binding on the employer and remains operative until the debt is cleared. 54,662 attachment orders were granted in 1977.

16. For details, see the two Joint Memoranda of Guidance for Scotland, *Assistance in Cash 1978* and *Fuel Debts 1978*. Both are available from the Social Work Services Group.

17. Part of the problem is that these valuations necessarily reflect the exchange value of the articles concerned. This is likely to be considerably less than the use value of the articles or their replacement cost. According to Michele Myers ("A Study of Warrant Sale Procedures." Unpublished M.Sc. thesis, University of Glasgow 1976) the valuations are often considerably less than what the articles could fetch on the open market.

18. For a recent critique, see the series of articles in the *Glasgow Herald*, 27-29/10/77.

19. David Lassels (Faculty of Law, University of Aberdeen) has analysed the records of all Warrant Sales carried out in Aberdeen between 1970 and 1976. Out of ninety-six Sales, only six produced a net surplus for the debtor (by a net surplus is meant a sum exceeding the total of the creditor's claim, together with Court expenses and the expenses of poinding and sale) while in thirty-nine cases the proceeds of the Sale were less than the expenses incurred in poinding and Sale alone.

20. It is very doubtful that even repeated arrestments would, on their own, justify dismissal under the Employment Protection (Consolidation) Act 1978, but an employer might be prepared to risk a finding of unfair dismissal and pay compensation if he really wished to get rid of an employee.

21. A total of 1195 actions were brought. Of these 490 (41%) were dismissed, 100 (8.5%) resulted in decrees for expenses only and 605 (50.6%) in decrees for the debt and expenses. Offers to pay by instalments were made in ninety-one cases and accepted in the majority

of cases. See *Interim Report on Social Aspects of Diligence,* Scottish Office Central Research Unit, May 1977, Vol. 1. Table 6.

22. The small number of actions raised in the Court for sums of less than £20 can also be attributed to the high costs of debt collection and enforcement.

23. See, for example, HC-Deb 30th November 1977 Cols. 501-502.

24. Actively supported by Dennis Canavan, Labour MP for West Stirlingshire, James Dempsey, Labour MP for Airdrie and Coatbridge and Willie Hamilton, Labour MP for Central Fife.

25. See the series of articles in *Glasgow Herald,* op. cit.

26. See *The Sunday Times,* 11/7/76.

27. Sheriff Nigel Thompson, then of Hamilton Sheriff Court. See, e.g. John Temple Ltd. v Logan (1973 S.L.T. (Sh.Ct) 41 at 47), British Relays vs Keay (1976 S.L.T. (Sh.Ct) and Lawrence Jack Collections vs Hamilton (1976 S.L.T. (Sh.Ct) 18).

28. See statements of British Association of Social Workers, Scottish Social Policy and Social Action Group.

29. Scottish Legal Action Group, Debt Conference 15th May 1976.

30. See R. A. McCreadie, "Debtors 1" *Scolag Bulletin,* 5/6/76; "Debtors 2" *Scolag Bulletin,* 6 August/September 1976; "Debtors 3: Poinding and Sale" *Scolag Bulletin,* 7 Oct./Nov. 1976; "Debtors 4: Arrestment" *Scolag Bulletin,* 9 March/April 1977; "Debtors 5: Conclusions" Scolag Bulletin 10 May/June 1977. Anyone who has read these articles will see how heavily we have drawn on them in this paper.

31. An account of this programme of research can be found in the *Interim Report on Social Aspects of Diligence,* op. cit.

32. The Consumer Credit Act 1974 does impose some controls on the granting of credit and gives some protection to customers — it is now a criminal offence to provide credit without a licence and consumers must be given full details of the cost of any credit offered to them. Although this legislation may succeed in curbing the most flagrant abuses of power by creditors, it will not substantially alter the scope of credit or the terms on which it is offered. Providers of credit are not required to ascertain whether the customer can afford the terms offered or to insure themselves against loss.

33. *Scottish Law Commission Thirteenth Annual Report, 1977-78.*

34. Philip Lewis "Unmet Legal Needs" in Pauline Morris et al. *Social Needs and Legal Action,* Martin Robertson, 1973, p. 79.

35. Very few debtors dispute their debts in Court. Equally, few debtors from the sample of default debtors whom we interviewed disputed their debts in practice.

36. Most default debtors would thus appear to subscribe to the dominant value system, based on the commercial morality of the market place, while relatively few seem to be committed to subordinate or radical value systems. See Frank Parkin *Class Inequality and Political Order,* Paladin, 1972.

37. This point has been very forcibly made by Bill Jordan in *Poor Parents,* Routledge and Kegan Paul, 1974 and elsewhere.

38. This argument has frequently been made by David Donnison. See, for example, "Supplementary Benefits: Dilemmas and Priorities" *Journal of Social Policy* 5:4, October 1976.
39. Under present procedures, creditors are often granted instalment decrees based on unrealistic offers of repayment on which the debtor subsequently defaults.
40. Members of the public would be able to check whether their name is on the register and, if so, whether the entry is correct.
41. Scottish editions of *Stubbs Weekly Gazette* and *Kemp's Mercantile Gazette* are published weekly and circulated privately to banks and other organisations granting credit.
42. Phillipe Nonet *Administrative Justice*. Russell Sage 1969.
43. No doubt some self-employed people do keep their money under their beds, but they are probably a very small minority.
44. The claim that our proposals would benefit debtors *and* creditors has been received with some incredulity. However, reform of procedures for debt enforcement is *not* a zero-sum game — we maintain that debtors would benefit from our proposed procedures even if they had to repay more of their debts.
45. This analysis owes a great deal to an unpublished paper by Robert Kagan and John Scholtz of the University of California, Berkeley, entitled "The 'Criminology' of the Corporation' and Regulatory Enforcement Strategies". This paper can be obtained from Michael Adler on request.
46. Although each model of debt enforcement has its defining characteristics, individual enforcement agents nevertheless discriminate between default debtors. Default debtors whose circumstances are seen to conflict with the assumptions made by the system of debt enforcement may be "cooled out". See Paul Rock *op. cit.*

N

11

THE SCOTTISH FISHING INDUSTRY: TECHNICAL OPPORTUNITIES AND POLITICAL CONSTRAINTS

JOHN GODFREY
Department of Zoology, University of Edinburgh

NORMAN GODMAN
Department of Business Organisation, Heriot-Watt University

The sea fisheries of Scotland present a clear challenge to political wisdom. The fish on which the industry depends have been severely depleted by the combination of a series of improvements in the efficiency of fishing technology and inadequate political control over the access of competing fishermen to the common resource. Only rising prices due to scarcity have sheltered the industry from feeling the full effects of the crisis. Legal changes offer the opportunity for rational solutions to the problem, but at the time of writing, there is still no Common Fisheries Policy and meanwhile the problem gets worse and its solution more difficult.

The interim arrangements for fisheries among the EEC states which were hastily put together on the eve of the enlargement of the Community in 1972 to include the UK, Ireland and Denmark are weak. They run only to 1982 when, in the absence of an agreed alternative policy, there is to be free competition among all fishermen of the EEC member states in what would become their joint waters. It was mainly because of this prospect that Norway decided, following a referendum, not to join the EEC, and it has been consistently opposed by fishing interests in both the United Kingdom and the Irish Republic. We wish to outline the problem and suggest the framework of a realistic answer to it.

Change and Continuity in the Scottish Fisheries

Historically, the Scottish fishing industry has shown considerable adaptability whilst undergoing comprehensive change.

For example, the latter half of the nineteenth century saw a major shift in emphasis from the traditional methods of long-line and drift-net fishing to trawl-fishing. Change was facilitated by the expansion of the railways in mid-nineteenth century and by the growing use of ice to preserve the fish. These developments encouraged the growth of the white-fish industry which was to become more important than the drift-net fisheries for herring. Towards the end of the century more changes took place with the introduction of steam-propelled trawlers and drifters.

The twentieth century has seen the virtual disappearance of the once-thriving Scottish herring industry with its hundreds of vessels and many thousands of men and with its Scottish fisher-girls who were once employed itinerantly to follow the seasonal movement of herring around the coast to North Shields, Hull, Great Yarmouth and Lowestoft. This fishery reached its peak before the first world war and has collapsed since the second. One of the most important developments in the Scottish fishing industry over the past fifty years has been the growth in the number of seine-net vessels. Apart from Aberdeen, which is still the major Scottish trawler-port, seine-net gear is now responsible for a high percentage of landings in the Scottish fishing districts. Trawling involves towing a net along the sea bed with the mouth of it held open by two boards, one on each side of the net. A seine net has large wings but no boards. A further development is the purse-seine net, the use of which allows the encirclement of a shoal of fish. The net can measure 1200 metres long with a depth of up to 240 metres and as the name suggests, the net is shaped like a purse. By using electronic equipment the skipper can tell exactly where his net and the fish shoal are with respect of one another. He can surround a shoal, or, if it is so large as to endanger his gear, take a chosen proportion of it.

Other innovations, such as the power block for lifting the net and catch aboard, and pair-trawling, have increased the catching efficiency of many vessels. In pair-trawling two vessels tow the net between them. The net can have a much larger mouth than a single vessel can handle. The inevitable results of these changes, with unrestricted entry to fishing grounds and free competition among fishermen, is a severe depletion of stocks of commercially valuable fish.

Intense fishing with fine mesh nets means that fish are usually caught young around Western Europe. So more and more effort goes into catching smaller and smaller fish, which if left to grow would provide far more food. Most species suffer from this type of overfishing although some, such as cod, have such a great reproductive potential that even when considerably overfished are still unlikely to be exterminated.

More serious still, overfishing may cut down the number of fish available to breed, and thus further reduce the harvestable population. This has already happened to herring in the North, the Irish, and the Celtic Seas, and in the waters West of Scotland.

And even extinction is no idle fear. The sardine industry of California collapsed as a result of this kind of overfishing long ago — and has never recovered. Species with low reproductive potential and those that shoal so as to be economically caught even when at a low population density are most likely to suffer extinction.

It is not only excessive catching for the table that has caused the present crisis. Since supplies of fishmeal and fertiliser from South America have decreased, industrial fishing has grown so much around Europe that more than two million tons have lately been taken from the North Sea each year to feed to animals.

Fish we spurn as food are the targets of this operation. But a fine net is not a precision tool, and the young of valuable species like herring are caught in large quantities together with the intended sprats. In some years more than 100,000 tons of young haddock have been turned into fish meal together with the pout that were being fished for. Pout fishing has been excluded from a "box" off the east coast of the UK to protect the breeding of haddock and whiting. Only part of the nursery grounds are protected, but a still inadequate extension of this protection is leading to the UK being taken to the European Court by the Commission of the EEC. The Commission is doing this to establish whether the measure is both necessary and non-discriminatory as between nations. Denmark is the nation doing most industrial fishing which would be most affected, but its vessels could not be excluded, in the British area, on the basis of nationality. British measures to conserve stocks by prohibiting the use of mesh sizes that were previously allowed are leading to similar action by the Commission.

Haddock caught for the table have to be above a minimum size, and if young fish are caught they must be thrown back. But it has been hard to enforce this regulation when huge quantities of the same infants are grist to the industrial mill because of the loophole of an allowable "bye-catch".

There have been a few examples of attempts at conservation by the voluntary action of fishermen. One case in point is that of the Shetland herring fishermen who adopted conservation measures some three years before the final collapse of the North Sea herring. The overall ban on herring fishing, introduced by the British government, came only after the stocks had been severely depleted mainly by the rapid growth of the Norwegian purse seine fleet and also the damage done to young herring by the industrial fisheries of Denmark in particular. This ban is particularly harsh on the Shetland herring boats which were voluntarily conserving herring by about 50% until banned from catching herring altogether. They did this by setting a daily quota based on how many fish could be bought locally for human consumption, and so none went for reduction to fish meal at a lower price. The six vessels implemented the quota by keeping in touch by radio. As soon as the quota had been reached by any combination of boats, fishing stopped. Each boat took an equal share of the money from selling the fish irrespective of how many it had caught. These Shetlanders have had no benefit from their own co-operative innovation, which in itself is remarkable for such traditionally competitive fishermen. (The Norwegian purse seiner fleet is now itself in grave difficulty. Many vessels are being taken out of fishing, in part by aid from the Norwegian Government. Some are being sold to Scottish owners).

With the failure of the herring fishery, many Scottish purse-seiners among others have turned to mackerel off the west coast of Scotland in the autumn and off Cornwall in the winter. The western mackerel is now the most important stock to the British fishing industry in volume terms. It is not properly controlled internationally and the recommended Total Allowable Catch set by the International Council for the Exploration of the Seas has been grossly exceeded. The mackerel faces the prospect of collapse in the S.W. Its management, because it is migratory, demands common action by Norway and the Community.

Overfishing, depletion of stocks and extension of state

control over traditional fishing grounds were major features in the protracted fisheries dispute between Iceland and the United Kingdom. Whilst the exclusion of British trawlers from their traditional and once rich Icelandic fishing grounds was of less immediate significance to Scotland than to Fleetwood, it had important implications for the whole of the United Kingdom industry. The resolution of this fisheries squabble, rightly in Iceland's favour, encouraged the growing demands for coastal-state control of fishing grounds, particularly by the trawler companies and the Transport and General Workers' Union which represents their employees.

As far as the North Atlantic is concerned, Iceland simply established an arbitrary lead with its decision to extend its control over the surrounding fishing grounds. The Icelandic government's actions demand sympathy because of Iceland's overwhelming dependence on fish. Similarly, the Faroe Islands face major economic problems associated with overfishing. So the Faroese have very effectively restricted fishing operations in their waters and this action has had a direct bearing on the activities of a large sector of the Aberdeen trawler fleet. In addition to the decisions taken by these two nations in the North Atlantic, the Norwegian, Russian and Canadian governments have also severely restricted the activities of foreign trawlers around their coastlines.

"The general move that is now taking shape towards 200 mile exclusive Economic Zones (EEZ) recognises that a nation state is likely to provide the best mechanism for protecting the resource and for ensuring its renewable character."[1] The declaration, at the end of 1976, of 200-mile zones by the member states of the European Community was welcomed by most pople in the Scottish fishing industry but it has not stilled the demand for an exclusive British zone of at least fifty miles. This was reflected in a recommendation contained in a House of Commons Trade and Industry Sub-Committee's Report:

> "We recommend that it should be the object of the UK policy
> to secure agreement that each EEC Member State should have
> exclusive fishing access to a 50-mile wide zone from its own
> coasts."[2]

There remains a considerable hostility towards the activities of European Community fishing vessels in what are regarded as traditional British fishing grounds. John Silkin, Minister of Agriculture, Fisheries and Food in the outgoing Labour Administration epitomised this view. In Hull in March 1979 he argued: "Other member states have been very reluctant to accept the need for adequate conservation. The Commission has been much too prone to take account of the reservations of some member states unconnected with the scientific evidence. In all the circumstances I find it extremely odd that it is the United Kingdom that the Commission has seen fit to take to Court on conservation matters. But then, burglars are not known for their respect for property rights."[3]

The Scottish Fishing Industry Today

Scotland has now only a few large trawlers but she has a huge fleet of the smaller fishing vessels, with trawlers of all sizes being now built for fishing over the stern rather than the side.[4]

The Scottish fishing fleet has increased in importance in recent years with respect to that of the rest of the United Kingdom. The fleet consists mainly of near water vessels.

Table 1 shows the weight and value of landings of all fish including shellfish in the UK in 1978. It can be seen that landings by Scottish vessels in Scotland and elsewhere in Britain now account for as much as 60% of the weight and 53% of the total value of UK landings by all UK vessels.

Table 1

WEIGHT AND VALUE OF LANDINGS IN 1978 BY
SCOTTISH AND OTHER UK VESSELS

	'000 Tonnes	%	£m	%
Landings of UK vessels in UK	956.5	100	254.7	100
Landings of UK vessels in Scotland	426.2	45	122.2	48
Landings of UK vessels in Northern Ireland	11.5	1	4.8	2
Landings of UK vessels in England and Wales	518.8	54	127.7	50
Landings of Scottish vessels in England and Wales	150.9	16	13.6	5
Landings of Scottish vessels in Scotland	*420.6	44	*121.1	48
Landings of Scottish vessels in UK	571.5	60	134.7	53

* Estimated figure

Figures kindly supplied by the Department of Agriculture and Fisheries for Scotland

In contrast to the declining fortunes of the distant-water fleet, the inshore fleet has prospered, due largely to rising prices, particularly for species not previously highly valued for human consumption, some of which are exported to new markets in Africa and Australia as well as America and Europe.

The fishing industry has only a very minor role to play in the United Kingdom's gross domestic product but it is of considerable importance in a number of regions of Scotland (see Map 1). For example, in the Shetland Islands, the industry has been responsible for almost 30% of the employment and in other Scottish communities there are few employment opportunities outwith the industry. In terms of the actual number of jobs, the Grampian Region with over 50% of the industry's workforce is a most important area. Recent evidence suggests that some 8.0% (14,986 for 1978) of the employed population in the region is dependent on fishing.[5]

There has been little overall decline in the numbers of employed fishermen in recent years, but the pattern has changed. There has been development in a number of Highland ports due to the positive policies of the Highlands and Islands Development Board. Within the industry there appears to be a general belief that the ratio of fishermen to ancillary workers is at least 1: 4 and possibly 1: 7. Just as the catching sector has undergone change so too has the onshore side of the industry. We have already mentioned the decline in employment in herring processing and ancillary work but there has also been widespread contraction of employment in fish processing. In 1978, there were approximately 8000 full-time employees in fish processing, some 2,500 of whom were based in Aberdeen which is still the main Scottish centre for white-fish processing. In the same year there were upwards of 1000 employees in herring processing. One can contrast these figures with those obtaining in the early part of the century when, as J. Coull has shown, Shetland alone employed some 13,000 people to process the herring catches.[6]

In remote areas such as Shetland, boats may "trip" to a more central port, such as Aberdeen, to get a better market. This makes it difficult to maintain adequate local processing. The most hopeful developments are processing co-operatives, such as that on Westray, where the fishermen are part owners of the processing factory.

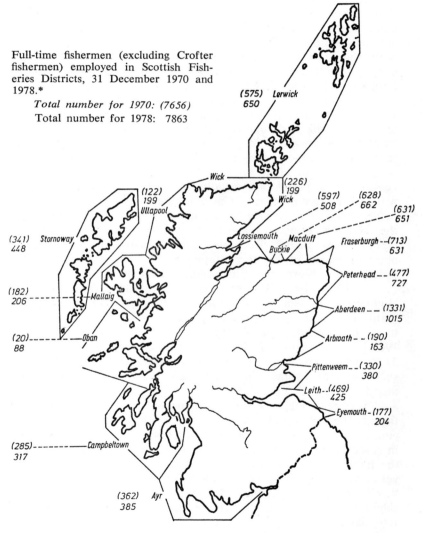

Full-time fishermen (excluding Crofter fishermen) employed in Scottish Fisheries Districts, 31 December 1970 and 1978.*

Total number for 1970: (7656)
Total number for 1978: 7863

(575) Lerwick
650

Wick (226)
199
Wick

(122)
199
Ullapool

(597) (628)
508   662

(631)
651

(341) Stornoway
448

Lossiemouth Macduff
Buckie

Fraserburgh --(713)
631

Peterhead __ (477)
727

(182)
206 ------- Mallaig

Aberdeen __ (1331)
1015

(20) ------ Oban
88

Arbroath -- (190)
163

Pittenweem __ (330)
380

Leith..(469)
425

Eyemouth - (177)
204

(285) -------- Campbeltown
317

(362) Ayr
385

*Department of Agriculture and Fisheries of Scotland Statistics, Hansard, 3 April 1979.

Share Fishermen

In Scotland, the majority of the sea-going workforce are share fishermen and they crew the smaller vessels. They receive equal shares of the crew's allocation of the total earnings and are classified by the Department of Employment as self-employed even though they obtain unemployment benefit if they can demonstrate that they are prevented from working due to reasons outwith their control, e.g. harsh weather conditions or vessels under repair. The size and composition of the crews of these vessels varies in terms of the species hunted, fishing methods (e.g. creel fishing, dredging, great lining, seine-net fishing, pair-trawling and trawling) length of voyage, fishing conditions, and so on, but in general they range from two or three men on the smaller boats to eight and up to eleven men on the largest vessels. These vessels are usually owned by the skippers jointly with other crew members. The purchase of a vessel is generally helped by a grant and/or loan from the White Fish Authority, the Herring Industry Board or the Highlands and Islands Development Board. Recently some Scottish fishermen have obtained loans, at very low interest, from Norwegian sources in order to buy Norwegian purse-seiners with no grant aid.

In 1977, the HIDB provided the fishing industry in the Highlands and Islands with the sum of £1,950,000 by way of grants and loans, an increase of some £417,000 over the 1976 total. The overall sum of money approved by the Board since 1965 is in the region of £13 million and it is estimated that over 3,000 jobs have been established or retained and that, with such assistance, some 450 vessels have been acquired by fishermen in the area.[7]

A large number of the vessel owners have formed associations, often co-operatives, and these help by selling gear and equipment and fuel to members, auctioning their catches, and in some cases, processing the fish. Assistance is also given with the financial needs and administrative functions associated with vessel ownership. A survey of Scottish skipper-owners found that "while in one place some older members seemed to exert considerable influence in conserving old habits, in another the Association had been more successful in stimulating technical progress and efficiency among others by building its own ice factory to the profit of its members. In general, the fishermen seemed to be reasonably satisfied by the functioning of their associations, and they had no objections against running part of the business themselves."[8]

Many of these share fishermen and skipper-owners live in small and remote communities in which there is a long, historical tradition of fishing. J. Tunstall, a sociologist, has argued:

"The basic economic set-up is similar to that in a smaller family-run farm. It is a dangerous job under bad conditions for very low pay per hour. But inshore men choose to do it, because they presumably do not want to leave the region to work for more money in factories in Glasgow (sic). In this type of fishing there is a genuine family tradition."[9]

One could add that the financial rewards, though varied in the extreme, can be high.

It is of some interest to note that a number of the distant-water trawler companies and other companies in the food-processing industry have taken a financial interest in the near-water sector. For example, it has been reported that one firm alone has invested several million pounds in a number of these vessels. The growing interest shown by the large trawler companies in fishing operations around the Scottish and English coastline is now causing disquiet among the traditional near-water fishermen.

Wage-earning Fishermen

The wage-earning fishermen in Scotland are based in Aberdeen and are employed by a small number of trawler companies on a variety of craft (see Table 2). The smaller trawlers have crews of from nine to twelve men and the very small number of larger trawlers have crews of twelve to fourteen men. The skippers and mates of most trawlers receive 5.33% and 4.33% respectively of the gross earnings of the vessel and the skipper gets an additional 5% of the net proceeds. The rest of the crew receive both a basic weekly wage and a share of the gross earnings of the voyage. In their evidence to the Trade and Industry Sub-Committee inquiry into the fishing industry, representatives of the Aberdeen Fishing Vessels Owners' Association claimed that average total earnings for deckhands in January 1978 was £113.75 for seven days at sea.[10]

Table 2

OWNERSHIP OF SCOTTISH DEEP SEA FLEET

As at 31 December 1977

	Number of Owners	Number of Vessels	Cumulative Percentage of Fleet
Over 10 vessels	2	23	27
5-10 vessels	5	35	69
4 vessels	—	—	—
3 vessels	—	—	—
2 vessels	1	2	71
1 vessel	24	24	100
TOTAL	32	84	—

White Fish Authority, Annual Report and Accounts 1977-8

It will be seen from Table 2 that seven companies own approximately 70% of the Scottish deep-sea fleet. For example, Associated Fisheries, through British United Trawlers Limited, own companies in Aberdeen, Hull, Grimsby and Fleetwood. In England and Wales, three companies own more than 50% of the deep-sea fleet. Despite the concentration and rationalisation of trawler companies, assisted by interlocking directorships between holding companies and subsidiaries, they remain fairly small organisations when compared with firms in the manufacturing industries.

To date most trawler fishermen remain casual employees, and so they receive little or no protection under the provisions of the Redundancy Payments Act 1965 and other industrial legislation, and even although the Merchant Shipping Acts ensure that trawler crews sign articles of agreement, this does not guarantee security of employment, since crews are employed for only one voyage at a time. It follows that, given this casual employment relationship, the extended absence from home and community, the hazardous nature of the work, the long work hours, the somewhat cramped living conditions on many of the trawlers, the brief leave entitlement, few fishermen have a record of continuous service with a particular trawler company.[11]

Wage-earning fishermen are members of the T & GWU, which has officers in the main fishing ports and a National Fishing Officer. In Aberdeen, Hull and Grimsby, skippers and mates have their own Trawler Officers' Guilds and they, along with the T & GWU, negotiate with the Fishing Vessels Owners' Association in each of the major ports. Trade unionism is virtually 100% in Aberdeen but almost nil elsewhere in Scotland. (In view of the role of the union in the politics of fisheries, it is unfortunate that most of the Scottish fishermen are un-represented by the union because of their non-membership).

The union has become increasingly involved in the industry in terms of the resources given to its fishermen-members, and its involvement with the fishermen's registration scheme in each port, ensuring fairer discipline and grievance procedures. Union representatives have been appointed to a number of Department of Trade (Maritime Division) working groups concerned with the safety of fishermen, fishing vessels and safe working practices. In addition, the union in recent years has vigorously argued the case for a different and more equitable employment scheme which has led in 1979 to an agreement in principle on a modest scheme of decasualisation.[12] A key aspect of the scheme[13] is the "topping up" of unemployment benefit by payments from employers.

A Community Fishing Policy

Many of the fish stocks on which Scottish fishermen depend move long distances during their lifetimes. Adequate management in the interests of the Scottish fishing industry depends on agreed policies for these shared stocks. England, Ireland, other Community countries and Norway share many Scottish problems as well as stages in the life cycle of her fish.

A Community Fishing Policy requires broad agreement on principles and objectives. The following objectives should be taken into account:

1. To sustain an economic use of marine fish.

2. To maximise the supply of food at a reasonable and stable price for the consumer, bearing in mind the likely long-term requirements for first-class protein which is likely to become more expensive in world markets.

3. To assist in resolving social and regional problems by providing jobs for communities that have few other economic options for employment.

4. To guarantee to those employed in the industry good
    conditions of employment and training and educational
    opportunities.

These aims will often conflict to some extent, and fisheries
management should be compatible with energy conservation (a
distant-water freezer trawler uses roughly a ton of oil for each
ton of fish landed) and pollution policies. (These, too, can cause
problems. Regulations have recently had to be made to control
the mackerel industry in Loch Broom where major sales to
Russian processing ships take place seasonally). In addition,
as we have argued elsewhere, European fisheries have a contribution to make to the fisheries development of the Third World.[14]
    When there will finally be an agreed Common Fisheries
Policy remains uncertain. The negotiations have got stuck
because of the incompatability between the British demand for
a national preference that will reflect the fact that 60% or so
of EEC fish swim in the UK sector of the seas of the Community
states and the fact that the UK fishermen have lost the right
to fish in distant waters that used to contribute 40% of their
catches; and the demand of most of the other states that
competition should be more free. In the view of many Europeans
with no particular interest in fish, the UK position runs counter
to the spirit of the Treaty of Rome, and if acted on might set a
very dangerous precedent.
    As the collapse of fish stocks has been the clear result
of the free play of the competitive market forces up till now,
Mr Silkin's stand was acclaimed by everyone in this country
connected with fishing. The deadlock has now become so bitter
that it threatens negotiations over issues like currency stability
and whether Community funds should be used mainly to
diminish regional inequalities rather than to subsidise some
sectors of agriculture indiscriminately.
    Such issues are vital to Scotland. Fishing is not a major
industry for the UK nor for any of the EEC states. It is, however,
extremely important to particular localities, where the industry
provides up to one-third of the economic input. The Ministers
could resolve their deadlock by recognising the local nature of
the problem and basing policy on this fact. Given that the
exclusive rights approach is anathema to most of the Member
States of the Community, it will not be acceptable. Local

dominant preference could provide the foundation for an agreement, particularly on the basis of forward fishing plans, an idea acceptable to the Community. Given that Scotland, and to a lesser extent the UK as a whole, has so many fishing ports near fishing grounds, local preference along these lines should add up to a fair share in fishing from the national point of view. It would go some way towards solving conflicts between different types of fishing vessel, but would not solve the conflicts between the catching, and the marketing and processing sectors.

Co-operative ownership of the kind that is relatively common in agriculture is probably the main hope here. It should be encouraged by the EEC Commission as well as by national and local governments. For any scheme to succeed, the fish stocks must be allowed to recover and a European policy for conservation would make more biological sense than a series of national policies.

This means less fishing while the fish breed and grow. EEC funds should be used to make this period bearable. When stocks have recovered more fish will be available in the shops at lower prices, employment in fishing will be secure with higher incomes, and there will be more jobs in fish processing as the quantity of fish increases. But if there is no sound agreement, no one will get what they want.

Among the proposed objectives of Community fishing plans put forward by the Commission (COM(78) 39 final, of 30 January 1978) are:

1. To promote rational exploitation of the biological resources bearing in mind the social and economic needs of certain categories of fishermen in specific regions of the Community.

2. To assure, in regard to these regions, the enjoyment of the natural geographic advantage in catch possibilities within a few hours steaming time from home ports so as to favour balanced development in line with the progressive improvement of fish stocks.

As fishing plans could eventually extend to all waters beyond twelve miles from baselines within the 200-mile Exclusive Economic Zone, it seems appropriate for EEC fishing interests to think out and argue for components of such plans that seem desirable in local circumstances.

This idea of fishing plans is catching on in Scotland.[15][16] Fishermen's associations are considering making local plans, and already the Shetland Islands Council with the Shetland Fishermen's Association are behind the development of a local fishing plan for the sea between 59 degrees North and 61 degrees 50 minutes North, and between 1 degree East and 3 degrees West. The plan shows how modest are the needs for preference to local boats. Between 1970 and 1977 Shetland boats took 11% of bottom-feeding fish. In this period, the USSR fleet took 26%, Scottish vessels 20%, the Danes 16%, the French 8% and English boats 4%. In 1977 information produced by the International Council for the Exploration of the Seas shows that Scotland landed only 14% of the fish taken from their statistical area that includes Shetland (IVa). Shetland's share was 3% compared with Denmark's 36% and Norway's 29%. The Russians are now excluded, as they are from all EEC waters. The patterns of fishing for sand-eels, pout, and herring vary, but for not one of these did Shetland take more than one-quarter of the total catch. The plan should anticipate the need for growth of the fishing sector to replace the temporary employment in oil-related activities in Shetland. We believe that most local communities of fishermen and the related shore-based workers would benefit from a fishing plan for the maritime areas in which they operate. Plans would need to extend to all waters for their full benefit to be realised for mobile fishermen and migratory fish. Fishing plans might be based on the following principles:

1. Local dominant preference, reflected in guaranteed percentages, based on the proximity to the fishing grounds, should be the basis for management policy. This could be achieved by dividing the waters of all the EEC countries into maritime areas that take account of our knowledge of fish stocks. Priority of access would be based on (a) first call to local boats, particularly when individual or co-operatively owned so as to maximise the economic and employment benefits to the communities of peripheral maritime areas. Preference for local owners would tend to control the movement into biologically rich inshore and middle-water fisheries by fleet owners whose main interest has previously been in distant waters. This is happening on a rapidly

increasing scale in Scotland; (b) favourable treatment for other areas with few employment options apart from fishing; (c) temporary allowance for vessels from ports whose home maritime area has fewer fish than normal; (d) allowance for mobility between areas for vessels designed for fishing migratory species; (e) diminishing priority on the basis of historic rights, and on the basis of exclusion of vessels, such as those of Humberside and West German ports, from waters outwith the EEC.

2. Implementation of fishing plans should be based, in the main, on effort limitation. This would require a licensing system for boats linked to an appropriate definition of fishing effort, an increase in mesh size of nets phased over a period and seasonal and area controls to protect fish when spawning or while of poor quality. Some use of catch quotas would also be necessary. Boats would be prohibited from carrying industrial fishing gear together with normal trawls.

3. Exclusion from most controls of boats below a certain size, varying with local circumstances. This might refer, say, to boats under ten or twelve metres in length. The catch of these boats would be recorded and count towards the total catch allowed for a given species.

4. Relatively relaxed limitations to be imposed on boats of intermediate size, up to perhaps twenty-five metres. "Size" is related to fishing capacity, but a more effective measure might involve several factors including length of vessel, engine power (including auxiliary power), gear, etc. Gross Registered tonnage is a crude but simple alternative.

5. Vessels capable of very high fishing capacity must be limited to certain areas and subject to relatively stringent limitations. Both Faroe and Iceland have successful experience in enforcing regulations along these lines.

Allocation by licensing of fishing effort has the following advantages over allocation by catch quota:

1. It is more certain, and therefore can be seen to be fair.

O

2. It is more flexible in operation, and therefore a more effective tool of management and conservation.

3. It reduces costs to the industry and makes them more predictable.

4. It is easier to enforce, and more economical given that enforcement at sea can be combined with the other "civil power" duties of the coastal state concerned (e.g. oil and gas installation and pipeline protection, regulation of sand and gravel extraction, traffic control, environmental monitoring), some of which can be best done by suitable aircraft. The licence numbers of vessels could be detected from the air in poor visibility by putting a transponder on each vessel.

5. It is relatively easy for fishermen to know who is licensed and whether a vessel is breaking the rules, which will encourage self-discipline.

6. It tends to be self-regulating in that the effort permitted will result in larger catches when there are more fish than had been predicted when the Total Allowable Catch (TAC) was set. With a catch quota alone, there is a tendency for fishing effort to be increased if fish are scarce.

7. It will reduce discards as well as controlling landings. Discards of ineligible fish are a majority consequence of the catch-quota system; they cause high mortality to young fish which the regime seeks to protect. Controlling effort by the use of larger mesh sizes will help to protect young fish.

8. It allows licence holders more flexibility to fish at times of their own choosing. This will tend to remove one of the factors that forces fishermen to work in bad weather. This should lead not only to a reduction in the numbers of fishermen lost or injured at sea but also to an improvement in their working conditions.

9. Whilst not discriminating between nations, it enables regional and local interests to be protected.

The two most serious objections to this proposal are:

1. That local preference would act to the disadvantage of fishing interests prepared to operate at a distance from their home ports. For instance, Scottish fishermen would only fish for mackerel on the south west coast of England by agreement on the same basis as fishermen from other EEC states. In Britain, the trawler companies would have reason to object strongly to our proposal. West Germany with least coastline in relation to the size of her fishing fleet would presumably raise similar objections. These objections could preclude local preference unless interests in those localities most in need of preference unite to press their case. Ireland has already obtained substantial advantages in negotiation within the EEC. Her case was based on economic need. With rich local fishing grounds and a relatively small fishing fleet, Ireland shares some characteristics and problems with Scotland, and, for instance, the south west of England. The other current member state in need of regional preference, partly on the grounds of low *per capita G.D.P.* and partly on the grounds of doing rather badly where the Common Agricultural Policy is concerned, is Italy. By a happy chance, Italy's fishing interests, though considerable, do not impinge upon those of the United Kingdom.

2. This proposal would entail much greater regulation of fishing. Fishermen have been long accustomed to operating under conditions of competition with regulations that can be evaded with relative impunity. Our scheme would have to be administered by an authority that some would decry as yet another bureaucracy. This disadvantage should be minimised by decentralising the administration as far as possible. Only the overall conservation framework should be centrally co-ordinated.

Some Possible Effects of a Common Fisheries Policy

Appropriate reduction in fishing effort will allow fish stocks to recover, as they did during two World Wars, so that most species of fish will be harvested at a larger size, when they are economically more rewarding. Some species, particularly among the pelagic forms, such as herring, will reproduce more effectively so that greater numbers of fish will be caught, to the considerable benefit of the industry and those many communities dependent on fishing. This will give greater profitability to those licensed to fish. A reduction in scarcity may lead to a fall in fish prices, though this in its turn may lead to an increase in consumption of fish on a *per capita* basis. Such extra revenue could be subjected to some form of taxation or licence fee to provide revenue for fisheries policing. The fee might be varied to take account of policy objectives and regional factors.

While the stocks recover, considerably less fishing, and hence fish processing, distribution and marketing, can be done, except insofar as:

1. Underexploited species can be utilised. There are important possibilities for developing fisheries, of which the most promising are the horse mackerel which has export potential, and the blue whiting, whose breeding stock is so large that possibly around 1 million tonnes might be taken annually on a continuing basis. The easiest way to use the stock is for fish meal production. The project to develop fish meal processing in the Outer Hebrides, as elsewhere, has the severe problem that once established a fish meal factory exerts pressure for supply, and this too often is found at the expense of fish stocks that could better be fished for human consumption. Blue whiting could be caught by vessels of the distant-water fleet during part of the year and so assist the fleet to adapt itself during a critical phase. The standing stock of some other species is also very large, but not enough is known of their productivity to assess the harvesting rate that could be adopted safely. The grenadier, for instance, has a very large population size but the productivity of the population is low.

2. There are still some important opportunities in Third World economic zones available for fishing under licence from the coastal state, for agency fishing under contract from the coastal state, and perhaps for joint enterprise fishing with local fishing interests, as a form of aid to encourage the appropriate development of their fisheries by the states concerned.

3. Agency and joint enterprise fishing is also possible in the fisheries of advanced nations. Where schemes are marginally viable Community incentives could well be given during the hard period when EEC stocks must be allowed to recover. The expertise of Scottish fishermen is widely recognised. Canadian and Newfoundland fishing interests have sought to recruit Peterhead skippers of advanced dual purpose seine net-pair trawlers with their vessels to fish to their maximum capacity in their waters while local skippers learn their techniques

In the long term, job opportunities in the catching sector should become stable at a level rather lower than at present unless part of the surplus value from improved profitability that can be expected is used to promote employment among fishermen. This would entail a deliberate reduction in efficiency. Controlled fishing will mean a larger harvest of fish. The long-term prospects for the fish processing, storage and marketing side of the industry are therefore excellent. If human consumption fisheries are given preference over industrial fisheries where these conflict this will foster jobs in both the catching and processing sectors because industrial fishing employs few people. The fish that are harvested by present fisheries management techniques are only a small fraction of the primary productivity of the sea. There are exciting possibilities for technological improvement that could increase the scale of fisheries, given successful research and development and appropriate training. A better understanding of the interaction between species may have great practical value.

Filter feeding shellfish offer great scope for improved yields. They subsist directly on the plankton micro-organisms that are more or less the marine equivalent of grass. In the relatively cool waters of Scotland mussel culture offers the best prospects. Natural mussel beds can often be made more productive, but, as they are limited in numbers by the shortage of suitable places to live, the most exciting possibility is to provide them with artificial sites from which they can be easily harvested.

The future for the Scottish fisheries will be calamitous without effective management but given far-sighted policies, that are rigorously enforced, prospects are extremely good. If a Common Fisheries Policy has been agreed by the date of publication, this paper, we believe, offers a yardstick by which the policy can be judged. The penalty of an inadequate policy will become severe indeed when the Community is enlarged to include the huge fleets of the applicant nations.

REFERENCES

1. *White Fish Authority Annual Report and Accounts 1975-6.* Edinburgh: White Fish Authority, 1976, p.3.
2. *The Fishing Industry: Vol 1 — Report and Appendix 1 to the Minutes of Evidence, Trade and Industry Sub-Committee, House of Commons.* HMSO, April 1978, p.75.
3. *Hull Daily Mail,* 16/3/79.
4. Steel, D. I. A., and Buchanan, N., "Meaningful Effort Limitation: The British Case", in *Fisheries of the European Community.* Edinburgh: White Fish Authority, 1977, p.7.
5. *op. cit.* p.33 and information supplied by Department of Agriculture and Fisheries for Scotland.
6. Coull, J. R., "Modern Trends in Scottish Fisheries." *Scottish Geographical Magazine* 84:1, 1968, p.27.
7. *Highlands and Islands Development Board Annual Report, 1978.*
8. Postel-Coster, E., and Neijmerink, J. J. M., *"Fishing Communities on the Scottish East Coast."* University of Leiden, 1972.
9. Tunstall, J., "Fish: an antiquated industry". Fabian Tract 380, 1968, p.2.
10. *op. cit..* p.38.
11. Godman, N. A., "Scottish Fishermen — Their Employment and Trade Union Membership". *Scottish Trade Union Review* No. 2, Summer, 1978.
12. *T & GWU Policy Statement on the De-casualisation of Employment in the Fishing Industry.* Hull: T & GWU, 1975.
13. D.A.F.S. 1979, personal communication.
14. *Fishing into the 80s.* Octagon Press, 1978.
15. Godfrey, J., *The Times,* 7/9/77.
16. Godfrey, J., *The Shetland Times,* 7/10/77.

12

ENERGY DEMAND AND ENERGY POLICY
IN SCOTLAND

G. A. MACKAY
Aberdeen University

Over the last few years there has been a very marked increase in interest in energy issues and energy policy. The immediate cause was the success of OPEC (the Organisation of Petroleum Exporting Countries) in quadrupling crude oil prices in 1973 and 1974. This has had a profound effect on the state of the world economy and international relations, and has resulted in attempts by most countries to find alternative sources of energy. One other source, nuclear power, has itself generated further controversy, particularly in the light of accidents in a few countries.

Scotland is no exception to this renewed interest in energy policy. Like all industrialised countries, we have suffered the deflationary effects of the huge rises in oil prices. However, we have the tremendous fortune of our own indigenous oil and gas resources in the North Sea, and thus have benefited from the oil price rises. The nuclear debate has been particularly keen in Scotland because of the electricity authorities' wish to build a new nuclear station at Torness in East Lothian, problems with an existing station at Hunterston in Ayrshire, the possibility of building a commercial fast breeder reactor at Dounreay in Caithness, and the argument over mining for uranium in various parts of the country.

It seems an opportune time therefore to examine energy needs and energy policy, and the purpose of this paper is to discuss the various options open to Scotland and the likely pattern of events over the next few years.

Recent Experience

Before discussing the future it is necessary to consider in some detail events over the past decade. The best starting point is the pattern of demand, both in aggregate terms and from the point of view of individual fuels. In the current Scottish context five fuels can be distinguished usefully: coal, oil, natural gas, hydro-electricity and nuclear electricity. It may be that in future other energy sources — such as peat, solar energy, wind and wave power — may become important, but at the present time they make a tiny contribution.

Table 1 shows energy consumption for each year since 1970[1]. The latest available figures are for 1977 but those for 1978 and 1979, when published, are unlikely to show significant changes. The unit of measurement in the table is the petajoule, which is a measure of primary fuel input. There are alternative measures of fuel production and consumption — such as tons of coal equivalent or therms — but in the present context it does not matter which is used. There are also various different definitions of production and consumption — such as primary fuel input, heat supplied and useful heat — which are of more significance, but this aspect can also be ignored, although the related aspect of energy efficiency is discussed below[2].

Table 1

SCOTTISH FUEL CONSUMPTION (IN PETAJOULES)

	1970	1971	1972	1973	1974	1975	1976	1977
Coal*	352.1	309.1	299.6	344.2	290.6	306.9	313.7	311.8
Petroleum	381.8	400.7	424.0	448.4	424.9	375.7	376.1	382.6
Natural gas	2.4	26.3	38.5	47.0	59.2	64.6	70.7	76.7
Nuclear electricity	38.6	38.6	38.6	36.0	37.5	37.8	50.4	64.4
Hydro-electricity**	53.5	45.1	38.3	34.3	49.4	55.9	52.1	45.4
Total	828.4	819.8	837.3	909.8	861.5	840.9	863.0	880.9

* Including other solid fuels.
** Including some imports of electricity.

The table shows that over the seven years Scottish energy consumption has increased by 6.3%, equivalent to about 0.9% per year. There have been fluctuations in aggregate demand, however: consumption declined slightly in 1971 and more markedly in 1974 and 1975 but since then there appears to have been a reversion to the steady growth experienced in the 1950s and 1960s. Over the 20 years to 1970 the average annual rate of growth was just over 2%.

The fall in 1971 was a consequence of the industrial problems in that year and the 1973 and 1974 declines are an obvious consequence of the OPEC price rises. It is possible that the 1979 price rises will have a similar short-term effect. It is interesting to note that energy consumption in 1977 was still less than the 1973 figure.

Of more importance, however, are the changes in the composition of demand. These can be seen from Table 1 and also from the % shares in Table 2. Four main trends are clear. Firstly, there is the sharp decline in coal consumption, both in absolute quantity and % share: consumption declined from 13.3 million tons in 1970 to 11.3 in 1974, with a subsequent increase to 12.3 million in 1977; coal's % share fell from 42.5% in 1970 to 33.7% in 1974 and although there was an increase in 1975 it has again been falling to its 1977 level of 35.4%. Twenty years ago coal provided more than three-quarters of our energy needs so the industry's decline has been very rapid. It is little consolation that there has been a similar decline in the rest of the UK and in most other Western European countries.

Table 2

PERCENTAGE SHARES OF TOTAL CONSUMPTION

	1970	1971	1972	1973	1974	1975	1976	1977
Coal	42.5	37.7	35.6	37.8	33.7	36.5	36.4	35.4
Petroleum	46.1	48.9	50.6	49.3	49.3	44.7	43.6	43.4
Natural gas	0.3	3.2	4.6	5.2	6.9	7.7	8.2	8.7
Nuclear electricity	4.7	4.7	4.6	4.0	4.4	4.5	5.8	7.3
Hydro-electricity	6.5	5.5	4.6	3.8	5.7	6.7	6.0	5.2
Total	100	100	100	100	100	100	100	100

Secondly, there has been a contrasting rise in natural gas consumption. Since the replacement of manufactured town gas by North Sea gas, its share has risen sharply from less than 1% to 8.7% in 1977 and later figures will certainly show a continuation of than trend. Most of the increase has been in the domestic sector.

Thirdly, there has been the reversal in the growth record of the oil industry: in 1970 oil overtook coal as our major fuel but the OPEC price rises have checked the almost inexorable growth, and consumption has been static since 1975.

Finally, there is the slow growth in the production of hydro and nuclear electricity. Hydro's share has fluctuated between 3.8% and 6.5% over the period; nuclear's production and % share were static in the early 1970s but the commissioning of the Hunterston B station brought increases in 1976 and 1977. This growth should be seen, however, in the context of official predictions of a tenfold increase in nuclear production during the 1970s and the continuing delays and problems of the nuclear industry are discussed in more detail below.

These changes are all self-evident and need little further explanation. There is one point I would like to consider in more detail, however, because of its future importance and that is the relationship between economic growth and energy demand. Most energy authorities and government departments use the concept of an energy coefficient in forecasting demand. The energy coefficient is the ratio of the growth of demand for energy to the growth in GDP (gross domestic product) or some other similar measure of economic output. Given that the latter is much easier to forecast (or so most economists allege) it is a simple — and useful — means of obtaining a rough picture of energy growth. In the UK since the 1950s an average annual growth in GDP of about 2.7% has been associated with an annual growth of primary energy consumption of about 1.7% — giving a crude energy coefficient of about 0.7. There are some drawbacks in using such a coefficient for forecasting purposes, but they are not important in the present context. If we assume an annual rate of growth in Scottish GDP of around 3% over the next decade, total energy consumption would rise from its 1977 level of 880.9 petajoules to around 1,040 in 1985 and 1,155 in 1990.

Is this energy coefficient and its implied relationship acceptable? This is really the crucial question and its implications for the future are discussed in more detail below. In the context of what has happened since 1970 it is impossible to be dogmatic because there have been a lot of strange happenings. For example, industrial production in Scotland has increased by (only) 6.0% over the period 1970-77; despite the oil price rises energy consumption has risen by 6.3%. In the years when there were declines in industrial production (1971, 1974 and 1975) there were also declines in energy consumption and in the other years of increased industrial output there was increased energy consumption. Certainly for 1971, 1972 and 1973 there is a very close correlation between industrial output and energy consumption; but in 1974 industrial production fell by 2.0% and energy consumption by 5.8%; in 1976 industrial production increased by 0.6% and energy consumption by 2.7%; and in 1977 industrial production increased by 0.4% and energy consumption by 2.1%. One possible explanation of the divergence in experience in 1976 and 1977 is that there has been a time-lag in operation, but we would need data for the period 1978-80 before we could be reasonably certain of that.

Some useful additional evidence is given in the paper by Hampson and Thomson[3] where they disaggregate consumption by sector and show significantly different responses to the events of 1973 and 1974. In the domestic sector there was no significant decline whereas the drop in industrial consumption was almost double that in all other sectors. There was a small decline in the transport sector, with private motorists reducing petrol consumption more than commercial road transport but still by not much. Given the importance of the industrial sector it should be remembered that the industrial recession itself was caused in part by the OPEC price rises so the disentangling of cause and effect is difficult.

A crucial point to bear in mind at the outset is that the demand for energy is a derived demand. In other words, the primary demand is for appliances and energy-using goods and it is the stocks of these and their utilisation which determine the demand for energy. One implication of this is that in the short run the price elasticity of demand for energy — and, to a lesser extent, for individual fuels — is not very important because changes in the stocks of goods and appliances are very slow. An obvious example is the domestic heating sector, where the initial capital costs are substantially greater than the running costs and to change from oil to gas is not a short-term choice. Another example is the demand for petrol, which has fallen surprisingly little since the OPEC price rises, simply because petrol represents a relatively small part of the cost of motoring. The longer the time period, however, the easier it is to change the pattern of demand and it may well be that the real effects of the oil revolution will not be felt until the early 1980s.

Forecasting Future Consumption

Some rough estimates were given above: if an energy

coefficient of 0.7 was used and Scottish GDP grew 3% per year, total energy consumption would increase from its 1977 level of 881 petajoules to 1,040 in 1985. In million tons coal equivalent the rise would be from 31.7 in 1977 to about 37.5 in 1985.

This provides a reasonable starting point and luckily more detailed forecasts have been made by the South of Scotland Electricity Board (SSEB)[4]. These are shown in Table 3 and are of particular interest because they represent the "official" picture based on existing UK policies. Two points should be made at the outset regarding these forecasts. Firstly, the SSEB are an interested party and it is in their interest that electricity's share of the energy market should continue to grow. Secondly, the SSEB have been strongly committed to a substantial nuclear power programme. They were the main proponents of the steam-generating heavy-water reactor (SGHWR) but have recently accepted the Government's preference for an advanced gas-cooled reactor (AGR) programme. In May 1978 the Secretary of State for Scotland announced that Torness would go ahead, but based on an AGR system rather than a SGHWR.

Table 3

SSEB FORECASTS OF ENERGY CONSUMPTION

(million tons coal equivalent)

	1974 tons (%)	1980 tons (%)	1984 tons (%)
Oil	12.0 (38.7)	14.0 (36.8)	15.0 (35.7)
Coal	4.0 (12.9)	4.0 (10.5)	4.0 (9.5)
Gas	2.0 (6.5)	3.0 (7.9)	4.0 (9.5)
Electricity	13.0 (41.9)	17.0 (44.7)	19.0 (45.2)
— of which oil	2.0	3.0	4.0
— coal	7.0	8.0	8.0
— hydro	2.0	2.0	2.0
— nuclear	2.0	4.0	5.0
TOTAL	31.0	38.0	42.0
Total coal	11.0 (35.5)	12.0 (31.6)	12.0 (28.6)
Total oil	14.0 (45.2)	17.0 (44.7)	19.0 (45.2)
Total gas	2.0 (6.5)	3.0 (7.9)	4.0 (9.5)
Total hydro	2.0 (6.5)	2.0 (5.3)	2.0 (4.8)
Total nuclear	2.0 (6.5)	4.0 (10.5)	5.0 (11.9)

Source: South of Scotland Electricity Board.

Note: The figures here are not directly comparable with those in Table 1 because of differing definitions.

With future policy there are two major issues: the total size of the energy market and the distribution of demand among the various competing fuels. Differences of opinion about the former have not been great and it has not been a major policy issue. Nevertheless, it would be sensible to repeat the doubts expressed tentatively above.

Given the events of 1973-75 it would be unwise to predict with great confidence that energy consumption will continue to grow in line with the rate of economic growth. It may, but it may not. It certainly did in the 1950s and 1960s, but the experience of the 1970s is so confused that we shall have to wait for another two or three years before we know if the relationship is likely to continue. Thus, it is rather unfair of the SSEB's Director and General Manager, Donald Miller, to say, as he did recently[5], that "What people are saying when they suggest that there will be no growth in electricity demand, is that there will be no economic growth and that they don't believe there is going to be increased standards of living." There is a valid point of view that energy growth may be less than the rate of economic growth — in other words that the old relationship has broken down. This is not my view — nor that of Mr Miller — but it may prove to be correct and certainly warrants careful consideration. There is also the valid point of view that electricity's share may fall and this is discussed in the next section.

In the light of this uncertainty, however, the sensible strategy is to be sufficiently flexible to cope for the maximum likely demand. Problems of overcapacity are much less than those of undercapacity and it is therefore much better to err on the side of optimism.

The Roles of the Different Fuels

This is the major policy issue and the one that has caused — and undoubtedly will continue to cause — the greatest debate. Taking electricity first, it is arguable that UK energy policy is too committed to electricity generation and that Scotland has an even greater dependence. The expectation for the UK is that although electricity may have difficulties in the period to 1980 the rate of growth over the period to 1990 should average between 3% and 4% per year. Given the great uncertainty about energy demand and energy policy, and the obvious need to make decisions on the basis of an acceptable range of forecasts, this view of the Department of Energy/SSEB could turn out to be correct. On the other hand, there is a good deal of evidence to suggest that it might be substantially awry and therefore it is necessary to examine the alternative case thoroughly. In the present context only a brief summary is possible but there appear to be four main points.

Firstly, electricity consumption in the UK as a proportion of GNP is much higher than any other country in the world, including those more industrialised such as the USA and West Germany. Some examples for 1975 are[6]:

Country	ratio
Australia	3.81
Canada	4.39
France	2.18
West Germany	1.79
Italy	2.87
Japan	2.99
Sweden	3.82
UK	5.13
USA	3.47

Secondly, the generation of electricity is a relatively inefficient way of producing energy, although for many consumers it has been a very convenient form. The important factor is the conversion of heat energy into mechanical energy. The level of efficiency depends upon the maximum and minimum temperatures of the working fluid used, usually steam. These temperatures are limited by engineering considerations and in practice the overall efficiency of even the most efficient power station is less than 35%. The average is about 30%. In practice, this means that only one-third of the heat energy latent in the primary fuel is released as electricity, with the rest of the heat being discharged to the environment, through the medium of cooling water, as waste heat. Also the further losses sustained in the transmission and distribution of electricity from power stations to consumers must be taken into account; in 1975, these losses amounted to approximately 10%; and the overall efficiency for the UK electricity industry was therefore around 27%. In contrast, the efficiency of other energy forms is usually substantially higher. Given the recent rises in energy prices, and the country's balance-of-payments problems it is not surprising that the Government is keen to increase the efficiency of energy use — as exemplified by the "Save Energy" campaign — and electricity must inevitably be the main target.

Thirdly, changes in relative prices will strengthen the above trends. The official view is that electricity will steadily increase its penetration of the energy market, to the extent that by the year 2025 it would account for about 60% of total energy supply to consumers, but this appears to ignore the effect of increasing prices on demand. Experience since the early 1950s shows that even modest rises in relative prices have had a depressing effect on demand, bearing in mind the time-lags involved because energy is a derived demand, the primary demand being that for energy-consuming appliances. The recent large increases in electricity prices have rendered it uncompetitive in many sectors in comparison with North Sea gas and this has given rise to a number of official complaints by the electricity industry. At least until the late 1980s gas should continue to be much more competitive for uses such as central heating.

Fourthly, some economists have been arguing that the current problems affecting the electricity industry are not simply a short-run consequence of the industrial recession, OPEC price rises, etc., but are in line with a long-run trend which implies that the growth in demand for electricity will continue to slow down and possibly even fall in the forseeable future. The basic argument is that in some markets a "saturation point" has been reached — for example, with many domestic appliances such as televisions, cookers, refrigerators, electric kettles, etc. The growth in electricity consumption since the 1950s correlates very closely with the growth in ownership of these domestic appliances. Now that most households have these appliances, the growth in demand for them must slow down and must therefore have an adverse effect on the demand for electricity, principally in the domestic market (already badly hit by the inroads made by natural gas into the central heating market).

A great deal of detailed work would have to be done to test the appropriateness and validity of the four points above, and unfortunately time is not available to do this, but to us there does appear to be sufficient justification in each of the four points to suggest that the official Department of Energy/SSEB forecasts of electricity demand are too optimistic.

216   SCOTTISH GOVERNMENT YEARBOOK 1980

On present plans, the excess electricity capacity will worsen rather than improve over the next few years. In 1978 the SSEB had an installed capacity of 7,572 MW (megowatts) and the maximum demand was 4,228 MW. The average thermal efficiency of the conventional plant was 33%[7]. The NSHEB had an installed capacity of 2,109 MW and the peak demand (on the mainland system) was 1,576 MW. In addition the North Board also takes some electricity from the Atomic Energy Authority's prototype fast reactor at Dounreay[8]. Thus at the present time there is substantial excess capacity — about 45% — although both Boards probably need 25-30% spare capacity as a safety margin in case of plant breakdowns. The bad winters of 1977/78 and 1978/79 caused particular problems in that respect for the North Board and the South Board has had problems with the Hunterston B nuclear station.

This installed capacity of just under 9,600 MW (plus Dounreay) will increase in 1979 with the commissioning of the third unit at the Inverkip oil-fired station (680 MW) and in 1980 with the Peterhead oil/gas-fired station (1,320 MW). Approval has also been given for the Torness nuclear station (1,320 MW) for commissioning in the late 1980s and the North Board are keen to build a pump storage scheme (of up to 3,200 MW) at Craigroyston on Loch Lomond. There are also tentative plans for a new coal-fired station in Fife and a third nuclear station at Hunterston, and, on a smaller scale, the North Board are considering expansions in Shetland, Orkney and the Western Isles.

Even if the SSEB's forecasts of electricity demand in Table 3 proved correct, the implication is that this surplus or spare capacity will continue, even taking into account the phasing out of older, less efficient coal stations. There is little doubt that this argument will be a common one in the public inquiries and related discussions about the proposed new stations.

Nevertheless, it is more a matter of timing than anything else because at some stage in the future the excess will disappear. Leaving aside the nuclear versus non-nuclear debate, a station at Torness will be needed in the near future: the SSEB say by the late 1980s, whereas the above figures suggest by the mid-1990s at the earliest. The cynics among us will probably say that this is therefore rather an unnecessary debate because our performance in building power stations is so bad that Torness will not be completed by the late 1980s in any case!

The Craigroyston pump storage scheme is in a different category because of its nature as a "cheap reserve" for use only in terms of peak demand. Nuclear (or other) stations which have low running costs and pump storage schemes are sensible complements and the argument of excess capacity does not really apply to Craigroyston.

The final point on electricity concerns the nuclear debate and this is not the place to discuss it. Suffice to say that there is increasing public concern about the dangers of nuclear stations — both conventional and fast breeder — and it is obvious that the Department of Energy and the electricity authorities will have to do a great deal to satisfy the majority of the public that an expansion of our nuclear capacity is safe. Only the nuclear enclave in Caithness seems to welcome uranium mining and/or a commercial fast breeder station and in the light of the increasing sophistication of environmental groups the planning process will undoubtedly take a long time.

In the short run, this would leave the choice for electricity of oil, gas and coal, and here again I have some doubts about existing policies. Oil and gas are attractive sources of fuel because of the North Sea discoveries, although oil-fired power stations would continue to depend on imported oil from the Middle East and other countries, but to the extent to which North Sea oil and gas are used for power generation and similar uses, my strong view is that it is a misallocation of resources. From the Scottish point of view, the main benefits from these new indigenous sources would come from the establishment of a major refining and petro-chemical industry. The main reason for this is that the type of oil discovered in the North Sea has a much higher proportion of the "lighter fractions" than oil from the Middle East, for example, and is therefore better used for petrochemicals than industrial fuel; also, there have been large discoveries of associated gas in the northern North Sea, and these similarly offer opportunities for processing. In fact, gas processing is likely to be on a much greater scale than oil refining and processing, although at the present time there are few signs of the opportunities being grasped, and it could well be that much of the oil and gas will be used for other purposes or exported, either to England or Wales or overseas[9]. It is rather ironic that Shell-Esso have been experiencing planning problems in their attempts to build petrochemical

P

plants in Fife as severe as the electricity boards in their attempts to build power stations at Torness and Craigroyston.

With gas, there are some added considerations because of the current arguments within the energy industry that the price of gas is too low. The real price of energy is now what it was in 1951/52, with the exception of gas which in real terms has fallen steadily over the last twenty years. A consequence of this is the pressure for rapid depletion of the North Sea fields which is undesirable not only in its own right, but also because of the problems it creates for the coal and electricity industries. There is certainly a case for setting a higher selling price in order to allow gas to concentrate on two very important markets — the premium domestic market and the petrochemical feedstock market. Another reason is that if, as seems likely, a transition from natural gas to synthetic natural gas is required in the foreseeable future, then the pricing of the natural material should increasingly take account of the long-run cost of the substitute material.

This then leaves coal with a more important role in the Scottish energy market. Coal consumption and production are currently running at around 11 million tons per year, of which 8 million tons go to power stations in Scotland. It is difficult to believe other than that the non-power station use will continue to decline steadily in the future, and therefore the crucial issue is coal's use for electricity generation. Traditionally, Scottish coal has been high-cost, even within the UK industry: in the financial year 1974/75 the loss per ton to the National Coal Board of Scottish coal was £0.96, compared with £0.29 in Great Britain as a whole, presumably largely because productivity was lower in Scotland, 39.5 tons per man-shift compared with 45.0 tons in Great Britain. Rising oil prices have made coal much more competitive, however, and there is a strong economic case for re-examining the National Coal Board's plans for Scotland. On social grounds also, there is the usual argument that the real resource cost of coal is significantly lower than the market price because of the unemployment which would be created in the mining areas if closures took place, and this applies much more to Scotland than to England and Wales. To the economist this argument is not strong, but it should be borne in mind, particularly since the National Coal Board employ around 27,000 people in Scotland.

On the face of it, there appears to be a good case for some of the newer power stations to be coal-fired, which would allow the industry to maintain its sales to the SSEB at around 8 million tons per year plus about 0.5 million tons of slurry. A long-term commitment to do this would make forward planning much easier, and encourage the commercial exploitation of new discoveries.

The change in relative prices has given a similar boost to the prospects of alternative energy sources such as solar energy, wind and wave power, but it is very unlikely that these will make more than a minor contribution in the near future. At the local level there are some possibilities — such as district heating schemes — but otherwise the problems are much greater than the environmental lobby recognises and a great deal more planning is required. In the short run we have no alternative to the conventional fuels discussed above.

Conclusions

The two crucial questions which energy policy has to answer are:

1. What is the likely pattern of aggregate demand over the next 10-15 years?

2. What will be the role of the various fuels?

It should be clear from the above that there can be different answers to these questions, which implies that the energy debate will continue in Scotland for some time to come. The Torness confrontations may recur at fairly regular intervals.

I have tried to avoid the nuclear versus non-nuclear argument because it is outwith the scope of the present paper, but I have attempted to set out fairly the main arguments about the size and nature of the future energy market.

There is considerable agreement on the first question above. It seems reasonable to assume for planning purposes that total energy demand will grow at between 2% and 2.5% per year. Although there was an absolute fall in consumption in 1974 and 1975, Table 1 suggests that growth has started again and that these two years should be seen as a hiccup in a long-term trend rather than a major change.

On the other hand there is considerable disagreement about the second question and this has been the crux of the arguments in Scotland. In particular there is a body of opinion wishing to constrain the growth of nuclear electricity and to a lesser extent (and for different reasons) the domestic consumption of natural gas. The obverse of that is the encouragement of the Scottish coal industry and alternative energy sources. It is probably reasonable to conclude that an expansion of the coal industry is out of the question and that the best hope is to maintain production and consumption at roughly current levels. Many hopes for alternative sources are also over-optimistic at the national level.

There can be little doubt, however, that the more open discussion of needs and policies has been very beneficial in recent years and that the non-official lobby is acquiring increasing knowledge and expertise. The result must be slower but better policy decisions.

REFERENCES

1. *Scottish Economic Bulletin,* No. 17, Spring 1979.
2. For more detail see Hampson, S. F. and Thomson, L. H., *Recent trends in the Scottish energy market.* Scottish Economic Planning Department, 1978.
3. Ibid.
4. South of Scotland Electricity Board, *Energy and electricity in Scotland* in Department of Energy, *Energy paper No. 13, 1976.*
5. *The Scotsman,* 11/1/79.
6. Casper, D. A., "A less-electric future" *Energy Policy,* September 1976.
7. South of Scotland Electricity Board, *Report and accounts 1977-78.*
8. North of Scotland Hydro-Electric Board, *Report and accounts 1977-78.*
9. Mackay, G. A. et. al., *The economic impact of North Sea oil on Scotland,* HMSO, 1978.

REFERENCE SECTION

SECTION 1

SUMMARY OF SCOTTISH OPINION POLLS RELATING TO VOTING INTENTION AND CONSTITUTIONAL CHANGE

Dr ALLAN MACARTNEY
Staff Tutor in Politics,
the Open University in Scotland

It is probably true to say that there has been more interest in Scottish opinion polls this past year than ever before. Nowhere was this more obvious than in the run-up to the referendum on the Scotland Act. Indeed one poll on devolution commissioned by the *Scottish Daily Express* was not immediately published and did not appear until a subsequent poll had been taken; presumably the reasoning was that the publication of the poll completed on February 22 might have harmed that newspaper's anti-Assembly campaign. This rare event illustrates the strength of the belief that polls have an effect on voter behaviour — a controversy which looks like being with us for some time.

The exceptionally high number of opinion polls carried out over the twelve months since the last edition of the *Yearbook* reflects the important political events of 1979 — the referendum on March 1, the General Election on May 3 and the Euro-elections on June 7. The sheer volume of opinion-poll material has made it necessary to leave out some interesting subjects and concentrate on the major areas of interest, namely voting intention at a General Election, voting intention for the referendum, and preference for various constitutional options.

Tables 1 and *2* are derived from System Three's invaluable monthly polls on Scottish voting intentions (published in the *Glasgow Herald*); the former gives an overview of the period between the October 1974 and May 1979 General Elections, while the latter gives the monthly countdown to the recent General Election. *Table 3* gives figures produced by other polling organisations on voting intention in General Elections. *Tables 4* and *5* concern the attitude of voters towards the Labour Government's devolution proposals (*Table 4* covering the years 1976 to 1978), which later took concrete form in the Scotland Act. *Table 5* gives voting intentions in 1979 for the referendum on the Act. (The last poll, it should be noted, was carried out on voting day itself). Finally *Table 6* — which it will be noted, includes one done on referendum day and one taken, after the referendum dust had begun to settle — gives voters' views in 1979 on various constitutional options. Within the category shown as

222   SCOTTISH GOVERNMENT YEARBOOK 1980

"Devolution" the number of different schemes is shown in brackets, but it should be pointed out that the wording varied from one polling organisation to another.

Two polls, each *sui generis*, deserve special mention in this record. One asked interviewees simultaneously how they would vote in a British General Election and in an election for the proposed Scottish Assembly. The answers were:

	General Election	Scottish Assembly
	%	%
Labour	45	45
Conservative	30	26
Scottish National Party	23	25
Liberal	2	3

(Poll carried out 12-14 February 1979 by MORI for "Weekend World" [London Weekend Television].)

The other poll of interest concerned the election to the European Assembly and was carried out by System Three Scotland between 26 May and 2 June 1979 for the *Glasgow Herald*.

	Poll 2 June 1979	Actual Result 7 June 1979
	%	%
Labour	47	33
Conservative	25	34
Scottish National Party	19	19
Liberal	9	14

(The "Don't know" category was very high in the poll — 42%).

Technical notes on the tables.

The date shown is the last date on which the questions were asked rather than the date of publication, which was typically two or three days later. Following past practice, percentages have been rounded and "Don't knows", "Won't votes" and "Refusals" have been disregarded. In the light of the Cunningham Amendment (or 40% rule) this might seem odd, but it is a fact that polling organisations are no more uniform in their approach to the question of those who could not be contacted or would not answer than is British electoral organisation geared to producing accurate figures of those who could (in a legal and practical sense) vote. (It is however significant that two polling organisations produced figures for the views of non-voters, the net result of which is that they might as well be disregarded since their views are not markedly different from those of the intending voters.)

The following abbreviations are used in the tables:

DM	The *Daily Mail*
DR	The *Daily Record*
DT	The *Daily Telegraph*
Gall	Gallup
GH	The *Glasgow Herald*
ITN	Independent Television News
LWT	London Weekend Television
Mar	Marplan
MORI	Market & Opinion Research International
NOP	National Opinion Polls
ORC	Opinion Research Centre
PSL	Professional Studies Ltd.
S3	System Three Scotland
Sc/m	*The Scotsman*
SDE	The *Scottish Daily Express*
SM	The *Sunday Mail*
Sun	*The Sun*
WW	"Weekend World"

Acknowledgements:

We would like to thank all the above-mentioned polling organisations, newspapers and television company for their kind permission to reproduce data, and I would like to express a warm word of personal thanks to all the individuals concerned for their readiness to provide me with assistance in compiling this appendix.

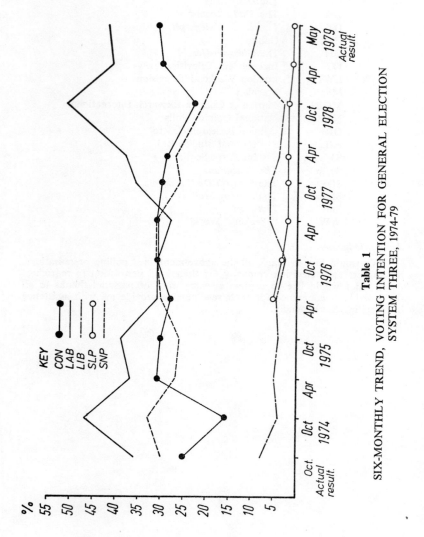

Table 1

SIX-MONTHLY TREND, VOTING INTENTION FOR GENERAL ELECTION
SYSTEM THREE, 1974-79

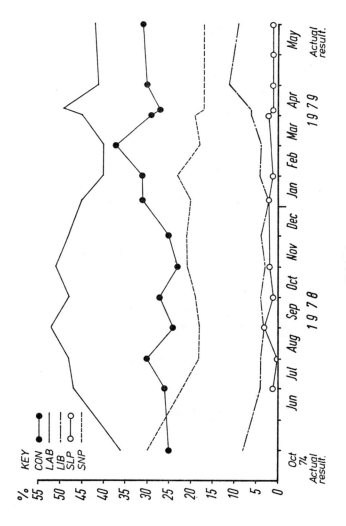

Table 2

VOTING INTENTION FOR GENERAL ELECTION, MONTHLY
SYSTEM THREE, 1978-79

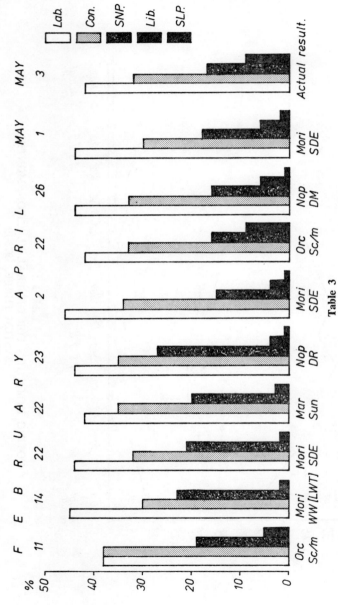

Table 3

VOTING INTENTION FOR GENERAL ELECTION 1979
POLLS UNDERTAKEN BY OTHER ORGANISATIONS

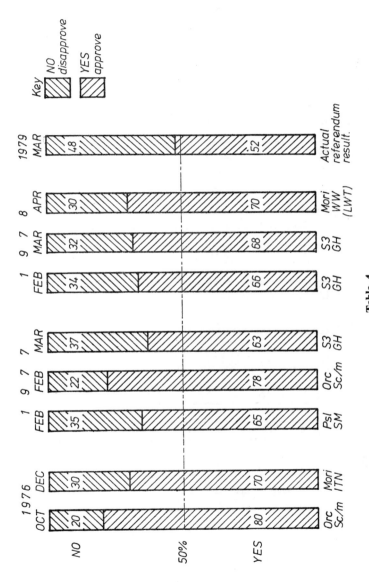

Table 4

ATTITUDE TOWARDS GOVERNMENT'S DEVOLUTION PROPOSALS: 1976-78

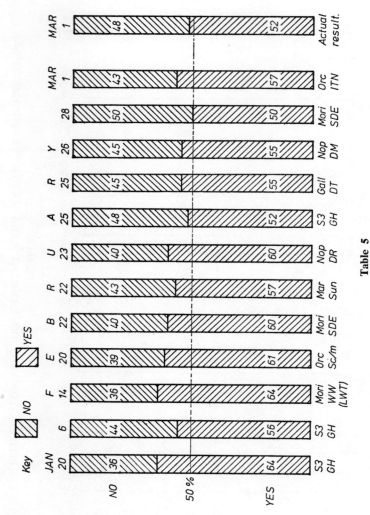

Table 5

VOTING INTENTION FOR REFERENDUM ON SCOTLAND ACT: 1979

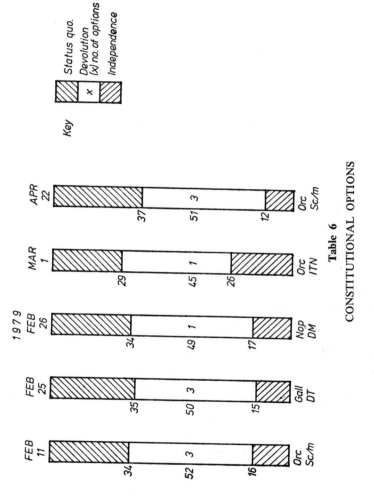

Table 6

CONSTITUTIONAL OPTIONS

SECTION 2

CHRONOLOGY OF DEVOLUTION

JUNE 1978 - JUNE 1979*

1978

7 June   Lords Report Stage of Scotland Bill begins. Main amendments inserted: Assembly committees required to reflect party balance; purchase grants for libraries, museums and art galleries reserved; requirement for fourteen days' interval followed by second vote if Bill not affecting Scotland carried by Commons only because of votes of Scottish MPs; new Government clause on Orkney and Shetland to replace "Grimond amendment".

20 June   Report Stage concluded.

29 June   Unopposed third reading.

4 July   Commons timetable motion for consideration of Lords amendments.

6 July   Consideration began. Alternative member voting system defeated.

26 July   Consideration concluded. Government defeated on committee balance, second vote in Commons and reservation of forestry.

27 July   Lords accepted Commons amendments.

31 July   Royal Assent.

1 Nov   Referendum date announced.

1979

1 March   Referendum held. Of those who voted, 51.6% voted "Yes" and 48.4% voted "No". Of the total electorate, 32.9% voted "Yes", 30.8% voted "No" and 36.3% did not vote.

22 March   Statement to Commons by Prime Minister Callaghan, declining to set date for vote on order to repeal Scotland Act and calling for all-party consultations. Motion of no-confidence put down by SNP.

28 March   Government defeated on Conservative motion of no-confidence.

20 June   Commons passed repeal order for Scotland Act by 301 votes to 206. Of the Scottish MPs, forty-three voted against repeal, nineteen in favour and nine were absent. Mr George Younger, Secretary of State for Scotland, offered all-party talks to consider "the scope for improving the handling of Scottish business in Parliament".

*The chronology of devolution 1885-1978 (May) was included in *The Scottish Government Yearbook 1979.*

SECTION 3

REFERENDUM RESULTS, MARCH 1, 1979

The question voters were asked was: "Do you want the provisions of the Scotland Act 1978 to be put into effect?"

Table 1:

Number and proportion of voters, by region, who voted "Yes", and who voted "No"; turnout

	Yes	%	No	%	Turnout %
Borders	20,746	40.3	30,780	59.7	66.4
Central	71,296	54.7	59,105	45.3	65.9
Dumfries & Galloway	27,162	40.3	40.239	59.7	64.1
Fife	86,252	53.7	74,436	46.3	65.3
Grampian	94,944	48.3	101,485	51.6	57.2
Highland	44,973	51.0	43,274	49.0	64.7
Lothian	187,221	50.1	186,421	49.9	65.9
Strathclyde	596,519	54.0	508,599	46.0	62.5
Tayside	91,482	49.5	93,325	50.5	63.0
Orkney	2,104	27.9	5,639	72.1	54.1
Shetland	2,020	27.0	5,466	73.0	50.3
Western Isles	6,218	55.8	4,933	44.2	49.9
SCOTLAND	1,230,937	51.6	1,153,502	48.4	62.9

Table 2:

Proportion of total electorate, by region, who voted "Yes", who voted "No" and who did not vote.

	Yes	No	Did not vote
Borders	26.7	39.7	33.6
Central	36.1	29.9	34.1
Dumfries & Galloway	25.8	38.3	35.9
Fife	35.1	30.3	34.7
Grampian	27.6	29.5	48.4
Highland	33.0	31.7	35.3
Lothian	33.0	32.9	34.1
Strathclyde	33.7	28.7	37.5
Tayside	31.2	31.8	37.0
Orkney	15.1	39.0	45.9
Shetland	13.6	36.7	49.7
Western Isles	27.8	22.1	50.1
Scotland	32.5	30.4	37.1

As % of electoral register *as adjusted by Secretary of State* (3,747,112):
Yes 32.9%   No 30.8%   Did not vote 36.3%

SECTION 4

SCOTTISH OFFICE: TRANSFER OF FUNCTIONS

1954 - 1978

1954   *Ministry of Fuel and Power to SHD:* electricity in southern Scotland.

1955   *MAFF to DAFS:* (1) agricultural price guarantee scheme; (2) animal health.
MAFF to SED: the school milk scheme.
Lord Chancellor's Office to SHD: the appointment of JPs.

1956   *Ministry of Transport to SHD:* roads and bridges.

1960   *SHD to DAS (DAFS):* (1) fisheries; (2) Highland ferry services.
SHD to SED: various responsibilities for children.
Local authorities to SED: student awards.
DAFS (DAS) to DHS: coast protection and flood prevention.
DAFS (DAS) to SHD: Highland township roads and roads in live-stock rearing areas.

1962   *SHD/DHS became SHHD/SDD*
SHHD's responsibilities were: (1) home affairs, i.e. prisons, police, fire, civil defence and criminal justice; (2) health services.
SDD's responsibilities were environmental and local government, i.e. planning, New Towns, housing, electricity, local authority finance and administration, tourism, water and sewerage, and clean air.
General Board of Control to SHHD: State Hospital at Carstairs.

1964   *Regional Development Division* set up in SDD reporting direct to the Permanent Under-Secretary of State.

1965   *SED to Scottish Certificate of Education Examination Board:* administration and running of SCE examinations.
SED to General Teaching Council: registration of teachers after probationary period.
SHHD to SED: National Galleries and National Museum of Antiquities.
SHHD to local probation committees: responsibility for after-care supervision of prisoners. Initially, responsibility shared with small central government staff but subsequently wholly transferred to probation service (now local authority social work department).

1966   *To SED:* training units from DAFS, SHHD and SDD setting up Scottish Office Training Unit.
Ministry of Public Buildings and Works to SDD: responsibility for the National Building Agency in Scotland, and for historic buildings.

1967   *Social Work Services Group* set up as a "joint unit" of SED and SHHD.

1968   *DAFS to Meat and Livestock Commission:* fatstock guarantee scheme.

DAFS to SDD: responsibility for HIDB and Highland transport.
Ministry of Transport to SDD: responsibility for bus and ferry services in Scotland.

1969 *Social Work Services Group* wholly responsibility of SED.
Ministry of Public Buildings and Works to SDD: policy responsibility for royal parks and gardens and ancient monuments.

1970 *DAFS to SDD:* responsibility for Highland piers.
To Central Services: (1) Permanent Under-Secretary of State's office; (2) chief statistician's office; (3) solicitor's office; (4) information office; (5) under-secretaries for finance and establishments; (6) Regional Development Division.
Civil Service Department to Central Services: Edinburgh Organisation and Management division.

1971 *To Central Services:* (1) establishment divisions from each department; (2) Scottish Office computer services and library from DAFS; (3) Scottish Office training unit from SED; (4) departmental liaison units in Dover House; (5) finance divisions from each department.
To SHHD: superannuation divisions to form Scottish Office superannuation division.
SHHD to Scottish Courts Administration: court services.
SED to Scottish Sports Council: certain grant-making powers for sport.

1972 *SDD:* appointment of chief reporter for public planning inquiries.
SHHD to Lord Advocate/Scottish Courts Administration: responsibility for Scottish Law Commission, Council on Tribunals and certain areas of law.

1973 *SEPD set up* with (1) RDD from Central Services; (2) responsibility for the HIDB, New Towns, electricity, transport, tourism and rural industries from SDD.
SHHD to DAFS: meat hygiene etc., milk and dairies hygiene.
SHHD to local authority social work departments: prison welfare service.
Central Services: management group formed.

1974 *SHHD to Common Services Agency (NHS):* health education, research and intelligence, supplies.

1975 *SDD to Central Services:* local authority finance (including Rate Support Grant).
SDD: urban renewal unit set up.
Central Services to Commission for Local Authority Accounts: some functions on local authority audit.
Department of Industry to SEPD: selective help to industry and responsibility for export services.
SDD to Scottish Development Agency: derelict land reclamation.
SEPD to SDA: Small Industries Council for Rural Areas of Scotland.
Local Authorities to Secretary of Commissions (Central Services): appointment of General Commissioners of Income Tax.

Q

234 SCOTTISH GOVERNMENT YEARBOOK 1980

1976 *DAFS to Health and Safety Executive:* agricultural safety inspectorate.
Directorate of Telecommunications responsible to Central Services as well as SHHD.

1977 *Department of Employment to SEPD:* Ministerial responsibility for the Manpower Services Commission in Scotland.
SEPD to SDD: transport.

1978 *Department of the Environment to SDD:* financial and management responsibility for royal parks, ancient monuments and rescue archaeology.

SECTION 5

THE SCOTTISH OFFICE —

SUMMARY OF RESPONSIBILITIES IN 1979

Central Services

Private office of Secretary of State and Ministers; office of Permanent Under-Secretary of State; management group support staff; amalgamated Scottish Office liaison units in Dover House, London; co-ordinating groups (urban policy, statutory planning).

Personnel management and services; training unit; welfare unit; manpower and organisation; office services. Library. Computer services.

Finance: public expenditure programmes; departmental votes; local government finance; payments, audit, accountancy services.

Solicitor's office.

Scottish Information Office. Statistics unit. Inquiry reporters.

Department of Agriculture and Fisheries for Scotland

Capital assistance to agriculture and horticulture including crofting development (with Crofters Commission), arterial drainage, agricultural land tenure. Policy on use of agricultural land. Liaison with Forestry Commission. Management of state-owned agricultural property (599,983 acres in 1975).

Crop improvement and marketing, plant health, pest control: policy and regulations.

Livestock products. Beef, sheep meat, pig meat, poultry and eggs: policy and regulations. Meat hygiene. Milk: policy, marketing and hygiene. Wool marketing.

Agricultural price support, hill farming and other subsidies: taking part in formulation of agricultural policy in UK and EEC contexts, operating the schemes, development of co-operation.

Animal health: policy and administration of control measures. Administration of livestock improvement schemes; enforcement of minimum wages for agricultural workers.

Conservation of fish stocks: taking part in international negotiations; protection of Scottish waters by fleet of cruisers (in co-operation with Royal Navy); management of white fish quota. Assistance to fishing and processing industries and fishery harbours.

Provision of agricultural education, research and development through three agricultural colleges and eight agricultural research institutes and an agricultural research station; provision of fisheries research services; assistance to the agricultural and fishing industries through local officers.

Administration of Royal Botanic Garden.

Scottish Development Department

Housing: policy; grants to local authorities and approval of housing plans; relations with Scottish Special Housing Association; research and development; improvement grants to private sector and modernisation subsidy to local authorities; rent registration services; servicing of rent assessment panel and rent tribunals.

Local government structure and areas: policy.

Land-use planing: approval of local authority structure plans; issue of guidelines; policy on community land scheme and compensation; land acquisition use and disposal for offshore petroleum development; countryside and conservancy policy; marine advice; graphic and photographic services.

Roads and transport: approval of local authorities' transport policies and programmes; specific grants; support for local authority bus services; assistance for Highlands and Islands shipping and transport piers; liaison with other forms of transport (airports, rail, etc.); road traffic regulations; road safety advisory unit; trunk road works.

Urban renewal: policy, aid programme and liaison.

Water supply, sewerage and pollution, etc.: policy; management of the water supply, sewerage, coast protection and flood prevention programmes; specific grants under the Regional Water and Sewerage and Local Employment Acts; research and development; refuse disposal; HM Industrial Pollution Inspectorate.

Historic buildings: policy, grants and casework; administration of ancient monuments and royal parks; rescue archaeology.

Building control: policy, review of regulations and some casework.

The SDD central research unit, building directorate and engineering division also provide services for other departments.

Scottish Economic Planning Department

Co-ordination of North Sea oil policy; oil research and intelligence; applications to European regional development fund; liaison with ports, aircraft, steel and shipbuilding industries; relations with Scottish Development Agency. Liaison with Manpower Services Commission; careers service, policy and administration. Economic and statistical advice. Selective financial assistance to industry — policy and casework; promotion of industrial expansion and inward investment; export promotion; information to small firms.

Electricity: relations with the two Scottish electricity boards. Energy policy.

New Towns: relations with the Development Corporations.

Highland development and tourism: policy; relations with Highlands and Islands Development Board and Scottish Tourist Board.

Co-ordination of Scottish Office interests in the Scottish construction industry.

Scottish Education Department

Primary and secondary education: policy and regulations; approval of local authority schemes of provision; issue of guidance; taking part in curriculum development; inspection of schools; grant aid to some secondary and residential special schools and promotion of special education; policy on school meals and milk.

Formal further education: approval of advanced courses provided at colleges maintained by education authorities; policy development; oversight and financing of central institutions (other than the three agricultural colleges — see DAFS).

Some Universities functions (but most are administered for Great Britain by the Department of Education and Science); awards to students.

Informal further education, sport, recreation and cultural activities: policy and grant aid.

Registration of educational endowments.

Oversight and financing of national museums and galleries.

Teacher demand and supply; pre-service and in-service training of teachers; teacher exchange; school staffing; teachers salaries and conditions of service; administration of colleges of education.

Educational building: capital expenditure allocations, project control and design guidance.

Social Work Services Group: formal and informal guidance to local authorities, voluntary organisations and others; review and evaluation of services provided by local authorities and voluntary organisations; central oversight of the Children's Panels system; central control of the List D schools system; making of regulations under the 1968 Act and associated legislation; central oversight of the local authority social work building programme; the making and control of grants under sections 8 and 10 of the 1968 Act (grants for research and to voluntary organisations for services provided).

Scottish Home and Health Department

Health services: guidance to, and collaboration with, health boards and the Common Services Agency in the planning and administration of services provided by the boards and the Agency, and development of health service planning; policy on major building programme, project control of major schemes and issue of building guidance; land transactions; procurement policy; participation in negotiations on pay and conditions of service for health service staff; manpower planning; commissioning of research; servicing health service consultative machinery; hospital advisory service; regional medical service; liaison with other bodies (e.g. international, university) concerned with health care.

Advice on telecommunications (health, police and fire).

Police: inspection; approval of establishments and capital expenditure; participation in negotiations on pay and conditions of service; servicing Police Advisory Board for Scotland and other bodies; administration of Scottish Police College and Police (Scotland) Examinations Board; complaints against the police and discipline appeals; common police services and other policy matters.

Fire Service: inspection; policy on pay and conditions of service; monitoring of capital expenditure; other policy questions, including fire prevention.

Home defence planning: co-ordination on major civil emergencies; warning and monitoring organisation.

Civil law and law reform; electoral arrangements; ceremonial.

Penal establishments: administration; capital building programme; personnel; industries and supplies; inmate casework; parole scheme.

Criminal justice (policy questions); Royal Prerogative of Mercy; licensing law; research in criminology.

Superannuation: local government fire and policy schemes (policy); teachers health service and legal aid schemes (policy and administration).

SECTION 6

SCOTTISH OFFICE MINISTERS

		Private Secretary
Secretary of State	Rt. Hon. George Younger, MP	Kenneth MacKenzie NSAH ext. 4001
Minister of State	Rt. Hon. Earl of Mansfield (Agriculture & Fisheries, Highlands & Islands affairs)	Adam Rennie NSAH ext. 4041
Parliamentary Under-Secretaries of State	Russell Fairgrieve, MP (Health & Social Work)	Ian Sneddon NSAH ext. 4024
	Alex Fletcher, MP (Industry & Education)	John Laydon NSAH ext. 4011
	Malcolm Rifkind, MP (Home Affairs & Environment)	Nigel Pittman NSAH ext. 4005

SECTION 7

SCOTTISH OFFICE DIRECTORY

Senior Scottish Office Staff:

The organisation and staffing of the Scottish Office down to divisional level are shown here. Heads of departments are graded as Deputy Secretaries Beneath them are Under-Secretaries. The heads of divisions who report to the latter are usually Assistant Secretaries; SP after a name indicates Senior Principal (one grade down). Telephone numbers quoted are enquiry points. Information correct as at June 1979.

Scottish Office Addresses (all Edinburgh except):*

NSAH   New St Andrew's House, EH1 3SX. 031-556 8400.
SAH   St Andrew's House, EH1 3DB. 031-556 8501.
CH   Chesser House, Gorgie Road, EH11 3AW. 031-443 4020.
WP   16 Waterloo Place, EH1 3DN. 031-556 8400.
JC   James Craig Walk, EH1 3BA. 031-556 8400.
AH   Argyle House, Lady Lawson Street, EH3 9SE. 031-229 9191.
BD   Broomhouse Drive, EH11 3XD. 031-443 4040.
PS   83 Princes Street, EH2 2HH. 031-226 3781.
PH   Pentland House, Robb's Loan, EH14 1TY. 031-443 8681.
AHG*   Alhambra House, Waterloo Street, Glasgow, G2 6AT. 041-248 2855.
JS   43 Jeffrey St., EH1 1DN. 031-556 9233.

THE SCOTTISH OFFICE

		Private Secretary
Permanent Under-Secretary of State	W. Kerr Fraser, C.B. (b. 1929, app. 1978)	C. M. A. Lugton, NSAH, ext. 4023

CENTRAL SERVICES

		Private Secretary
Deputy Secretary, Central Services	W. K. Reid (b. 1931, app. 1978)	D. J. Palmer, NSAH ext. 5896
Assistant Under-Secretary of State & Head of Liaison Division, London	J. F. McLellan	Dover House, Whitehall, London. 01-233-3440
Devolution Division; Under-Secretary	J. M. Ross	NSAH ext. 4242

CENTRAL SERVICES—*Continued*

Under-Secretary, Personnel
L. P. Hamilton

Head of Division

Personnel (General): Management information, manpower
planning, personnel planning
for devolution, industrial
relations   G. J. Murray, WP, ext. 4107

Personnel Management
(Administration Group)   J. Inglis, WP, ext. 4103

Personnel Management
(Professional, technical and
industrial staff)   J. Smith (SP), WP, ext. 4121

Personnel Services: pay,
pensions, security, hospitality,   R. D. M. Calder (SP), JC, ext.
VIP visits   4227

Under-Secretary, Management
Services
J. S. Gibson

Manpower and Organisation   H. Macnamara, WP, ext. 4465

Accommodation and Office   W. J. A. Scott (SP), JC, ext.
Services   5651

Computer Service   J. S. Robertson, BD, ext. 497

Telecommunications   A. F. Harrison

Library   H. A. Colquhoun
                                     (Chief Librarian)

Head of Division

Under-Secretary, Principal Finance
Officer
P. C. Rendle

Devolution and General   P. McKinlay, NSAH, ext. 4286
Accounting and Vote   F. B. Drysdale (SP), CH,
                                     ext. 2390

Audit   I. S. Scott (SP), 132 Rose
                                     Street. 031-226-5783, ext. 17

Accountancy Services   I. Nicholson (SP), JC, ext. 4566

CENTRAL SERVICES—Continued

Under-Secretary, Finance B
J. E. Fraser

Head of Division

Local Government Finance
Policy, Income & Statistics
(including valuation and
rating)   G. B. Baird, NSAH, ext. 5512

Local Government Expendi-
ture including Rate Support
Grant   D. A. Leitch, NSAH, ext. 5282

Public Expenditure: Trade,
Industry & Employment;
Nationalised Industries   H. H. Mills, NSAH, ext. 5340

Roads & Transport; Housing;
Other Environmental Services;
Procurement Policies   H. H. Mills, PS, ext. 274

Public Expenditure: Education,
Libraries, Science & Arts;
Forestry   W. A. M. Good, NSAH,
                                           ext. 5967
Agriculture & Fisheries   W. A. M. Good, CH, ext. 2341

Public Expenditure: Law,
Order and Protective Services   A. H. Mitchell, NSAH, ext.
                                           2153
Health & Personal Social
Services   A. H. Mitchell, SAH, ext. 2373

Director, Scottish Information
Office   Charles MacGregor

Deputy Director and Chief
Press Officer   D. C. M. Beveridge, NSAH,
                                           ext. 5652

Chief Publicity Officer   R. Marshall, NSAH, ext. 4450

Principal Information Officer   A. H. Sutherland, Dover
                                           House, 01-233-8520

Senior Information Officers:
    SEPD matters   J. F. Lindsay, NSAH,
                                           ext. 4432

CENTRAL SERVICES — *Continued*

Head of Division

SDD matters — C. M. McPhail, NSAH, ext. 5876

SED matters — M. Q. Jardine, NSAH, ext. 4128

DAFS matters & housing — D. W. Stewart, NSAH, ext. 5334

SHHD matters — A. N. Pagett, NSAH, ext. 4856

Manpower Services — W. H. Gunn, NSAH, ext. 5424

Chief Statistician — C. M. Glennie, NSAH, ext. 4425

Chief Inquiry Reporter — A. J. Hunt, 44 York Pl., EH1 3JJ, ext. 233

Solicitor — R. W. Deans, NSAH, ext. 4740

Deputy Solicitors — J. B. Allan, NSAH, ext. 5715

D. Cunningham, NSAH, ext. 5285

Divisional Solicitors and main responsibilities:

(SHHD) — J. L. Jamieson, NSAH, ext. 4244

(SED) — Miss M. Y. Walker, NSAH, ext. 5435

(DAFS) — R. Bland, NSAH, ext. 4662

(SDD) — J. A. Stewart, NSAH, ext. 4464

(DOE) — H. D. Glover, NSAH, ext. 5679

(HIDB) — J. E. Taylor, NSAH, ext. 4238

(DI) — E. S. Robertson, NSAH, ext. 5343

(SEPD) — A. A. McMillan, NSAH, ext. 4063

(CS) — A. A. McMillan, NSAH, ext. 5750

DEPARTMENT OF AGRICULTURE AND FISHERIES FOR SCOTLAND

Secretary
J. I. Smith, C.B., (b. 1924, app. 1972)

Private Secretary:
Mrs J. Jones, CH, ext. 2478

Head of Division

Under-Secretary, Agriculture I
W. W. Gauld

Capital Grants, Loans, Farm Structure — J. Glendinning, CH, ext. 2771

DEPARTMENT OF AGRICULTURE AND FISHERIES FOR
SCOTLAND — Continued

	Head of Division
Land Tenure, Land Use, Forestry	I. G. F. Gray, CH, ext. 2666
Agricultural Education, Advisory Services, Research Crofting Development	G. S. Murray, CH, ext. 2074
Estate Management	T. M. Brown (SP), CH, ext. 2722

Under-Secretary, Agriculture II
R. D. Cramond

Crops, Plant Health, Pest control	L. V. McEwan, CH, ext. 2527
General Agricultural Policy, EEC co-ordination, hill farming and other subsidies, co-operation and marketing	B. Gordon, CH, ext. 2450
Agricultural labour, animal health, epidemics, livestock improvements and animal welfare	A. I. Macdonald, CH, ext. 2270
Livestock products: fat-stock, milk, poultry, eggs, dairy hygiene, slaughterhouses	A. B. Scott, CH, ext. 2420

Under-Secretary, Fisheries
J. Cormack

Fisheries I: regimes (EEC and international); Law of the Sea; fish conservation	F. H. Orr, CH, ext. 2371
Fisheries II: salmon and freshwater fish, fisheries harbours, offshore oil and marine pollution of fish	H. G. Robertson, CH, ext. 2176
Fisheries III: fishing industry structure and finance, EEC marketing, protection and enforcement, DAFS fleet	J. F. Laing, CH, ext. 2580

DEPARTMENT OF AGRICULTURE AND FISHERIES FOR
SCOTLAND — *Continued*

Head of Division

Chief Agricultural Officer — C. Mackay, CH, ext. 2091

Director of Agricultural Scientific Services — J. M. Todd, East Craigs, EH12 8NJ. 031-339-2355

Chief Agricultural Economist — J. M. Dunn, CH, ext. 2540

Director of Fisheries Research — B. B. Parrish, Torry, Aberdeen. 0224-876544

Chief Inspector of Sea Fisheries — M. J. MacLeod, CH, ext. 2024

SCOTTISH DEVELOPMENT DEPARTMENT

Secretary
E. L. Gillett (b. 1920, app. 1976)

Private Secretary
S. Brotchie, NSAH, ext. 4015

Under-Secretary, Planning
T. L. Lister

Chief Planning Officer
W. D. C. Lyddon

Head of Division

Planning I: Grampian, Highlands regions, Islands areas. Oil-related planning — D. G. Mackay, NSAH, ext. 5445

Planning II: Borders and Dumfries & Galloway regions. Legislation, land, policy and procedures — J. Lonie, NSAH, ext. 4642

Planning III: Strathclyde, Tayside, Fife, Central and Lothian regions; planning appeals — N. G. Campbell, NSAH, ext. 4604

Building Control and Standards — N. E. Sharp, 125 George St. EH2 4LE. 031-226-6981, ext. 219

Ancient Monuments — N. E. Sharp, AH, ext. 5259

Historic Buildings and Conservation Areas — N. E. Sharp, 25 Drumsheugh Gardens, EH3 7RN, 031-226-3611

SCOTTISH DEVELOPMENT DEPARTMENT — *Continued*

Head of Division

Urban Renewal Unit (Glasgow
Eastern Area Renewal, Urban
Aid Programme)   J. Hamill, WP, ext. 5165

Under-Secretary
W. W. Scott

Roads and Transport I: Local
transport planning, local roads,
Greater Glasgow transport, bus   G. F. Hendry, NSAH,
support, freight grants   ext. 5966

Roads and Transport II:
Scottish Transport Group,
shipping, air, bridges, road   J. M. Currie, NSAH,
safety   ext. 4402

Roads and Transport III: J. Leithhead (SP), NSAH,
motorways and trunk roads   ext. 5357

Local Government (structures,
procedures, manpower)

Water, Sewerage and Pollution
(including coast protection,
waste disposal, noise, clean
air)   D. A. Campbell, PH, ext. 348

Under-Secretary, Housing
I. D. Penman

Housing I: local authority
finance management, rent
rebates, private building,
statistics and research   T. M. Bond, PS, ext. 296

Housing II: rehabilitation and
improvement, Housing
Associations, private rented
sector   S. C. Aldridge, PS, ext. 313

Housing III: local authority
standards, plans and project
approvals, housing for special
groups, Scottish Special
Housing Association   I. R. Duncan, PS, ext. 310

Chief Architect and Director of
Building   B. P. Beckett, NSAH, ext. 4329
Chief Research Officer   Miss B. D. Baker, NSAH,
                                    ext. 4518

SCOTTISH DEVELOPMENT DEPARTMENT — *Continued*

Head of Division

Chief Estates Officer	G. H. Lumb, NSAH, ext. 4843
Chief Quantity Surveyor	A. Y. Hamilton, PS, ext. 264
Chief Engineer	S. C. Agnew, PH, ext. 491
Chief Roads Engineer	J. A. M. MacKenzie, NSAH, ext. 4288
Chief Industrial Pollution Inspector	W. McCamley, PH, ext. 299

SCOTTISH ECONOMIC PLANNING DEPARTMENT

Secretary
T. R. H. Godden, C.B. (b. 1927, app. 1973)

Under-Secretary and Chief Economic Adviser
R. G. L. McCrone

Regional Development I: Oil development, regional policy, EEC co-ordination

Regional Development II: Industrial co-ordination (including shipbuilding, steel); Government dispersal

Regional Development III: Scottish Development Agency Manpower and Careers service policy

Under-Secretary
J. A. Scott

Electricity and Energy Policy

Highland tourism and construction industry

New Towns

Under-Secretary, Industrial Development
A. G. Manzie

Private Secretary
Miss S. M. Macnamara, NSAH, ext. 4038

Head of Division

Miss J. L. Ross, NSAH, ext. 5046

H. Morison, NSAH, ext. 4376

R. F. Butler, NSAH, ext. 5907

D. J. Essery, NSAH, ext. 5993

H. Robertson, NSAH, ext. 5823

NSAH, ext. 4455

SCOTTISH ECONOMIC PLANNING DEPARTMENT — *Continued*

Head of Division

Industrial Development I:
Steering of industry, inward
investment, financial assistance
policy, SDA liaison   R. Burns, AHG, ext. 386

Industrial Development II: L. C. Roberts (SP), AHG,
selective financial assistance   ext. 307

Industrial Development III:
industrial policy, oil technology,
planning agreements   J. W. Sinclair, AHG, ext. 476

Industrial Development IV:
export promotion   J. E. Milne, AHG, ext. 276

SCOTTISH EDUCATION DEPARTMENT

Secretary   Private Secretary
J. A. M. Mitchell (b. 1924 app. 1976) R. T. M. Berry, NSAH,
                                        ext. 5005
Under-Secretary
Miss P. A. Cox
                                       Head of Division

  I: Primary and Secondary
  Schools (Organisation, cur-
  riculum, religious education,
  Pack Committee)   A. K. Forbes, NSAH, ext. 5192

  II: Local government, special
  education, independent schools,
  meals and milk, employment
  of children   B. J. Fiddes, NSAH, ext. 5408

  III: Planning, research,
  technology, examinations,   W. J. Fearnley, NSAH,
  Munn and Dunning Reports   ext. 5074

Under-Secretary
I. L. Sharp

  IV: Formal Further Educa-   J. J. Farrell, 8 George St.
  tion   EH2 2PF. 031-226-3521,
                                        ext. 14

  V: Higher Education (Central   W. A. P. Weatherston,
  institutions, universities, and   8 George St. EH2 2PF.
  educational endowments)   031-226-3521, ext. 31

SCOTTISH EDUCATION DEPARTMENT — *Continued*

Head of Division

Student Awards

A. J. C. Mitchell (SP), Haymarket Ho., Clifton Terr., EH12 5DR, 031-337-2477, ext. 288

VI: Informal Further Education, adult and community education, arts, libraries, museums and galleries, sport and recreation

D. Connelly, 113 Rose St., EH2 3DT, 031-266-5016, ext. 25

Under-Secretary
I. M. Wilson

VII: Supply and training of teachers: recruitment, distribution, staffing standards, General Teaching Council

M. H. Orde, JS, ext. 262

VIII: Teachers' salaries and conditions of service; administration of Colleges of Education

J. Keeley, JS, ext. 270

IX: Educational building programme and approvals

I. D. Hamilton, AH, ext. 5494

Under-Secretary,
Social Work Services Group
A. F. Reid

X: Children's Panels, probation, after-care, research, training, staffing

G. Murray, JS, ext. 438

XI: List D Schools

R. J. W. Clark, JS, ext. 372

XII: Local authority social work services

R. D. Jackson, JS, ext. 339

XIII: Child care, adoption, fostering

Mrs E. Craghill (SP), JS, ext. 335

HM Senior Chief Inspector of Schools

J. F. McGarrity, NSAH, ext. 5459

R

SCOTTISH EDUCATION DEPARTMENT — *Continued*

Head of Division

Chief Social Work Adviser   Miss B. Jones, JS, ext. 332
Chief Statistician   D. Wishart, JS, ext. 281

SCOTTISH HOME AND HEALTH DEPARTMENT

Secretary   Private Secretary
A. L. Rennie, (b. 1924, app. 1977)   G. Mowat, NSAH, ext. 4014

Under-Secretary, Group I
W. Baird

                                 Head of Division

Scottish Office   Miss M. A. McPherson,
Superannuation   St. Margaret's Ho., 151
                                    London Rd., EH8 7TG,
                                    031-661-6181, ext. 432

Police   R. R. Hillhouse, NSAH,
                                    ext. 4373

Fire   G. P. H. Aitken, NSAH,
                                    ext. 5335

Home Defence and Civil
Emergencies

Under-Secretary, Group II
D. J. Cowperthwaite

Law and General (Land
tenure, civil law, legal aid,
Boundary Commission, minor   A. T. F. Ogilvie, NSAH,
regulatory matters)   ext. 4509

Prisons   J. Scrimgeour, St. Margaret's
                                    Ho., ext. 399

Criminal Justice, criminal
law, liquor licensing,
protection of birds   N. J. Shanks, NSAH, ext. 5897

Under-Secretary, Health Services
(Care)
J. B. Hume

Health Boards, administration
and planning   W. P. Lawrie, SAH, ext. 2200

SCOTTISH HOME AND HEALTH DEPARTMENT — *Continued*

Head of Division

Primary care: prevention;
environmental health; health
education; family planning,
maternity, adoption, patients'
interests   E. Redmond, SAH, ext. 2319

Mentally and physically
disabled; alcoholism, misuse
of drugs   G. Robertson, SAH, ext. 2378

Scientific and information
services; emergency services,
blood transfusion, liaison with
Common Services Agency,   A. M. MacPherson, SAH,
devolution (health questions)   ext. 2646

Under-Secretary, Health Services
(Resources) and Part III, emergency
services and blood transfusion
J. Walker

Doctors and dentists, medical   Miss M. Maclean, SAH,
and dental education   ext. 2305

Nursing, administrative and
professional staff   D. Stevenson, SAH, ext. 2558

Ancillary and domestic services
and staff, control of drugs,
food standards   F. H. Cowley, SAH, ext. 2289

Capital allocations and
approvals, project control,
land, building and design
guidance, supplies policy   A. H. Bishop, SAH, ext. 2370

HM Chief Inspector of Constabulary   D. Gray, NSAH, ext. 4149
Chief Medical Officer   J. J. A. Reid, SAH, ext. 2117
Chief Scientist   Sir Andrew Watt Kay, Trinity
                                         Park House, EH5 3SF,
                                         031-552-6255, ext. 2709
Chief Nursing Officer   Miss M. G. Auld, SAH,
                                         ext. 2219

SECTION 8

REGIONAL COUNCILS:
Names and addresses of Conveners and Chief Officers

	Convener/ Population	Chief Executive	Director of Administration	Director of Finance	Director of Education	Director of Social Work	Director of Planning	Director of Roads
BORDERS Newtown St Boswells TD6 0SA 083 52 3301	John Askew (Con) 99,000	K J Clark	A R Napier	H Hall	J McLean	D A Macdonald	D P Douglas	R I Hill
CENTRAL Viewforth Stirling 0786 3111	James Anderson (Lab) 270,000	E Geddes	P W Buchanan	J Broadfoot	I Collie	H M Garland	F Bracewell	J F Keith
DUMFRIES & GALLOWAY Council Offices Dumfries 0387 3141	John Niven (Ind) 144,000	L T Carnegie	D A Lyle	D Y Booth 0387 62323	J K Purves 30 Edinburgh Rd Dumfries 0387 63822	J W Barbour 8 Gordon St Dumfries 0387 63022	A H Dobbie	H D B Murray
FIFE Fife House North Street Glenrothes 0592 754411	Robert Gough (Lab) 339,000	J M Dunlop	J F Kennedy	R Venters	I S Flett Wemyssfield Kirkcaldy 0592 62351	M A Gillespie Queensway Glenrothes 0592 756901	M E Taylor County Bldgs Cupar 0334 3722	R J Stobie (Engineering) Craig Mitchell House Flemington Road Glenrothes 0592 756541
GRAMPIAN Woodhill House Ashgrove Road West Aberdeen AB9 2LU 0224 23401	Alexander Mutch (Con) 454,000	J D Macnaughton	I Miller	T E Carter	J A D Michie	Miss M Hartnoll	T F Sprott	W Turner
HIGHLAND Regional Buildings Glenurquhart Road Inverness 0463 34121	Ian Campbell (Ind) 186,000	F G Armstrong	F F Bruce R H Stevenson	J W Bremner	R Macdonald	J G Bailey	D W M Calder	G K M Macfarlane

	Convener/Population	Chief Executive	Director of Administration	Director of Finance	Director of Education	Director of Social Work	Director of Planning	Director of Roads
LOTHIAN George IV Bridge Edinburgh EH1 1UQ 031-229 9292	John Crichton (Lab) 755,000	R G E Peggie	A L McNicoll	B Grosset	W D C Semple 40 Torphichen St Edinburgh EH3 8JJ	R W Kent Shrubhill House Shrub Place Edinburgh EH7 4PD 031-554 4301	F P Tindall 1 Parliament Sq Edinburgh EH1 1TU	A S Crockett 19 Market St Edinburgh EH1 1BL
STRATHCLYDE Melrose House 19 Cadogan Street Glasgow G2 6HR 041-204 2900	Charles O'Halloran (Lab) 2,489,000	L Boyle	G Carlton	R Paterson	E Miller 25 Bothwell St Glasgow G2 6NR	F E Edwards McIver House 51 Cadogan St Glasgow G2 7QB 041-204 2727	H D B Torrance McIver House 51 Cadogan St Glasgow G2 7QB 041-204 2727	W S Mc-Alonan McIver House 51 Cadogan St Glasgow G2 7QB 041-204 2727
TAYSIDE Tayside House 26-28 Crichton Street Dundee 0382 23281	William Fitzgerald (Con) 402,000	A H Martin		G A McFee	D G Robertson	S O Moxley	H Ramsay	A R Mollison
ISLANDS COUNCILS								
ORKNEY County Offices Kirkwall 0856 3535	Edwin Eunson (Ind) 18,000	H A G Lapsley	R M Ross	R H Gilbert	A Bain	A R Mac-kinnon	M Sargent	
SHETLAND Town Hall Lerwick 0595 3535	Alexander Tulloch (Ind) 19,000	E Urquhart	P B Regan County Bldgs Lerwick	C V Ennis 4 Market St Lerwick	R A B Barnes Brentham Ho Harbour St Lerwick	P Malcolmson 64 St Olaf St Lerwick	J M Fenwick Victoria Bldgs Esplanade Lerwick	
WESTERN ISLES Council Offices South Beach Stornoway 0851 3773	Rev Donald Macaulay (Ind) 30,000	R MacIver	D Sinclair	D G Macleod	A Macleod 0851 3992	0851 3664	J R Haworth	

SECTION 9

DISTRICT COUNCILS

Names and address of Conveners and Chief Executives.
Population ('000s) in brackets after district name.

	Convener/ Provost	Chief Executive
BORDERS		
Berwickshire (17)	J R Ford	R Christie District Offices, Duns, TD11 3DU (03612 2331)
Ettrick & Lauderdale (32)	A L Tulley	D H Cowan Council Chambers, Paton Street Galashiels, TD1 3AS (0896 4751)
Roxburgh (36)	Rev R S Blakey	J F A Richardson District Offices, High Street Hawick TD9 9EF (0450 5991)
Tweeddale (14)	T Blyth	G Gardiner District Offices, Peebles (0721 20153)
CENTRAL		
Clackmannan (48)	J Clement	A E O'Neill The Whins, Alloa (0259 722160)
Falkirk (143)	A Crawford	J P H Paton Municipal Buildings Falkirk FK1 5RS (0324 24911)
Stirling (79)	Mrs L M McCaig	D M Bowie Municipal Buildings Corn Exchange Road Stirling FK8 2HU (0786 3131)
DUMFRIES & GALLOWAY		
Annandale & Eskdale (35)	R G Greenhow	G F Murray High Street, Annan (04612 3311)
Nithsdale (56)	W B Simpson	G D Grant Municipal Chambers Dumfries, DG1 2AD (0387 3166)
Stewartry (22)	J Nelson	W L Dick-Smith Council Offices Kircudbright DG6 4PJ (0557 30291)
Wigtown (30)	D R Robinson	J D Sharp Sun Street, Stranraer, DG9 3JJ (0776 2151)

	Convener/ Provost	Chief Executive
FIFE		
Dunfermline (125)	L G Wood	G Brown City Chambers, Dunfermline (0383 22711)
Kirkcaldy (149)	R King	W C Hogg Town House, Kirkcaldy KY1 1XW (0592 61144)
North-East Fife (65)	Mrs V D Purvis	H Farquhar County Buildings Cupar, KY15 4TA (0334 3722)
GRAMPIAN		
City of Aberdeen (210)	W J Fraser	J M Wilson Town House Aberdeen, AB9 1AQ (0224 23456)
Banff and Buchan (76)	W R Cruickshank	W S McAlister St Leonards Sandyhill Road, Banff (026 12 2521)
Gordon (51)	J B Presley	A C Kennedy 3 High Street Inverurie, AB5 9QA (0467 20981)
Kincardine & Deeside (36)	I M Frain	Miss E M G Cockburn Arduthie Road Stonehaven, AB3 2DQ (056 92 62001)
Moray (81)	J M Anderson	J P C Bell High Street, Elgin, IV30 13X (0343 3451)
HIGHLAND		
Badenoch & Strathspey (9)	A C Robertson	H G McCulloch High Street, Kingussie (054 02 555)
Caithness (29)	J M Young	A Beattie Council Offices, Wick (0955 3761)
Inverness (55)	I C Fraser	B Wilson Town House, Inverness IV1 1JJ (0463 39111)
Lochaber (20)	Miss Maclean	J McGhee Tweedale, Fort William (0397 3881)
Nairn (10)	H McLean	J R McCluskey 4 Court House Lane Nairn IV12 4DR (0667 52056)
Ross & Cromarty (42)	W S Fowlie	A Cuthbertson County Buildings Dingwall IV15 9QN (0349 3381)

	Convener/ Provost	Chief Executive
Skye & Lochalsh (10)	L Mackinnon	D H Noble Dunvegan Road, Portree (0478 2341)
Sutherland (12)	D F Mackay	D W Martin District Offices Golspie KW10 6RB (040 83392)
LOTHIAN		
City of Edinburgh (467)	K W Borthwick	E G Glendinning City Chambers, High Street Edinburgh, EH1 1YJ (031-225 2424)
East Lothian (79)	T Wilson	D B Miller Council Buildings Haddington EH41 3HA (062 082 4161)
Midlothian (85)	D R Smith	D W Duguid 1 White Hart Street, Dalkeith (031-663 2881)
West Lothian (124)	J Clark	D Morrison South Bridge Street, Bathgate (Bathgate 53631)
STRATHCLYDE		
Argyll & Bute (66)	E T F Spence	M A J Gossip Kilmory, Lochgilphead (0546 2127)
Bearsden & Milngavie (38)	T H N Young	A R Rae Boclair, Bearsden, G61 2TQ (041-942 2262)
Clydebank (56)	W Johnston	J M Brown Municipal Buildings Clydebank, G81 1XQ (041-952 1103)
Cumbernauld & Kilsyth (48)	G S Murray	R Kyle Bron Way, Cumbernauld (02367 22131)
Cumnock & Doon Valley (48)	J Paterson	D T Hemmings Lugar, Cumnock KA18 3JQ (0290 22111)
Cunninghame (133)	M Brown	J M Miller Cunninghame House Irvine, KA12 8EE (0294 74166)
Dumbarton (81)	W Petrie	L Mackinnon Crosslet House, Dunbarton (0389 65100)
East Kilbride (83)	J Marshall	W G McNay Civic Centre, East Kilbride (035 52 28777)
Eastwood (51)	I S Hutchison	M D Henry Cotton Street, Paisley (041-889 5454)

	Convener/ Provost	Chief Executive
City of Glasgow (856)	D Hodge	Vacant City Chambers Glasgow, G2 1DU (041-221 9600)
Hamilton (107)	C Brownlie	W Johnston 102 Cadzow Street Hamilton ML3 6HH (069 82 21188)
Inverclyde (104)	A D Fletcher	I C Wilson Municipal Buildings, Greenock (0475 24400)
Kilmarnock & Loudon (83)	Mrs M G Parker	J C W Nicol Civic Centre Kilmarnock, KA1 1BY (0563 21140)
Kyle & Carrick (112)	A D Paton	J R Hill Burns House, Ayr (0292 81511)
Lanark (55)	R C M Monteith	R G Dalkin District Offices Lanark, ML11 7JT (0555 61331)
Monklands (108)	T Clarke	J S Ness Dunbeth Road Coatbridge ML5 3LF (0236 24941)
Motherwell (161)	V Mathieson	F C Marks PO Box 14, Motherwell (0698 66166)
Renfrew (209)	R Cowper	W McIntosh Cotton Street, Paisley (041-889 5400)
Strathkelvin (81)	D Stark	A W Harrower PO Box 4 Kirkintilloch, G66 1PW (041-776 7171)
TAYSIDE Angus (90)	M Struthers	W S McCulloch County Buildings Forfar, DD8 3LG (0307 5101)
City of Dundee (194)	W C Vaughan	G S Watson City Chambers, Dundee (0382 23141)
Perth & Kinross (118)	N T Renfrew	R T Blair 1 - 3 High Street, Perth (0738 24241)

SECTION 10

NEW TOWN DEVELOPMENT CORPORATIONS
IN SCOTLAND

	Address	*Chief Executive*
Cumbernauld	12 Clyde Walk, Centre South, Cumbernauld, G67 1BP (023-67-23345)	Brig C. H. Cowan
East Kilbride	Atholl House, East Kilbride G74 1LU (035-52-41111)	G. B. Young
Glenrothes	New Glenrothes House, Town Centre, Glenrothes, Fife (0592-754343)	M. Cracknell
Irvine	Perceton House, Irvine, Ayrshire, KA11 2AL (0294-74100)	J. D. Marquis
Livingstone	Livingstone, West Lothian, EH54 7AD (0589-31177)	J. Wilson

SECTION 11

MAJOR POLITICAL AND SOCIAL ORGANISATIONS
IN SCOTLAND

1. *Political Parties*
   Communist Party, 44 Carlton Place, Glasgow, G5 (041-429-2558).

   Scottish Conservative Party, 11 Atholl Crescent, Edinburgh, EH3 8HG.

   The Labour Party (Scottish Council), Keir Hardie House, 1 Lynedoch Place, Glasgow, G3 6AB (041-332-8946).

   Scottish Liberal Party, 2 Atholl Place, Edinburgh, EH3 8HP (031-229-7484).

   Scottish National Party, 6 North Charlotte Street, Edinburgh, EH2 4JH (031-226-3661).

2. *Government Agencies*
   Glasgow Eastern Area Renewal Project (GEAR), Gear Centre, 596 London Road, Glasgow, G40 (041-551-0011).

   Highlands and Islands Development Board, 27 Bank Street, Inverness, IV1 1QR (0463-34171).

   Manpower Services Commission Office for Scotland, 4 Jeffrey Street, Edinburgh, EH1 IUU (031-556-0233).

   Scottish Development Agency, 120 Bothwell Street, Glasgow, G2 7JP (041-248-2700).

   Scottish Special Housing Association, 37-41 Manor Place, Edinburgh, EH3 7EE (031-226-4401).

3. *Industrial and Social Organisations*
   Church of Scotland, 121 George Street, Edinburgh, EH2 (031-225-5722).

   Confederation of British Industry (Scottish Office), 5 Claremont Terrace,, Glasgow, G3 (041-332-8661).

   Scottish Consumer Council, 4 Somerset Place, Glasgow, G3 (041-332-8858).

   Scottish Council (Development and Industry), 1 Castle Street, Edinburgh, EH2 3AJ (031-225-7911).

   Scottish Council of Social Service, 18/19 Claremont Crescent, Edinburgh, EH7 4QD (031-556-3882).

   Scottish Trades Union Congress, 16 Woodlands Terrace, Glasgow, G3 6DF (041-332-4946).

SECTION 12

MAIN SCOTTISH ECONOMIC INDICATORS

1. *Gross Domestic Product:* factor cost, current prices, £m

	1970	1971	1972	1973	1974	1975	1976
Scotland	3.76	4.24	4.75	5.53	6.38	8.24	9.76
UK	43.79	48.86	55.29	63.30	72.52	91.95	108.19
Scotland as % of UK, per capita basis	91.2	92.4	92.0	93.7	94.2	96.2	97.3

Source: *Regional Statistics,* 1979 edition, Table 15.1

2. *Total Personal Income:* £m

	1971	1972	1973	1974	1975	1976
Scotland	4.05	4.59	5.46	6.61	8.50	10.01
UK	47.74	54.23	63.12	76.16	96.46	112.22
Scotland as % of UK, per capita basis	90.4	90.6	92.8	93.0	94.6	95.8

Source: *Regional Statistics,* 1976 edition, Table 15.8; 1979 edition, Table 15.8

3. *Average weekly earnings:* full-time male manual workers over 21, £

	1970	1971	1972	1973	1974	1975	1976	1977
Scotland	27.04	29.83	34.93	40.35	48.37	60.71	67.88	73.53
UK	28.05	30.93	35.82	40.92	48.63	59.58	66.97	72.89
Scotland as % of UK	96.4	96.4	97.5	98.6	99.5	101.9	101.4	100.9

Source: *Regional Statistics,* 1974, Table 82; 1976, Table 13.7; 1979, Table 13.6

4. *Average household income:* per week, Family Expenditure Survey data (average of two annual surveys, liable to sampling error)

	1970/71	1972/73	1974/75	1976/77
Scotland	34.92	43.20	63.60	85.00
UK	37.04	46.16	65.87	87.64
Scotland as % of UK	92.3	93.6	96.6	97.0

Source: *Regional Statistics,* 1973, Table 86; 1974, Table 87; 1976, Table 13.8; 1979, Table 13.2

5. *Unemployment:* annual average %

	1970	1971	1972	1973	1974	1975	1976	1977
Scotland	4.2	5.8	6.4	4.5	4.0	5.2	7.0	8.3
UK	2.6	3.5	3.8	2.7	2.6	4.2	5.8	6.2
Scotland as % of UK	162	166	168	167	154	124	121	134

Source: *Regional Statistics,* 1979, Table 8.4; 1976, Table 8.4

6. *Public expenditure:* identifiable public expenditure per head

	1972/73	1973/74	1974/75	1975/76	1976/77
Scotland	447	496	658	856	948
England	335	408	543	686	754
Wales	386	439	583	776	875
Northern Ireland	446	523	759	983	1,122
Scotland as % of England	133	122	121	125	126

Source: House of Commons *Hansard,* 24 November 1977, Vol. 939 Col. 852

SECTION 13

SCOTTISH PARLIAMENTARY BY-ELECTIONS SINCE 1974*

Percentage poll for each party

	Con	Lab	SNP	Lib	Others	Turnout %
General Election of Oct. 1974, seats	16	41	11	3		
13.4.78 Glasgow, Garscadden	18.2	45.4	32.0	—	3.1	72.0
31.5.78 Hamilton	13.0	51.0	33.4	2.6		72.0
26.10.78 Berwick and East Lothian	40.2	47.4	8.8	3.6		**71.9**

* A Table giving Scottish by-election results from 1945 can be found in the 1979 *Yearbook*.

SECTION 14

GENERAL ELECTION RESULTS SCOTLAND,
MAY, 1979*

	% vote	seats
Labour (Lab)	41.5	44
Conservative (Con)	31.4	22
SNP (SNP)	17.3	2
Liberal (Lib)	9.0	3
Others	0.8	0

* See *The Scottish Government Yearbook 1979*, p.260, for General Election results in Scotland since 1945.

		%	Change since Oct. 1974
ABERDEEN			

North 64,747

R. Hughes (Lab)	26,771	59.3	+8.4
G. Adams (Con)	7,657	17.0	+5.7
Miss M. Watt (SNP)	5,796	12.9	−16.8
Miss L. Macmillan (Lib)	4,887	10.8	+2.7

No change.   Lab maj.: 19,114   Turnout 69.67%

South 65,090

I. Sproat (Con)	20,820	40.7	+5.2
N. Godman (Lab)	20,048	39.2	+4.4
Mrs H. Pitt-Watson (Lib)	5,901	11.5	+1.9
A. Stronach (SNP)	4,361	8.5	−11.6

No change.   Con maj.:   772   Turnout 78.55%

DUNDEE

Dundee East 64,330

G. Wilson (SNP)	20,497	41.0	−6.7
J. Reid (Lab)	17,978	36.0	+3.3
B. Townsend (Con)	9,072	18.2	+1.4
G. Brodie (Lib)	2,317	4.6	+1.8
R. Battersby (Workers Revolutionary)	95	0.2	

No change.   SNP maj.: 2,519   Turnout 77.66%

		%	Change since Oct. 1974
Dundee West 63,883			
E. Ross (Lab)	23,654	47.3	+6.2
J. Fairlie (SNP)	13,197	26.4	−8.7
I. Stevenson (Con)	12,892	25.8	+7.3
R. Mennie (Comm)	316	0.6	

No change.   Lab maj.: 10,457   Turnout 78.36%

		%	
EDINBURGH			
Central 37,740			
R. Cook (Lab)	12,191	47.8	+7.5
D. McLetchie (Con)	7,530	29.6	+3.6
S. Donaldson (Lib)	3,096	12.2	+3.3
G. Kennedy (SNP)	2,486	9.8	−15.0
C. Boyd (SLP)	176	0.7	

No change.   Lab maj.: 4,661   Turnout 67.51%

		%	
East 57,473			
G. Strang (Lab)	23,477	53.7	+8.8
G. Campbell (Con)	14,660	33.5	+10.4
G. MacDougall (SNP)	5,296	12.1	−13.5
Miss C. Downs (Comm)	173	0.4	
T. Brotherstone (Workers Rev)	124	0.3	

No change.   Lab maj.: 8,817   Turnout 76.09%

		%	
Leith 37,204			
R. Brown (Lab)	12,961	46.3	+6.6
A. McLernan (Con)	8,944	31.9	+3.9
K. Aitken (Lib)	3,382	12.1	+5.9
W. Platt (SNP)	2,706	9.7	−16.4

No change.   Lab maj.: 4,017   Turnout 75.24%

		%	
North 45,303			
A. Fletcher (Con)	14,170	43.6	+4.3
N. Lindsay (Lab)	9,773	30.1	+4.2
R. Guild (Lib)	5,045	15.5	+4.2
N. MacCormick (SNP)	3,521	10.8	−12.7

No change.   Con maj.: 4,397   Turnout 71.76%

		%	
Pentlands 58,652			
M. Rifkind (Con)	17,684	39.3	+5.4
A. Johnstone (Lab)	16,486	36.6	+5.7
C. Luckhurst (Lib)	5,919	13.2	+2.6
S. Maxwell (SNP)	4,934	11.0	−13.6

No change.   Con maj.: 1,198   Turnout 76.76%

		%	Change since Oct. 1974

South 58,556

M. Ancram (Con)	17,986	39.7	+3.8
G. Brown (Lab)	15,526	34.3	+6.1
B. Lovell (Lib)	7,400	16.3	+2.1
R. Shirley (SNP)	3,800	8.4	−13.3
S. Biggar (Ecology Party)	552	1.2	

No change. Con maj.: 2,460 Turnout 77.30%

West 54,727

Lord J. Douglas-Hamilton (Con)	19,360	45.4	+7.2
M. McGregor (Lab)	12,009	28.2	+3.0
Mrs R. Callender (Lib)	7,330	17.2	+0.8
C. Bell (SNP)	3,904	9.2	−11.0

No change. Con maj.: 7,351 Turnout 77.85%

GLASGOW

Cathcart 48,574

J. Maxton (Lab)	17,550	45.9	+7.8
E. Taylor (Con)	15,950	41.7	−1.0
A. Ewing (SNP)	2,653	6.9	−9.6
H. Wills (Lib)	2,042	5.3	+2.6

Lab gain from Con. Lab maj.: 1,600 Turnout 78.63%

Central 19,826

T. McMillan (Lab)	8,542	72.5	+8.9
F. Saleem (Con)	1,937	16.4	+3.4
S. Bird (SNP)	1,308	11.1	−8.1

No change. Lab maj.: 6,605 Turnout 59.45%

Craigton 44,326

B. Millan (Lab)	19,952	59.9	+9.4
J. Mair (Con)	9,480	28.5	+8.4
R. Silver (SNP)	3,881	11.6	−12.7

No change. Lab maj.: 10,472 Turnout 75.15%

Garscadden 52,440

D. Dewar (Lab)	23,591	61.5	+10.6
I. Lawson (Con)	8,393	21.9	+9.0
J. Bain (SNP)	6,012	15.7	−15.5
S. Barr (Comm)	374	1.0	

No change. Lab maj.: 15,198 Turnout 73.17%

S

		%	Change since Oct. 1974
Govan 24,894			
A. McMahon (Lab)	11,676	67.9	+18.0
J. Walker (Con)	3,188	18.5	+11.4
T. Wilson (SNP)	2,340	13.6	−27.4

No change.   Lab maj.:   8,488   Turnout 69.11%

Hillhead 39,793			
T. Galbraith (Con)	12,368	41.0	+3.9
R. Mowbray (Lab)	10,366	34.4	+6.2
M. Harris (Lib)	4,349	14.4	+3.5
G. Borthwick (SNP)	3,050	10.1	−12.7

No change.   Con maj.:   2,002   Turnout 75.72%

Kelvingrove 33,701			
N. Carmichael (Lab)	11,133	50.3	+7.5
A. Macdougall (Con)	6,374	28.9	+1.3
E. Bennett (Lib)	2,412	10.9	+4.5
I. Bayne (SNP)	2,199	9.9	−13.3

No change.   Lab maj.:   4,759   Turnout 65.63%

Maryhill 50,434			
J. Craigen (Lab Co-op)	22,602	66.2	+8.5
M. White (Con)	5,106	15.0	+5.7
D. McGlashan (SNP)	3,812	11.2	−18.7
Miss E. Attwooll (Lib)	2,332	6.8	+3.7
P. Smith (Comm)	287	0.8	

No change.   Lab maj.: 17,496   Turnout 67.69%

Pollok 59,032			
J. White (Lab)	21,420	49.2	+5.9
D. Roser (Con)	12,928	29.7	+2.7
A. McIntosh (SNP)	4,187	9.6	−14.7
G. McKell (Lib)	3,946	9.1	+3.8
Miss N. Armstrong (Ind Lab)	869	2.0	
Mrs I. Skinner (Nat Front)	104	0.1	
R. Hilton (Ind Dem)	41		

No change.   Lab maj.:   8,492   Turnout 73.68%

Provan 52,482			
H. Brown (Lab)	24,083	69.5	+10.9
S. Langdon (Con)	5,239	15.1	+5.3
R. Cunning (SNP)	4,767	13.8	−16.5
J. Jackson (Comm)	377	1.6	+0.2
M. Campbell (Workers Rev)	193	0.8	

No change.   Lab maj.: 18,844   Turnout 66.04%

		%	Change since Oct. 1974

Queen's Park 34,332

F. McElhone (Lab)	15,120	64.4	+8.3
J. Collins (Con)	5,642	24.0	+7.0
P. Greene (SNP)	2,276	9.7	−12.1
J. Kay (Comm)	263	1.1	−0.3
Miss J. Kerrigan (Workers Rev)	99	0.4	
W. MacLellan (Soc. Unity)	92	0.4	

No change.   Lab maj.:   9,478   Turnout 68.43%

Shettleston 31,910

D. Marshall (Lab)	13,955	64.1	+9.8
Miss M. McLure (Con)	4,794	22.0	+7.6
M. MacDonald (SNP)	3,022	13.9	−14.6

No change.   Lab maj.:   9,161   Turnout 68.23%

Springburn 42,118

M. Martin (Lab)	18,871	66.1	+11.5
G. McKay (Con)	6,100	21.4	+8.1
W. Morton (SNP)	3,587	12.6	−15.7

No change.   Lab maj.: 12,771   Turnout 67.81%

A

Aberdeenshire East 54,292

A. McQuarrie (Con)	16,827	42.8	+7.3
D. Henderson (SNP)	16,259	41.4	−7.1
N. Bonney (Lab)	6,201	15.8	+6.4

Con gain from SNP.   Con maj.:   558   Turnout 72.38%

Aberdeenshire West 67,915

R. Fairgrieve (Con)	21,086	40.9	+5.2
M. Bruce (Lib)	18,320	35.5	+5.6
G. Grant (Lab)	7,907	15.3	+3.1
J. Hulbert (SNP)	4,260	8.3	−13.9

No change.   Con maj.:   2,766   Turnout 75.39%

Angus North and Mearns 43,122

A. Buchanan-Smith (Con)	18,302	57.5	+13.9
I. Murray (SNP)	7,387	23.2	−11.0
H. McMahon (Lab)	6,132	19.3	+7.0

No change.   Con maj.: 10,915   Turnout 73.79%

		%	Change since Oct. 1974
Angus South 57,513			
P. Fraser (Con)	20,029	43.6	+4.4
A. Welsh (SNP)	19,066	41.5	−2.3
I. Philip (Lab)	4,623	10.1	−0.4
H. Will (Lib)	2,218	4.8	−1.7

Con gain from SNP.   Con maj.: 963   Turnout 79.87%

		%	
Argyll 43,527			
J. MacKay (Con)	12,191	36.8	+0.1
I. MacCormick (SNP)	10,545	31.8	−17.9
M. MacGregor (Lab)	5,283	15.9	+2.3
Mrs J. Michie (Lib)	5,113	15.4	

Con gain from SNP.   Con maj.: 1,646   Turnout 76.11%

		%	
Ayr 54,753			
G. Younger (Con)	18,907	43.3	+1.2
K. MacDonald (Lab)	16,139	36.9	+2.3
R. Mabon (Lib)	4,656	10.6	+4.3
J. McGill (SNP)	3,998	9.2	−7.5

No change.   Con maj.: 2,768   Turnout 79.81%

		%	
Ayrshire Central 67,288			
D. Lambie (Lab)	27,438	51.2	+6.1
R. Wilkinson (Con)	15,734	29.3	+4.5
I. Macdonald (SNP)	5,596	10.4	−14.1
I. Clarkson (Lib)	4,896	9.1	+3.5

No change.   Lab maj.: 11,704   Turnout 79.75%

		%	
Ayrshire South 50,727			
G. Foulkes (Lab)	14,271	35.2	−21.0
J. Sillars (SLP)	12,750	31.4	
G. Young (Con)	10,287	25.4	+6.8
C. Cameron (SNP)	3,233	8.0	−11.8

Lab gain from SLP.   Lab maj.: 1,521   Turnout 77.92%

B

		%	
Banff 32,768			
D. Myles (Con)	10.580	44.4	+6.5
H. Watt (SNP)	9,781	41.4	−4.5
R. Duncan (Lab)	3,381	14.2	+6.9

Con gain from SNP   Con maj.: 799   Turnout 72.45%

		%	Change since Oct. 1974

Berwick and East Lothian 60,919

J. Home Robertson (Lab)	21,977	43.5	+0.2
Miss M. Marshall (Con)	20,304	40.2	+2.6
T. Glen (Lib)	4,948	9.8	+3.9
A. Macartney (SNP)	3,300	6.5	−6.7

No change. Lab maj.: 1,673 Turnout 82.94%

Bothwell 61,309

J. Hamilton (Lab)	26,492	55.0	+6.3
J. Scott (Con)	11,275	23.4	+5.5
T. Grieve (Lib)	5,225	10.8	+1.9
J. McCool (SNP)	5,202	10.8	−13.7

No change. Lab maj.: 15,217 Turnout 78.61%

Bute and North Ayrshire 49,931

J. Corrie (Con)	17,317	45.7	+6.8
M. Smith (Lab)	13,004	34.3	+5.4
M. Brown (SNP)	5,272	13.9	−12.0
P. Giffney (Lib)	2,280	6.0	−0.3

No change. Con maj.: 4,313 Turnout 75.85%

C

Caithness and Sutherland 29,564

R. MacLennan (Lab)	9,613	41.5	+6.2
R. Wardrop (Con)	7,074	30.5	+11.7
R. Shaw (SNP)	6.487	28.0	+4.1

No change. Lab maj.: 2,539 Turnout 78.11%

Clackmannan and Stirlingshire East 66,535

M. O'Neill (Lab)	22,780	41.9	+5.5
G. Reid (SNP)	21,796	40.1	−10.6
T. Begg (Con)	9,778	18.0	+7.6

Lab gain from SNP. Lab maj.: 984 Turnout 81.69%

Coatbridge and Airdrie 60,133

J. Dempsey (Lab)	27,598	60.9	+9.3
J. Love (Con)	12,442	27.5	+10.3
Mrs M. Johnston (SNP)	5,260	11.6	−16.3

No change. Lab maj.: 15,156 Turnout 75.33%

D		%	Change since Oct. 1974
Dumfries 64,311			
H. Munro (Con)	22,704	45.2	+6.4
A. Wood (Lab)	13,700	27.3	+0.8
J. Wallis (Lib)	7,169	14.3	+6.0
E. Gibson (SNP)	6,647	13.2	−13.2

No change.   Con maj.: 9,004   Turnout 78.09%

Dunbartonshire Central 49,381			
H. McCartney (Lab)	20,515	51.9	+12.9
N. Soames (Con)	8,512	21.5	+4.9
W. Lindsay (SNP)	6,055	15.3	−13.4
Mrs L. McCreadie (Lib)	3,099	7.8	+3.0
D. McCafferty (Comm)	1,017	2.6	−6.1
R. Darroch (CD)	312	0.8	

No change.   Lab maj.: 12,033   Turnout 73.73%

Dunbartonshire East 73,261			
N. Hogg (Lab)	23,268	37.9	+7.6
M. Hirst (Con)	20,944	34.1	+2.9
Mrs M. Bain (SNP)	12,654	20.6	−10.6
R. Waddell (Lib)	4,600	7.5	+0.2

Lab gain from SNP.   Lab maj.: 2,324   Turnout 83.90%

Dunbartonshire West 54,507			
I. Campbell (Lab)	21,166	48.4	+10.3
C. Munro (Con)	14,709	33.7	+10.5
S. Stratton (SNP)	7,835	17.9	−15.8

No change.   Lab maj.: 6,457   Turnout 80.19%

Dunfermline 64,868			
R. Douglas (Lab Co-op)	22,803	44.3	+4.2
A. Lester (Con)	15,490	30.1	+7.1
Miss A. Cameron (SNP)	7,351	14.3	−14.3
G. Whitelaw (Lib)	5,803	11.3	+3.0

No change.   Lab maj.: 7,313   Turnout 79.31%

E

East Kilbride 73,094			
Dr M. S. Miller (Lab)	31,401	53.9	+12.0
W. Hodgson (Con)	17,128	29.4	+13.1
G. Murray (SNP)	9,090	15.6	−21.1
D. McDowall (Comm)	658	1.1	

No change.   Lab maj.: 14,273   Turnout 79.73%

F			%	Change since Oct. 1974
Fife Central 61,476				
W. Hamilton (Lab)		27,619	58.0	+6.1
I. McCrone (Con)		9,597	20.2	+7.8
J. Lynch (SNP)		9,208	19.3	−14.1
A. Maxwell (Comm)		1,172	2.5	+0.1
No change.	Lab maj.:	18,022		Turnout 77.42%
Fife East 59,291				
B. Henderson (Con)		20,117	43.0	+4.2
M. Campbell (Lib)		10,762	23.0	+10.3
H. McLeish (Lab)		9,339	19.9	+3.1
J. Marshall (SNP)		6,612	14.1	−17.6
No change.	Con maj.:	9,355		Turnout 78.97%
G				
Galloway 41,110				
I. Lang (Con)		15,306	45.8	+5.7
G. Thompson (SNP)		12,384	37.1	−3.2
D. Hannay (Lib)		2,852	8.5	−2.0
D. Johnston (Lab)		2,841	8.5	−0.5
Con gain from SNP.	Con maj.:	2,922		Turnout 81.20%
Greenock & Port Glasgow 61,610				
J. D. Mabon (Lab Co-op)		24,071	53.0	+4.8
J. Boyd (Lib)		12,789	28.2	+8.8
R. Glasgow (Con)		4,926	10.9	−0.5
K. Wright (SNP)		3,435	7.6	−13.5
Mrs I. Mathieson (Workers Rev)		176	0.4	
No change.	Lab maj.:	11,282		Turnout 73.68%
H				
Hamilton 51,802				
G. Robertson (Lab)		24,593	59.6	+12.1
P. Davison (Con)		9,794	23.8	+14.3
C. Stoddart (SNP)		6,842	16.6	−22.4
No change.	Lab maj.:	14,799		Turnout 79.60%
I				
Inverness 62,571				
R. Johnston (Lib)		15,716	33.7	+1.4
R. Gordon (Con)		11,559	24.8	+2.8
D. Barr (SNP)		9,603	20.6	−9.0
B. Wilson (Lab)		9,586	20.6	+5.0
U. Bell (Fine Gh)		112	0.2	
No change.	Lib maj.:	4,157		Turnout 74.43%

	%	Change since Oct. 1974

K

Kilmarnock 60,351

W. McKelvie (Lab)	25,718	52.6	+6.9
J. Corbett (Con)	14,251	29.1	+10.2
A. McInnes (SNP)	8,963	18.3	−11.9

No change.   Lab maj.: 11,467   Turnout 81.08%

Kinross & West Perthshire 38,591

N. Fairbairn (Con)	15,523	50.5	+8.8
I. Smith (SNP)	9,045	29.4	−12.1
Mrs J. Chapman (Lib)	3,572	11.6	+2.5
D. MacLeod (Lab)	2,593	8.4	+0.7

No change.   Con maj.: 6,478   Turnout 79.64%

Kirkcaldy 61,057

H. Gourlay (Lab)	25,449	53.9	+8.5
Mrs J. Stewart (Con)	12,386	26.2	+9.7
A. Currie (SNP)	9,416	19.9	−12.1

No change.   Lab maj.: 13,063   Turnout 77.39%

L

Lanark 51,320

Mrs J. Hart (Lab)	18,118	43.2	+5.6
A. Bell (Con)	12,979	30.9	+7.7
T. McAlpine (SNP)	7,902	18.8	−17.0
F. McDermid (Lib)	2,967	7.1	+3.7

No change.   Lab maj.: 5,139   Turnout 81.77%

Lanarkshire North 56,565

J. Smith (Lab)	25,015	55.5	+9.3
G. Robertson (Con)	14,195	31.5	+9.0
J. Ralston (SNP)	5,887	13.1	−13.8

No change.   Lab maj.: 10,820   Turnout 79.73%

M

Midlothian 101,482

A. Eadie (Lab)	37,733	47.8	+6.3
H. Mann (Con)	20,797	26.4	−10.4
G. Spiers (SNP)	13,260	16.8	−18.8
A. Brodie (Lib)	7,129	9.0	+2.1

No change.   Lab maj.: 16,936   Turnout 77.77%

		%	Change since Oct. 1974

Moray and Nairn 45,802

A. Pollock (Con)	14,220	40.1	+0.1
Mrs W. Ewing (SNP)	13,800	38.9	−2.3
S. Rodan (Lib)	4,361	12.3	+3.2
G. Scobie (Lab)	3,104	8.7	−1.0

Con gain from SNP.   Con maj.:   420   Turnout 77.47%

Motherwell and Wishaw 50,317

J. Bray (Lab)	22,263	56.9	+12.3
J. Thomson (Con)	11,326	28.9	+10.7
J. McKay (SNP)	4,817	12.3	−19.6
J. Sneddon (Comm)	740	1.9	

No change.   Lab maj.:   10,937   Turnout 77.80%

O

Orkney and Shetland 28,884

J. Grimond (Lib)	10,950	56.4	+0.2
C. Donaldson (Con)	4,140	21.3	+7.1
Miss R. Goodlad (Lab)	3,385	17.4	+5.0
M. Spens (SNP)	935	4.8	−12.4

No change.   Lib maj.:   6,810   Turnout 67.20%

P

Paisley 63,765

A. Adams (Lab)	25,894	55.8	+11.0
G. Wills (Con)	12,139	26.2	+10.5
D. Rollo (SNP)	7,305	15.7	−17.4
B. Monaghan (SLP)	811	1.7	
Mrs J. Tait (Comm)	145	0.3	
T. White (Workers Rev)	122	0.3	

Lab gain from SLP.   Lab maj.:   13,755   Turnout 72.79%

Perth and East Perthshire 62,142

W. Walker (Con)	20,153	41.9	+3.0
D. Crawford (SNP)	17,050	35.5	−5.3
W. McKenzie (Lab)	6,432	13.4	−0.2
B. Goudie (Lib)	4,410	9.2	+2.5

Con gain from SNP.   Con maj.:   3,103   Turnout 77.31%

		%	Change since Oct. 1974

R

Renfrewshire East 64,456

A. Stewart (Con)	25,910	49.9	+8.5
Mrs E. Sullivan (Lab)	12,672	24.4	+3.6
W. Craig (Lib)	9,366	18.0	+3.4
J. Pow (SNP)	3,989	7.7	−15.5

No change.   Con maj.: 13,238   Turnout 80.58%

Renfrewshire West 78,218

N. Buchan (Lab)	28,236	44.5	+6.0
W. Boyle (Con)	19,664	31.0	+4.2
C. Cameron (SNP)	8,333	13.1	−15.1
J. Finnie (Lib)	7,256	11.4	+5.3

No change.   Lab maj.: 8,572   Turnout 81.17%

Ross and Cromarty 32,892

H. Gray (Con)	10,650	42.4	+3.5
W. McRae (SNP)	5,915	23.6	−12.1
K. Bloomer (Lab)	5,055	20.1	+3.3
H. Morrison (Lib)	3,496	13.9	+5.3

No change.   Con maj.: 4,735   Turnout 76.36%

Roxburgh, Selkirk and Peebles 59,691

D. Steel (Lib)	25,993	53.1	+9.4
G. Malone (Con)	15,303	31.3	+3.9
D. Heald (Lab)	4,150	8.5	−0.4
A. Stewart (SNP)	3,502	7.2	−12.9

No change.   Lib. maj.: 10,690   Turnout 82.00%

Rutherglen 49,397

G. MacKenzie (Lab)	18,546	46.7	+2.3
P. Burns (Con)	10,523	26.5	+2.5
R. Brown (Lib)	7,315	18.4	+12.1
M. Grieve (SNP)	3,325	8.4	−16.9

No change.   Lab maj.: 8,023   Turnout 80.42%

S

Stirling, Falkirk and Grangemouth 66,164

H. Ewing (Lab)	29,499	56.5	+13.3
W. Boyles (Con)	13,881	26.6	+12.5
J. Donachy (SNP)	8,856	17.0	−22.2

No change.   Lab maj.: 15,618   Turnout 78.95%

		%	Change since Oct. 1974
Stirlingshire West 57,602			
D. A. Canavan (Lab)	22,516	47.7	+8.7
Mrs A. McCurley (Con)	12,160	25.8	+7.4
Mrs J. T. Jones (SNP)	8,627	18.3	−19.9
D. Cant (Lib)	3,905	8.3	+3.9

No change. Lab maj.: 10,356 Turnout 81.95%

W

Western Isles 22,393			
D. Stewart (SNP)	7,941	52.5	−9.0
A. Matheson (Lab)	4,878	32.3	+7.6
M. Morrison (Con)	1,600	10.6	+2.3
N. MacLeod (Lib)	700	4.6	−0.9

No change. SNP maj.: 3,063 Turnout 67.52%

West Lothian 85,645			
T. Dalyell (Lab)	36,713	54.9	+9.6
W. Wolfe (SNP)	16,631	24.9	−16.1
J. Whyte (Con)	13,162	19.7	+9.7
W. Sneddon (Comm)	404		

No change. Lab maj.: 20,082 Turnout 78.12%

Source: Social Statistics Laboratory, University of Strathclyde.

SECTION 15

RETIRING, DEFEATED AND NEW MPs,

MAY, 1979

MPs retiring
Labour

Peter Doig — Dundee West
Ronald King Murray —
    Edinburgh Leith
Harry Selby — Glasgow Govan
Sir Myer Galpern —
    Glasgow Shettleston
Richard Buchanan —
    Glasgow Springburn
Adam Hunter — Dunfermline
William Ross — Kilmarnock

Con

Michael Clark Hutchison —
    Edinburgh South
Sir John Gilmour — Fife East
Betty Harvie Anderson —
    Renfrewshire East

SNP

None

SLP

John Robertson — Paisley

MPs defeated
Lab

None

Con

Teddy Taylor — Glasgow Cathcart

SNP

Douglas Henderson —
    Aberdeenshire East
Andrew Welsh — Angus South
Iain MacCormick — Argyll
Hamish Watt — Banff
Margaret Bain —
    Dunbartonshire East
George Reid —
    Clackmannan & Stirlingshire East
George Thompson — Galloway
Winifred Ewing — Moray & Nairn
Douglas Crawford —
    Perth & East Perthshire

SLP

Jim Sillars — Ayrshire South

New MPs

Lab

Ernie Ross — Dundee West
Ron Brown — Edinburgh Leith
Andy McMahon — Glasgow Govan
John Maxton — Glasgow Cathcart
David Marshall —
  Glasgow Shettleston
Michael Martin —
  Glasgow Springburn
George Foulkes — Ayrshire South
Martin O'Neil —
  Clackmannan & Stirlingshire East
Norman Hogg —
  Dunbartonshire East
*Dick Douglas — Dunfermline
Willie McKelvie — Kilmarnock
Allan Adams — Paisley

Con

*Michael Ancram —
  Edinburgh South
Albert McQuarrie —
  Aberdeenshire East
Peter Fraser — Angus South
John MacKay — Argyll
David Myles — Banff
*Barry Henderson — Fife East
Ian Lang — Galloway
Alex Pollock — Moray & Nairn
Bill Walker —
  Perth & East Perthshire
Allan Stewart —
  Renfrewshire East

*formerly MP but not during last Parliament

SECTION 16

EUROPEAN ELECTIONS JUNE 7, 1979
SCOTTISH SEATS

May 1979: result in Parliamentary constituencies included in European constituency. SLP counted with Labour.

			%	May 1979 %	Change
GLASGOW Electorate 534,414					
Mrs J. Buchan	Lab	73,846	49.0	58.2	−9.2
Mrs B. Vaughan	Con	41,144	27.3	25.9	+1.4
G. Leslie	SNP	24,776	16.4	11.5	+4.9
Miss E. Attwool	Lib	11,073	7.3	4.0	+3.3

Lab maj.: 32,702   Turnout 28.3%

HIGHLANDS & ISLANDS Electorate 298,802					
Mrs W. Ewing	SNP	39,991	34.0	29.3	+4.7
R. Johnston	Lib	36,109	30.7	18.2	+12.5
M. Joughlin	Con	30,776	26.1	32.5	−6.4
J. Watson	Lab	10,846	9.2	20.0	−10.8

SNP maj.: 3,882   Turnout 39.4%

LOTHIANS Electorate 537,420					
I. Dalziel	Con	66,761	35.6	32.9	+2.7
A. Mackie	Lab	61,180	32.6	43.3	−10.7
D. Stevenson	SNP	29,935	16.0	13.8	+2.2
R. Smith	Lib	29,518	15.8	9.6	+6.2

Con maj.: 5,581   Turnout 34.9%

SCOTLAND MID & FIFE Electorate 538,483					
J. Purvis	Con	66,255	35.1	30.3	+4.8
Mrs M. Panko	Lab	58,768	31.2	39.7	−8.5
R. McIntyre	SNP	45,426	24.1	23.0	+1.1
J. Calder	Lib	18,112	9.6	6.7	+2.9

Con maj.: 7,487   Turnout 35.0%

SCOTLAND NORTH EAST   Electorate 481,680

J. Provan	Con	51,930	33.0	34.7	−1.7
Lord Mackie	Lib	38,516	24.5	9.2	+15.3
D. Clyne	Lab	38,139	24.2	31.1	−6.9
C. Bell	SNP	28,886	18.3	24.9	−6.6

Con maj.: 13,414   Turnout 32.7%

SCOTLAND SOUTH   Electorate 450,761

A. Hutton	Con	66,816	43.0	36.2	+6.8
P. Foy	Lab	43,145	27.7	36.2	−8.5
I. MacGibbon	SNP	28,694	18.5	12.8	+5.7
J. Wallace	Lib	16,825	10.8	14.7	−3.9

Con. maj 23,671   Turnout 34.4%

STRATHCLYDE EAST   Electorate 463,656

K. Collins	Lab	72,263	49.8	55.1	−5.3
Miss M. Carse	Con	41,482	28.6	27.6	+1.0
G. Murray	SNP	21,013	14.5	13.5	+1.0
D. Watts	Lib	10,325	7.1	3.4	+3.7

Lab maj.: 30,781   Turnout 31.3%

STRATHCLYDE WEST   Electorate 495,799

A. Fergusson	Con	65,608	37.2	31.9	+5.3
Miss V. Friel	Lab	63,781	36.1	43.4	−7.3
M. Slesser	SNP	29,115	16.5	14.1	+2.4
T. Fraser	Lib	17,955	10.2	10.1	+0.1

Con maj.: 1,827   Turnout 35.6%

SCOTLAND

		%	MAY 79 %	Change
Conservative	430,762	33.7	31.4	+1.7
Labour	421,968	33.0	41.5	−8.5
SNP	247,926	19.4	17.3	+2.1
Liberal	178,433	14.0	9.0	+5.0

Source: EUROVOTE NOP

SECTION 17

RECENT PUBLICATIONS IN SCOTTISH GOVERNMENT AND POLITICS

C. H. ALLEN

Department of Politics, University of Edinburgh

The lists below cover material omitted from earlier lists, and material published since then, in the period 1.6.78 to 31.5.79. As before, I would be grateful for notification of missing items.

The items are once again divided into two lists, the first covering books, pamphlets, long articles and major sets of newspaper features; and the second covering brief articles and newspaper features. There is a break in the numbering, with the second list beginning at 500, to allow for easier identification of longer pieces in the Index at the end of the lists.

Certain periodicals have been abbreviated thus:

CCN	*Community Council News*
DR	*Daily Record*
EN	*Evening News*
FT	*The Financial Times*
G	*Guardian*
GH	*Glasgow Herald*
New Stat.	*New Statesman*
Obs.	*The Observer*
Orc.	*The Orcadian*
S	*The Scotsman*
SDE	*Scottish Daily Express*
Shet. T.	*Shetland Times*
SI	*Scots Independent*
S. Mail	*Sunday Mail*
Spec.	*Spectator*
WHFP	*West Highland Free Press*

PART 1: BOOKS PAMPHLETS AND LONGER ARTICLES

1 Aberdeen University, *A physical and economic evaluation of loss of access to fishing grounds due to oil and gas installations in the North Sea.* Aberdeen: Department of Political Economy/Institute for the Study of Sparsely Populated Areas, 1978.

2 Aims for Freedom, *Attitudes of Scottish industry towards a Scottish Assembly.* London, 1978, 8pp.

3 Algar, P., "Aberdeen and the impact of oil". *Petroleum Review* 31: 382 (1977), pp. 25-33.

4 Allen, C. H., "Recent publications in Scottish government and politics". *The Scottish Government Yearbook 1979.* Edinburgh: Paul Harris, 1978, pp. 158-97.

5 Anonymous, "Annual gross changes in manufacturing employment in the Scottish New Towns and the rest of Scotland 1950-70". *Scottish Economic Bulletin* 14 (1978), pp. 10-11.
6 "Family expenditure survey Scotland 1968-77". *Quarterly Economic Commentary* 4:3 (1979), pp. 27-32.
7 "Occupational shifts in the Scottish working population 1851-71". *Quarterly Economic Commentary* 4:1 (1978), pp. 39-44.
8 "Recent trends in earnings in Scotland". *Scottish Economic Bulletin* 15 (1978), pp. 10-19.
9 "Regional profiles". *Scottish Economic Bulletin* 15 (1978), pp. 29-43.
10 "Survey of North Sea oil-related industry: employment aspect". *Scottish Economic Bulletin* 17 (1979), pp. 9-13.
11 "The electronics industry in Scotland: current issues and future prospects". *Scottish Economic Bulletin* 16 (1978), pp. 23-30.
12 "Trends in the residential land market 1966-76". *Scottish Economic Bulletin* 15 (1978), pp. 20-27.
13 "Wages and earnings". *Quarterly Economic Commentary* 4:2 (1978), pp. 29-33.
14 Arnold, G., *Britain's Oil*. London: Hamish Hamilton, 1978, 360pp.
15 Ashton, J., "After the referendum: Scotland". *Marxism Today* 24:5 (1979), pp. 148-51.
16 Assist, *A discussion paper on repairs and maintenance, Ferguslie Park, Paisley*. Glasgow: Strathclyde University Department of Architecture, 1977, 26pp.
17 *The internal condition survey, Ferguslie Park*. Glasgow: Strathclyde University Department of Architecture, 1977, 26pp.
18 Bain, D., "Scotland: the referendum campaign and beyond". *Marxism Today* 22:8 (1978), pp. 240-45.
19 Balneaves, E., "Fortunes of the Shetlands". *Geographical Magazine* Aug. 1978, pp. 723-29.
20 Baster, J., *The Scottish textile and clothing industry*. Edinburgh: SCRI, 1978, 15pp. plus appendices.
21 Baur, C., "Who runs Scotland?" *The Scotsman* 11-18/9/78.
22 Beaumont, P. B., "The extent of compliance with minimum wage regulation: the West of Scotland record". *Industrial Relations Journal* 9:2 (1978), pp. 4-14.
23 Begg, H. M. et. al., "Economic policy in the context of a Scottish Region". *Built Environment* 5:1 (1979).
24 Belding, R. K., and Hutchison, D. A., "Home or away: why do qualified leavers from Scottish schools move away from home?". *Tijdschrift voor Economische en Sociale Geografie* 69:4 (1978), pp. 216-24.
25 Bell, D. N. F., *Household savings in Scotland*. Glasgow: Fraser of Allander Institute Discussion Paper 12, 1978, 34pp.
26 *Regional output, employment and unemployment fluctuations*. Glasgow: Fraser of Allander Institute Discussion Paper 10, 1978, 29pp.
28 *Wage inflation in Scotland*. Glasgow: Fraser of Allender Institute Discussion Paper 9, 1978, 23pp.

T

28   Benyon, J., "Some political implications of airport location: the case of Edinburgh airport". *Political Administration* 56 (1978), pp. 439-58.

29   Bernath, M., "Il regionalismo in Gran Bretagno". *Amministrare* 1977/4, pp. 477-508.

30   Birch, A. H., "Minority nationalist movements and theories of political integration". *World Politics* 30:3 (1978), pp. 325-44.

31   Birks, S. and Sewel, J., "A typology of oil-stimulated population movements in Scotland: implications for the future". *Town Planning Review* 50:1 (1979), pp. 94-110.

32   Birrell, W. D., "The mechanics of devolution: Northern Ireland experience and the Scotland & Wales Bill". *Political Quarterly* 49:3 (1978), pp. 304-21.

33   Bloor, M. et al., *Island health care: access to primary services in the Western Isles.* Aberdeen: Institute of Medical Sociology, 1978, 65pp.

34   Bochel, D. and Maclaren, M., "Local health councils: the consumers voice". *The Scottish Government Yearbook 1979.* Edinburgh: Paul Harris, 1978, pp. 78-98.

35   Bochel, J. M. and Denver, D. T., "The regional council elections of May 1978". *The Scottish Government Yearbook 1979.* Edinburgh: Paul Harris, 1978, pp. 140-57.

36   Bogdanor, V., *Devolution.* Oxford: Oxford University Press, 1979, 246pp.

37   "Devolution and the constitution". *Parliamentary Affairs* 31:3 (1978), pp. 252-67.

38   "The English constitution and devolution". *Political Quarterly* 50:1 (1979), pp. 36-49.

39   Bonomi, C., "I due 'bills" per Scozia e Gallo: un passo avanti per la 'devolution of powers' ". *Rivista trimestrale di Diritto pubblico,* 1978/1, pp. 210-215.

40   Borders Regional Council, *Borders Region Structure Plan: report of survey and consultative report.* Newtown St. Boswells, 1978.

41   Bradley, A. W. and Christie, D. J., *The Scotland Act 1978.* Edinburgh: Green, 1979.

42   Bradley, K., "Worker control as a state managerial device: a study of the Scottish Daily News workers co-op". Ph.D. thesis, Essex University, 1978, 304pp.

43   Bradley, K. and Gleb, A., *The role of workers co-ops in relaxing constraints on government intervention: the case of the 'Scottish Daily News'.* Essex University Department of Economics Discussion Paper 110, 1978, 46pp.

44   "The political economy of 'radical' policy: an analysis of Scottish Daily News workers co-operative". *British Journal of Political Science* 9:1 (1979), pp. 1-20.

45   Brand, J., *The national movement in Scotland.* London: Routledge & Kegan Paul, 1978, 330pp.

46   Bruce, G., "Flying the saltire". *Scottish Review* 11 (1978), pp. 39-43.

47   Bryant, R., "Local authorities and voluntary organisations: a Scottish review". *Social Service Quarterly* Dec. 1978, pp. 51-54.

48   "Conflict and community work: a case study". *Community Development Journal* 14:2 (1979), pp. 128-34 (Gorbals, Govanhill).

49   Buchanan-Smith, A. (MP): "The Executive". *Scotland: the framework for change*. (Ed. by D. Mackay). Edinburgh: Paul Harris, 1979, pp. 80-87.

50   Bull, P. J., "The spatial components of intra-urban manufacturing change: suburbanisation in Clydeside 1958-68". *Transactions of the Institute of British Geographers* 3:1 (1978), pp. 91-100.

51   Bulmer-Thomas, V., *Income, expenditure and the balance of payments in Scotland: an input-output approach*. Glasgow: Fraser of Allander Research Monograph 6, 1977, 39pp.

52   "The Scottish balance of payments". *Structure, system and economic policy*. (Ed. by W. Leontief). Cambridge: Cambridge University Press, 1977, pp. 123-41.

53   Bulpitt, J., *Conservatism, unionism and the problems of territorial management*. Glasgow: PSA Workgroup on UK Politics, 1978, 17pp.

54   Burdekin, R., *The construction of the 1973 Scottish input-output tables*. London: IBM (UK), 1978, 76pp.

55   Business Scotland, "Strathclyde Region special survey". *Business Scotland* March 1979, pp. 13-35.

56   Butt, J., "Working class housing in Glasgow 1900-39". *Essays in Scottish labour history*. (Ed. by MacDougall). pp. 143-69.

57   Butt-Philip, A., *Creating new jobs: a report on long term job creation in Britain and Sweden*. London: Policy Studies Institute, 1978, 63pp.

58   "Devolution and regionalism". *Trends in British politics since 1945*. (Ed. by C. Cook and J. Ramsden). London: Macmillan, 1978, pp. 157-80.

59   Buxton, N. K., *Economic growth in Scotland between the wars: the role of production structure and rationalisation*. Edinburgh: Heriot-Watt University, Economics Department Working Paper 3, 1977, 28pp.

60   Caldwell, J. T., "Guy Alfred Aldred, antiparliamentarian 1886-1963: a memoir". *Essays in Scottish labour history*. (Ed. by MacDougall). pp. 225-46.

61   Campbell, D., "Scottish literature and the Scottish Assembly". *New Edinburgh Review* 45 (1979), pp. 3-5.

62   Campbell, R. H., "The Scottish Office and the Special Areas in the 1930s". *Historical Journal* 22:1 (1979), pp. 167-83.

63   Carney, J. G. and Hudson, R., "The SDA", *Town and Country Planning* 46 (Nov. 1978), pp. 507-509.

64   Central Regional Council, *Central Region economic review 1977*. Stirling, 1978.

65   Centre for Environmental Studies, *Parliamentary constituencies: a socioeconomic classification*. London: Office of Population Census, 1978.

66   Chapman, M., *The myth of Scottish culture: the Gaelic influence on Scottish consciousness*. London: Croom Helm, 1978, 224pp.

67 Coats, A. W., "The changing role of economists in Scottish government since 1960". *Public Administration* 56 (1978), pp. 399-424.
68 Cohen, A. P., "Oil and the cultural account: reflections on a Shetland community". *Scottish Journal of Sociology* 3:1 (1978), pp. 129-41.
69 Commissioner for Local Administration, *Report of discontinuation of the investigation of a complaint against Hamilton District Council.* Edinburgh, July 1978, 3pp.
70 . . . *Inverness DC.* Edinburgh, June 1978, 2pp.
71 . . . *Renfrew DC.* Edinburgh, March 1979, 1pp.
72 . . . *Stirling DC.* Edinburgh, Aug. 1978, 1pp.
73 . . . *West Lothian DC.* Edinburgh, Sept. 1978, 2pp.
74 . . . *Report of investigation of a complaint against Banff & Buchan DC.* Edinburgh, Dec. 1978, 8pp.
75 . . . *Banff & Buchan DC.* Edinburgh, Feb. 1979, 7pp.
76 . . . *Caithness DC.* Edinburgh, Aug. 1978, 12pp.
77 . . . *Central RC.* Edinburgh, July 1978, 6pp.
78 . . . *City of Aberdeen DC.* Edinburgh, 1978, 18pp.
79 . . . *City of Aberdeen DC.* Edinburgh, 1979, 2pp.
80 . . . *City of Dundee DC.* Edinburgh, Aug. 1978, 5pp.
81 . . . *City of Dundee.* Edinburgh, Dec. 1978, 14pp.
82 . . . *City of Edinburgh DC.* Edinburgh, 1978, 22pp.
83 . . . *City of Glasgow DC.* Edinburgh, Aug. 1978, 5pp.
84 . . . *City of Glasgow DC.* Edinburgh, Aug. 1978, 13pp.
85 . . . *City of Glasgow DC.* Edinburgh, Nov. 1978, 4pp.
86 . . . *City of Glasgow DC.* Edinburgh, Nov. 1978, 9pp.
87 . . . *City of Glasgow DC.* Edinburgh, Feb. 1979, 13pp.
88 . . . *City of Glasgow DC.* Edinburgh, 26/3/78, 10pp.
89 . . . *City of Glasgow DC.* Edinburgh, 19/3/78, 3pp.
90 . . . *City of Glasgow DC.* Edinburgh, Apr. 1979, 7pp.
91 . . . *Clydebank DC.* Edinburgh. April 1978, 11pp.
92 . . . *Cunninghame DC.* Edinburgh, March 1979, 3pp.
93 . . . *Cunninghame DC.* Edinburgh, March 1979, 5pp.
94 . . . *Dumbarton DC.* Edinburgh, 7/2/79, 11pp.
95 . . . *Dumbarton DC.* Edinburgh, 22/2/79, 7pp.
96 . . . *Dumbarton DC.* Edinburgh, 27/2/79, 23pp.
97 . . . *Dunfermline DC.* Edinburgh, Jan. 1979, 4pp.
98 . . . *Dunfermline DC.* Edinburgh, Jan. 1979, 9pp.
99 . . . *Dunfermline DC.* Edinburgh, April 1979, 6pp.
100 . . . *Ettrick and Lauderdale DC.* Edinburgh, 1978, 8pp.
101 . . . *Falkirk DC.* Edinburgh, March 1979, 11pp.
102 . . . *Fife RC.* Edinburgh, Aug. 1978, 8pp. plus app.
103 . . . *Fife RC.* Edinburgh, Nov. 1978, 6pp.
104 . . . *Fife RC.* Edinburgh, April 1979, 9pp.
105 . . . *Fife RC.* Edinburgh, May 1979, 6pp.
106 . . . *Gordon DC.* Edinburgh, Nov. 1978, 8pp.
107 . . . *Hamilton DC.* Edinburgh, Feb. 1979, 10pp.
108 . . . *Inverclyde DC.* Edinburgh, Aug. 1978, 10pp.
109 . . . *Inverness DC.* Edinburgh, Jan. 1979, 16pp. plus app.
110 . . . *Kirkcaldy DC.* Edinburgh, Feb. 1979, 15pp.
111 . . . *Kyle and Carrick DC.* Edinburgh, 1/11/78, 7pp.

112   ... *Kyle and Carrick DC*. Edinburgh, 23/11/78, 7pp. plus app.
113   ... *Kyle and Carrick DC*. Edinburgh, Dec. 1978, 10pp.
114   ... *Kyle and Carrick DC*. Edinburgh, Feb. 1979, 12pp.
115   ... *Lanark DC*. Edinburgh, July 1978, 32pp. plus app.
116   ... *Lanark DC*. Edinburgh, 12/3/79, 9pp.
117   ... *Lanark DC*. Edinburgh, 26/3/79, 22pp.
118   ... *Lothian RC*. Edinburgh, Sept. 1978, 5pp.
119   ... *Midlothian DC*. Edinburgh, March 1979, 16pp.
120   ... *Midlothian DC*. Edinburgh, April 1979. 15pp.
121   ... *Monklands DC*. Edinburgh, Sept. 1978, 11pp.
122   ... *Monklands DC*. Edinburgh, Feb. 1979, 11pp.
123   ... *North East Fife DC*. Edinburgh, Aug. 1978, 15pp. plus app.
124   ... *Orkney Islands Council*. Edinburgh, Oct. 1978, 8pp.
125   ... *Perth and Kinross DC*. Edinburgh, Nov. 1978, 8pp.
126   ... *Ross and Cromarty DC*. Edinburgh, Jan. 1979, 10pp.
127   ... *Shetland Islands Council*. Edinburgh, March 1979, 8pp.
128   ... *Stirling DC*. Edinburgh, Aug. 1978, 3pp.
129   ... *Stirling DC*. Edinburgh, Sept. 1978, 9pp.
130   ... *Strathclyde RC*. Edinburgh, 1978, 2pp.
131   ... *Strathclyde RC*. Edinburgh, 26/3/79, 12pp.
132   ... *Strathclyde RC*. Edinburgh, 29/3/79, 12pp. plus app.
133   ... *Strathclyde RC*. Edinburgh, April 1979, 10pp.
134   ... *Strathkelvin DC*. Edinburgh, April 1979, 6pp.
135   ... *Sutherland DC*. Edinburgh, July 1978, 16pp.
136   ... *Tayside RC*. Edinburgh, March 1979, 13pp.
137   ... *West Lothian DC*. Edinburgh, Dec. 1978, 13pp. plus app.
138   ... *West Lothian DC*. Edinburgh, March 1979, 6pp.
139   *Report of the Commissioner for Local Administration in Scotland for the year ended 31/3/78*. Edinburgh, 1978, 17pp. plus app.
140   Conservative Research Department, *Scotland Act 1978: a guide for the 1979 referendum campaign*. Edinburgh, 1978, 23pp.
141   Cosgrove, D. F. and Sheldon, H. N., *Community councillors in East Kilbride*. Paisley College of Technology Local Government Research Unit, 1977.
142   "Interim research report of the Strathclyde project". *Community councils research project interim reports*. Edinburgh: SDD, 1978, pp. 33-62.
143   Craig, C., "The powers of the Scottish assembly and executive". *Scotland: the framework for change*. (Ed. by D. Mackay). Edinburgh: Paul Harris, 1979, pp. 26-46.
144   Craigmillar Festival Society, *Craigmillar: comprehensive plan for action*. Edinburgh, 1978, 160pp.
145   Criddle, B., "Scotland, the EEC and devolution". *Divided loyalties: British regional assertion and European integration*. (Ed. by M. Kolinsky). Manchester: Manchester University Press, 1978, pp. 44-69.
146   Crofters Commission, *Annual report for 1977*. Edinburgh: HMSO, 1978.

147 Cunningham, S. M., "The entry of girls to higher education — a Scottish perspective". Ph.D. thesis, Aberdeen University, 1978, 599pp.
148 Davis, J. R., "The industrial investment policy of the SDA". *Quarterly Economic Commentary* 4:2 (1978), pp. 34-46.
149 Department of Town Planning, Oxford Polytechnic, *Planning for rapid development: oil related development in the North of Scotland and the Shetlands.* Oxford, 1976, 166pp.
150 Derby, C., "Housing in Scotland". *Local Government Chronicle* 22/9/78, pp. 1023-28.
151 Diamond, D. et al., "The use of strategic planning: the example of the national planning guidelines in Scotland". *Town Planning Review* 50:1 (1979), pp. 18-35.
152 Dickinson, I. A., "The Scotland Act 1978: some distinctive features". *Journal of the Law Society of Scotland* 24:1 (1979), pp. 5-10.
153 Dickson, S., "Class and nationalism in Scotland". *Scottish Journal of Sociology* 2:2 (1978), pp. 143-62.
154 Donald, D., *Modelling social deprivation.* Glasgow College of Technology Policy Analysis Research Unit, 1977, 17pp.
155 Drucker, H. M., "The political parties". *Scotland: the framework for change.* (Ed. by D. Mackay). Edinburgh: Paul Harris, 1979, pp. 88-108.
156 Drucker, H. M. and N. L., "Introduction: towards a Scottish politics". *The Scottish Government Yearbook 1979.* Edinburgh: Paul Harris, 1978, pp. 1-8.
157 *The Scottish Government Yearbook 1979.* Edinburgh: Paul Harris, 1978.
158 Dumfries and Galloway Regional Council, *Dumfries and Galloway Structure Plan: report of survey.* Dumfries, 5 vols, 1978.
159 *Dumfries and Galloway Structure Plan: interim statement.* Dumfries, 1979.
160 *Transport policies and programme 1978-83.* Dumfries, 1978.
161 *Transport policies and programme 1979-84.* Dumfries, 1979.
162 Duncan, T., "Housing in the wake of the Green Paper: view from Scotland". *Town and Country Planning* June 1978, pp. 298-300.
163 Edinburgh SHAC, *Submission to the Secretary of State for Scotland on Edinburgh District Council's scheme to sell council houses.* Edinburgh: Shelter Housing Advisory Centre, 1979, 5pp.
164 English, J., *A profile of Ferguslie Park.* Glasgow: Paisley CDP, 1977, 22pp.
165 Ennew, J., "Gaelic as the language of industrial relations". *Scottish Journal of Sociology* 3:1 (1978), pp. 51-68.
166 Ferguson, R., *Geoff. The life of Geoffrey M. Shaw.* Gartochan: Famedram, 1979, 285pp.
167 Firn, J. R., *Devolution: an exit-voice model of regional policy.* Glasgow University Department of Urban and Regional Studies Discussion Paper 25, 1978, 25pp.
168 Firth, H., "Orkney". *Scotia Review* 18 (1978), pp. 2-14.
169 Fletcher, A. and Mackay, J., *Scottish education: regaining a lost reputation.* Edinburgh: Scottish Conservative Party, 1978, 8pp.

170   Fry, M. and Cooney, J., *Scotland in the new Europe.* Dublin: Dublin
      University Press, 1979, 119pp.
171   Gibson, P., "How Scotland got the Housing (Homeless Persons)
      Act". *The Scottish Government Yearbook 1979.* Edinburgh: Paul
      Harris, 1978, pp. 36-47.
172   Glasgow District Council, *Glasgow: implications of population changes
      to 1983.* Glasgow, 1978, 40pp. plus app.
173   Glasgow East End Renewal, *Overall proposals 1. Working document
      1.* Glasgow: SDA, 1979.
174   *The future for GEAR: key issues and possible sources for action.*
      Glasgow: SDA, 1978.
175   Gostwick, M., "British road or national roads: hard choices ahead".
      Marxism Today 22:8 (1978), pp. 263-66.
176   Grampian Regional Council, *Aberdeen area structure plan: draft
      for consultation.* Aberdeen, 1979.
177   *Aberdeen area structure plan: report on consultation methods.*
      Aberdeen, 1978, 78pp.
178   Grant, W., "Industrialists and farmers: British interests and the
      European Community". *West European Politics* 1:1 (1978), pp.
      89-106.
179   Grasmuck, S. L., "Uneven regional development and Scottish
      nationalism: activists, ideology and North Sea oil". Ph.D. thesis,
      University of Texas (Austin), 1978.
180   Grieco, M., "Oil related development and Shetland: the institutional
      framework". *Scottish Journal of Sociology* 2:2 (1978), pp. 187-
      200.
181   Grigor, I., "Local authority accommodation of oil related develop-
      ments in Easter Ross". *Scottish Journal of Sociology* 3:1 (1978),
      pp. 69-84.
182   Gronneberg, R., Review of "Power and Manoeuvrability", by T.
      Carty and S. McCall Smith (Edinburgh 1978). *Nevis Quarterly* 1
      (1978), pp. 71-77.
183   *Island futures.* Sandwick: Thuleprint, 1978. 79pp.
184   Haddow, D., "Appointed and *ad hoc* agencies in the field of the
      Scottish Office". *The Scottish Government Yearbook 1979.* Edin-
      burgh: Paul Harris, 1978, pp. 115-26.
185   Hannay, D. R., *The symptom iceberg.* London: Routledge, 1979,
      207pp.
186   Harvie, C. and Brown, G., *A voters guide to the Scottish assembly
      and why you should support it.* Edinburgh: Studioscope, 1979,
      15pp.
187   Hatvany, D., "The general strike in Aberdeen". *Journal of the Scot-
      tish Labour History Society* 10 (1976), pp. 3-20.
188   Heald, D. and Keating M., *The impact of the devolution commitment
      on the Scottish body politic.* Sheffield: PSA conference, 1979,
      26pp.
189   Henderson, R. A., "Factors determining the location of immigrant
      industry within a UK assisted area: the Scottish experience
      1945-70". M. Litt. thesis, Glasgow University, 1978.

190   Heriot-Watt University, *Oil related activities in Scottish universities.* Edinburgh, 1978, 20pp.

191   Higgs, L., *New Town: social involvement in Livingston.* Glasgow: William McLellan, 1977.

192   Highland Regional Council, *Transport policies and programme 1979-84.* Inverness, 1979.

193   Highlands and Islands Development Board, *Proposals for changes in the Highlands and Islands Development (Scotland) Act 1965.* Inverness, 1978, 53pp.

194   *Twelfth report 1977.* Inverness, 1978.

195   Hill, D., *Devolution and local government.* PSA Workgroup on UK Politics, 1977.

196   Hogwood, B., *The primacy of politics in the economic policy of Scottish government.* Glasgow: Strathclyde University CSPP Study 14, 1977.

197   *The tartan fringe: quangos and other assorted animals in Scotland.* Glasgow: Strathclyde University CSPP Study 26, 1978.

198   Hood, C. C., *The Scottish Office in the UK context: some quantitative comparisons.* Glasgow: PSA Workgroup on UK Politics, 1978, 27pp.

199   House, J. D., "Oil companies in Aberdeen: the strategy of incorporation". *Scottish Journal of Sociology* 3:1 (1978), pp. 85-102.

200   Housing Centre Trust, *Scottish conference on housing plans: papers.* London, 1978, 57pp.

201   Housing Corporation, *The Housing Corporation in Scotland: development since 31/3/1978.* Edinburgh, 1978.

202   House of Commons, *Scotland Act 1978.* London: HMSO, 1978, 96pp.

203   House of Commons Library, *The devolution question: regional statistics.* Background Paper 67, London, 1978.

204   Hunt, D., *The engineering industry in the Grampian Region.* Aberdeen: NESDA, 1978, 27pp.

205   Hunter, E., *Scottish woman's place.* Edinburgh: Student Publications Board, 1979.

206   Hunter, J., "The crofter, the laird and the agrarian socialist: the Highland land question in the 1970s". *The Scottish Government Yearbook 1979.* Edinburgh: Paul Harris, 1978, pp. 48-60.

207   Hutchison, D. (Ed.), *Headlines. The media in Scotland.* Edinburgh: Student Publications Board, 1978, 112pp.

208   Jackson, B., *Westmark Action Group: a fight for improvement.* Glasgow: Paisley CDP, 1978, 59pp.

209   Jackson, P. M., "Financial control and responsibility". *Scotland: the framework for change.* (Ed. by D. Mackay). Edinburgh: Paul Harris, 1979, pp. 126-54.

210   Johnson, N., *In search of the constitution.* Oxford: Pergamon, 1977, 239pp. (See Chap. 7, "Devolution").

211   Johnston, R. (MP), *Scottish Liberal Party conference speeches.* Inverness: Bookmag, 1979.

212   Jones, B. and Kavanagh, D., *British politics today.* Manchester: Manchester University Press, 1979. 160pp. (See Chap. 4, "Devolution").

213 Jones, C., *Population decline and home ownership in Glasgow.* Glasgow University Department of Urban and Regional Studies Discussion Paper 26, 1978, 22pp.

214 Jones, G. W. and Norton, A., *Political leadership in local authorities.* Birmingham: INLOGOV, 1978, 243pp. (including Scottish rural authorities).

215 Jones, J. B. and Keating, M., *The British Labour Party as a centralising force.* Glasgow: PSA Workgroup on UK Politics, 1978, 53pp.

216 Jordan, G., *The committee stage of the Scotland and Wales Bill (1976-1977).* Edinburgh: Edinburgh University: Waverley Papers, Scottish Government Studies 1, 1979, 42pp.

217 Keating, M. J., "Parliamentary behaviour as a test of Scottish integration into the UK". *Legislative Studies Quarterly* 3:3 (1978).

218 *The battle of the Western approaches: a study in local pressure politics and amenity in Glasgow.* Glasgow College of Technology, Policy Analysis Research Unit Discussion Paper 4, 1978, 28pp.

219 *The Scottish Office: some issues for discussion.* PSA Local Politics Group: Scottish/English local government conference 1979, 14pp.

220 *The structure of the Scottish Assembly.* Glasgow: Scottish Council of Fabian Societies, 1979, 15pp.

221 Kellas, J. G., *Decentralisation and devolution: policy making in education and regional development in Scotland.* Berlin: European Consortium for Political Research Workshop, 1977, 20pp. plus tables.

222 *Policy-making in Scottish education.* PSA Workgroup on UK Politics, 1978, 11pp.

233 "Politics in a devolved Scotland". *Nevis Quarterly* 2 (1979), pp. 5-10.

224 "The policy process". *Scotland: the framework for change.* (Ed. by D. Mackay). Edinburgh: Paul Harris, 1979, pp. 155-63.

225 Kibblewhite, L. and Rigby, A., *Fascism in Aberdeen: street politics in the 1930s.* Aberdeen: Aberdeen People's Press, 1978, 48pp.

226 *Aberdeen in the General Strike.* Aberdeen: Aberdeen People's Press, 1977, 33pp.

227 King, D. N., "The price of independence". *Geographical Magazine,* July 1978, pp. 657-61.

228 Kirwan, F. X., "Aspects of migration between Scotland and the rest of Great Britain 1966-71". *Quarterly Economic Commentary* 3:3 (1978), pp. 42-53.

229 Knox, P. L., "Community councillors, electoral districts and social geography". *Area* 10:5 (1978), pp. 387-91.

230 Labour Movement Yes Campaign, *Speakers notes.* Glasgow, 1979, 24pp.

231 Lausen, P., *Letting in single people.* Edinburgh: Scottish Council for the Single Homeless, 1978.

232 Lazer, H., "Devolution, ethnic nationalism and populism in the UK". *Publius* 7:4 (1977), pp. 49-69.

233 Leruez, J., "La 'devolution' ecossaise". *Etudes,* July 1978, pp. 43-58.

290   SCOTTISH GOVERNMENT YEARBOOK 1980

234   "Partie politiques et elections dans l'Ecosse d'aujourd'hui". *Revue francaise des science politiques* 28:3 (1978), pp. 508-36.
235   Lewis, T. M. and McNicholl, I. H., *North Sea oil and Scotland's economic prospects.* London: Croom Helm, 1978, 147pp.
236   Lewis, T. M. et al., *Barriers to entry and technological change: oil related firms in Scotland.* Stirling University, Technological Economic Research Unit Discussion Paper 4, 1978, 33pp.
237   *Technological change as a strategy for growth: oil related firms in Scotland.* Stirling University, Technological Economics Research Unit Discussion Paper 3, 1978, 33pp.
238   Liddell, P., "The role of the Trades Council in the political and industrial life of Glasgow 1858-1976". M.Sc. thesis, Strathclyde University, 1978.
239   Liggett, E., *The community councillor.* Glasgow: Gressingham Press, 1978.
240   Lothian Regional Council, *Lothian Structure Plan: examination in public.* Edinburgh, 1978.
241   *Lothian Structure Plan: report of survey, information update.* Edinburgh, 1978.
242   Macartney, W. J. A., "Summary of Scottish opinion polls". *The Scottish Government Yearbook 1979.* Edinburgh: Paul Harris, 1978, pp. 198-203.
243   McCallum, J. D., *History of British regional policy to 1964.* Glasgow University Department of Urban and Regional Planning, Discussion Papers in Planning 5, 1976, 38pp.
244   McCluskey, Lord, "Legislative procedures for the Scottish Assembly". *Scolag Bulletin* 19 (1979), pp. 27-30.
245   McCormick, N., "Constitutional points". *Scotland: the framework for change.* (Ed. by D. Mackay). Edinburgh: Paul Harris, 1979, pp. 47-67.
246   MacDougall, I. (Ed.), *Essays in Scottish Labour History.* Edinburgh: John Donald, 1979, 265pp.
247   "Some aspects of the 1926 General Strike in Scotland". *Essays in Scottish Labour history.* Edinburgh: John Donald, 1979, pp. 170-206.
248   McGregor, A., "Family size and unemployment in a multiply-deprived urban area". *Regional Studies* 12:3 (1978), pp. 323-30.
249   McGuiness, J., "The administrative process". *Scotland: the framework for change.* (Ed. by D. Mackay). Edinburgh: Paul Harris, 1979, pp. 164-74.
250   McIntosh, J., "Pressure groups and law reform". *Scolag Bulletin* 29 (1979), pp. 20-23.
251   Mackay, D. I. (Ed.), *Scotland: the framework for change.* Paul Harris, 1979, 196pp.
252   "Scotland: the framework for change". *Scotland: the framework for change.* Edinburgh: Paul Harris, 1979, pp. 11-26.
253   Mackay, D. I. et al., *Scottish industrial property review.* Edinburgh: Kenneth Ryden and Partners, 1979, 7pp.
254   Mackay, G. A., *A study of the economic impact of the Invergordon aluminium smelter.* Inverness: HIDB, 1979.

255 Mackay, J. P. H., "Devolution and the Scottish Law Commission". *Scolag Bulletin* 29 (1979), pp. 24-27.
256 Mackie, A., "The Scottish Daily News". *The new workers co-operatives.* (Ed. by K. Coates). London: Spokesman, 1976.
257 Mackintosh, J. P., "Internal procedure and organisation". *Scotland: the framework for change.* (Ed. by D. Mackay). Edinburgh: Paul Harris, 1979, pp. 68-79.
258 "The killing of the Scotland Bill", *Political Quarterly* 49:2 (1978), pp. 127-32.
259 Mackinnon, D. M., "Return to Scotland". *Scottish Review* 11 (1978), pp. 16-20.
260 Mackinnon, K., *Gaelic in Scotland 1971.* Hatfield Polytechnic, 1978, 110pp.
261 McLennan, G., "The devolution referenda and after". *Scottish Marxist* 18 (1979), pp. 6-15.
262 McNicholl, I. H., "Some aspects of the impact of oil on the Shetland economy". Ph.D. thesis, Stirling University, 1977, 259pp.
263 McNicholl, I. H. and Walker, G., *The Shetland economy 1976/77: structure and performance.* Edinburgh University Department of Business Studies, 1978, 50pp.
264 MacQueen, H. L., *The Scotland Act 1978: a summary and some implications.* Edinburgh University Department of Extra Mural Studies, 1978, 8pp.
265 MacQueen, W. R., and Freeman, I. C., *Community councils in Scotland, an analysis of the approved schemes.* Edinburgh: SDD Central Research Unit, 1978, 38pp.
266 McWhirter, I., Review of *The breakup of Britain* by Tom Nairn (London 1977). *Capital and Class* 5 (1978), pp. 142-45.
267 McWilliam, C. G., *Policy committee report on 'Roads and transport with particular reference to rural areas'.* Edinburgh: Scottish Conservative Party, 1978, 4pp. plus app.
268 Manson, T. M. Y., *Annual report, Shetland Civic Society.* Lerwick, 1978.
269 Martin, M., *Concentrated unemployment and a local initiative.* Glasgow: Paisley CDP, 1978, 47pp.
270 Massie, A., "Scotland and Europe: responses to the decline of the nation state". *Nevis Quarterly* 1 (1978), pp. 37-48.
271 "Scotland and Europe: the representation of Scottish interests", *Nevis Quarterly* 2 (1979), pp. 34-46.
272 Massey, D., "Survey: regionalism, some current issues". *Capital and Class* 6 (1978), pp. 106-25.
273 Masterman, E. M., *Women in elected positions in Scotland.* Grenoble: European Consortium for Political Research, 1978, 15pp.
274 Masterson, M. P., "Forming community councils: East Kilbride". *Local Government Studies* 4:4 (1978), pp. 67-79.
275 Masterson, M. P., and Masterman, E. M., "Interim report of the Tayside and Fife research project". *Community Councils Research Projects: interim reports.* Edinburgh: SDD, 1978, pp. 1-31.
276 *Orkney's community councillors as schools councillors.* Dundee, 1977.

277   *Survey of community councillors in the Orkney Islands.* Dundee, 1977, 10pp.

278   Maxwell, S., "Implications of prospective independence: the problems of state power". *Nevis Quarterly* 2 (1979), pp. 11-20.

279   Midwinter, A. F., "Policy planning units in Scottish local government". *Public Administration Bulletin* 27 (1978), pp. 73-90.

279a Millan, B., "Geoff Shaw: an appreciation". *The Scottish Government Yearbook 1979.* Edinburgh: Paul Harris, 1978, pp. 11-15.

280   Miller, W., *Electoral dynamics.* London: Macmillan, 1977.

281   Mishler, W. and Mughan, A., "Representing the Celtic fringe: devolution and legislative behaviour in Scotland and Wales". *Legislative Studies Quarterly* 3:3 (1978), pp. 377-408.

282   Misselbrook, D., "Intermediate government". *Scotland: the framework for change.* (Ed. by D. Mackay). Edinburgh: Paul Harris, 1979, pp. 186-96.

283   Moore, R., "Northern notes towards a sociology of oil". *Scottish Journal of Sociology* 3:1 (1978), pp. 21-36.

284   Morrison, D. (Ed.), "Scotland special issue". *Resurgence* 69 (1978).

285   Motherwell District Council, *Public participation in local plans.* Motherwell, 1978.

286   Mullin, R., "Women in the SNP". M.A. thesis, Edinburgh University Sociology Department, 1977.

287   Nairn, T., "After the referendum". *New Edinburgh Review* 46 (1979), pp. 3-10.

288   Naughtie, J., "The Scotland Bill in the House of Commons". *The Scottish Government Yearbook 1979.* Edinburgh: Paul Harris, 1978, pp. 16-35.

289   Neilsen, M. J. and Sorensen, J. L., *The New Towns in West Central Scotland.* Copenhagen, 1978.

290   Nevin, E. (Ed.), *The economics of devolution.* Cardiff: University of Wales Press, 1978, 160pp.

291   Nevis Institute, *The Shetland Report.* Edinburgh, 1978, 233pp. (3 volume version also exists).

292   Nicholls, D. C., "Agencies for rural development in Scotland". *Regional and Rural Development.* (Ed. by P. J. Drudy). Chalfont St. Giles: Alpha Academics, 1976, pp. 69-90.

293   Nitschke, W., "Nationalismus in Schottland". *Offentliche Werwaltung* 30 (Oct. 1977), pp. 697-704.

294   Orkney Islands Council, *Orkney transport policies and programme 1978.* Kirkwall, 1978.

295   Page, E., "Local government and the Scottish Assembly". *Scotland: the framework for change.* (Ed. by D. Mackay). Edinburgh: Paul Harris, 1979, pp. 175-85.

296   "Michael Hechter's internal colonialism thesis: some theoretical and methodological problems". *European Journal of Political Research* 6:3 (1978), pp. 295-317.

297   *Why should local central relations in Scotland be any different from those in England?* Glasgow: Strathclyde University CSPP Paper 21, 1978, 46pp.

298 Page, S. A. B., "The value and distribution of the benefits from North Sea oil and gas 1970-85". *National Institute Economic Review* 82 (1977), pp. 41-58.

299 Paisley Community Development Project, *Housing allocations and social segregation*. Glasgow, 1978, 22pp.

300 Pearce, B., "Devolution, democracy and socialist advance". *Marxism Today* 21:12 (1977).

301 Penniman, H. R. (Ed.), *Britain at the polls: the parliamentary elections of 1974*. Washington: AEI, 1977, 256pp.

302 Perrott, R., "Shetland: a Klondyke among the crofts". *Sunday Times Magazine* 8/10/78, pp. 64-72.

303 Planning Aid (Dundee), *Report on progress in 1978*. Dundee, 1978.

304 Planning Aid (Glasgow), *Planning and the public: a guide to Scottish planning*. Glasgow: Planning Aid and SCSS, 1978.

305 Planning Exchange, *Planning aid: a report on Scottish experience*. Glasgow, 1978, 76pp.

305a *Scotland's travelling people: forum report 14*. Glasgow, 1978.

306 Popplewell, R., *Vacant Scotland: a Shelter report on empty housing*. Edinburgh: Shelter, 1978, 27pp.

307 Pottinger, G., *The Secretaries of State for Scotland 1926-76*. Edinburgh: Scottish Academic Press, 1979, 214pp.

308 Purves, A., "Scottish labour and British entry: labour movement attitudes to the European Community at Scottish and UK levels 1960-77". M.Phil. thesis, Edinburgh University, 1978, 180pp.

309 Pym, F. and Brittain, L., *The Conservatives and devolution: the realistic option*. London: Conservative Party, 1978, 53pp.

310 *The Conservative Party and devolution*. Edinburgh: Scottish Conservative Party, 1978, 32pp.

311 Radice, H., *The SDA and the contradictions of state entrepreneurship*. Stirling University Discussion Papers in Economics 59, 1978, 24pp.

312 Rawkins, P. M., "Outsiders as insiders: the implications of minority nationalism in Scotland and Wales". *Comparative Politics* 10:4 (1978), pp. 519-34.

313 Reich, G. G. C., "Symbols and sentiment in Scotland". Ph.D. thesis, Washington University, 1978, 365pp.

314 Robertson, E. (Ed.), *Socialist Scotland*. Edinburgh, No. 1 (1978).

315 Rodger, J. J., " 'Inauthentic' politics and the public inquiry system". *Scottish Journal of Sociology* 3:1 (1978), pp. 103-27.

316 Rose, R., *From steady state to fluid state: the unity of the Kingdom today*. Glasgow: Strathclyde University CSPP Paper, 1978, 38pp.

317 Rosie, G., *The Ludwig initiative: a cautionary tale of North Sea oil*. Edinburgh: Mainstream, 1978, 148pp.

318 Royale, T., "Behold the Hebrides". *Nevis Quarterly* 2 (1979), pp. 21-33.

319 Scottish Association for Public Transport, *Transport in Scotland: co-ordination and consumer representation*. Glasgow, 1978.

320 Scottish Conservative Party, *Conference '78*. Perth, 1978, 106pp.

321 *Conservative manifesto for Scotland 1979*. Edinburgh, 1979, 35pp.

322   *Food for thought: a policy for food and farming in Scotland.*
      Edinburgh, 1978(?), 7pp.
323   *Onward to victory: a statement of the Conservative approach for
      Scotland.* Edinburgh, 1978, 16pp.
324   *Report of the Discussion group on the social security system.*
      January 1978. Edinburgh, 5pp.
325   Scottish Conservative Crime Advisory Committee, *Crime and its
      remedies.* Edinburgh: Scottish Conservative Party, 1978, 32pp.
326   Scottish Conservative Women's Organisation, *How well is the health
      service?.* Edinburgh: Scottish Conservative Party, 1978, 8pp.
327   Scottish Consumer Council, *Houses to mend: a survey on council
      house repairs in Scotland.* Glasgow, 1978.
328   Scottish Council (Development and Industry), *Industrial position
      report.* Edinburgh, 1978, 11pp.
329   Scottish Council Research Institute, *Construction of a regional input-
      output table for Strathclyde.* Edinburgh, 1979.
330   *European manufacturing investment in Scotland.* Edinburgh, 1979,
      7pp.
331   *Labour supply and demand in Lochaber 1978-88.* Fort William:
      Lochaber District Council, 1978, 59 plus viii pp.
332   *Manpower shortages in Scottish manufacturing industry.* Edin-
      burgh, 1979, 52pp.
333   *Scotland's manufactured exports 1974-77.* Edinburgh, 1978, 6 plus
      vii pp.
334   Scottish Council of Social Service, *Annual review 1978.* Edinburgh,
      1978.
335   *Local plans and the public: Central, Fife and Tayside area.* Perth:
      SCSS,1978.
336   Scottish Development Agency, *SDA Report 1978.* Glasgow, 1978,
      80pp.
337   Scottish Development Department, *Circular 40/1978: the Morris
      Report on links between housing and social work.* Edinburgh,
      1978, 6pp.
338   *Code of practice for the examination in public of structure plans.*
      Edinburgh, 1977, 9pp.
339   *Environmental impact analysis: Scottish experience 1973-78.* Edin-
      burgh, 1978.
340   *Planning advice note 22: social surveys.* Edinburgh, 1978, 31pp.
341   *Planning advice note 23: Scottish economic monograph 1978.* Edin-
      burgh, 1978.
342   *Report for 1977.* Edinburgh: HMSO (Cmnd) 7270), 1978.
343   *Scottish housing statistics.* Edinburgh: HMSO, No. 1 (1978).
344   *Register of research.* Edinburgh: Central Research Unit, 1978,
      30pp.
345   *Social consequences of oil development.* Edinburgh, 1978, 18pp.
346   Scottish Economic Planning Department, *Circular 2/1978. Industrial
      strategy, the contribution of the local authorities.* Edinburgh,
      1978, 10pp.
347   "Report on activities 1977-78". *Scottish Economic Bulletin* 16
      (1978) pp. 9-15.

348 *The economic impact of North Sea oil on Scotland.* Edinburgh: HMSO, 1978.

349 Scottish Education for Action in Development, *The SNP and the developing world.* Edinburgh, 1978.

350 Scottish Home & Health Department, *Scottish Health Service Planning Council: report for 1977.* Edinburgh: HMSO, 1977, 27pp.

351 *Scottish Health Service Planning Council: report for 1978.* Edinburgh: HMSO, 1979, 30pp.

352 *The NHS in Scotland 1948-78.* Edinburgh, 1978.

353 Scottish Homeless Group, *Housing (Homeless Persons) Act 1977: a review of the first six months.* Edinburgh, 1978, 42pp.

354 Scottish Information Office, *The economy of Scotland.* Edinburgh (Factsheet RF 10), 1978, 17pp.

355 *The NHS in Scotland.* Edinburgh (Factsheet RF 8), 1978, 16pp.

356 Scottish Legal Action Group, *Memorandum of the Scottish Legal Action Group to the Royal Commission on Legal Services in Scotland. Part VI: the Judiciary.* Dundee, 1978, 15pp.

358 Scottish National Party, *Agricultural policy.* Edinburgh, 1978, 7pp.

359 *Draft policy statement on Gaelic.* Edinburgh, 1978, 7pp.

360 *Return to nationhood.* Edinburgh, 1978, 32pp.

361 *Scotland: facts and comparisons.* Edinburgh, 1978, 124pp.

362 *Special (one day) national conference.* Perth, 1979, Papers. Edinburgh, 1979, unpag.

363 Scottish National Party Research Department, *Multiple deprivation in Scotland. Research Bulletin 5:4,* Edinburgh, 1979, 31pp.

364 *Scotland and the EEC. Research Bulletin 5:3,* Edinburgh, 1979, 16pp.

365 Scottish Office, *Boundary Commission for Scotland report: European Assembly constituencies.* Edinburgh: HMSO, 1978 (Cmnd 7336).

366 Scottish Trades Union Congress, *81st Annual Report.* Glasgow, 1978, 772pp.

367 Secretary of State's Advisory Committee, *Scotland's travelling people 1975-78.* Edinburgh: HMSO, 1978, 42pp.

368 Shapiro, D., "Oil and Shetland: a comment". *Scottish Journal of Sociology* 2:2 (1978), pp. 210-203.

369 "The industrial relations of oil". *Scottish Journal of Sociology* 3:1 (1978), pp. 1-20.

370 Sharpe, R., *Raasay: a study in island history.* London: Grant and Cutler, 1978, 250pp.

371 Shelter (Scotland), *Empty housing in Gordon.* Edinburgh, 1979, 27 plus iv pp.

372 *No recourse for the homeless.* Edinburgh: Scottish Homeless Group, 1979, 13pp.

373 *Scotland's housing shambles.* Edinburgh, 1979, 28pp.

374 Shetland Islands Council, *Shetland Structure Plan: written statement, 4.* Lerwick, 1978, 128pp.

375 *Shetland's oil era, phase 2.* Lerwick: Research and Development Department, 1978, 107pp.

376   Short, J., "The regional distribution of public expenditure in Great Britain 1969/70-1973/74". *Regional Studies* 12:5 (1978), pp. 499-510.

377   Sinclair, D. J., "Scottish identity". *Geographical Magazine* Sept. 1978, pp. 803-807.

378   Smith, A. D., *Nationalism in the twentieth century*. London: Martin Robertson, 1979 (see pp. 150-65, "Ethnic resurgence in the West").

379   Smith, B., "The politics of devolution". *Public Administration Bulletin* 23 (1977), pp. 63-67.

380   Smith, G., "Westminster and the Assembly". *Scotland: the framework for change*. (Ed. by D. Mackay). Edinburgh: Paul Harris, 1979, pp. 110-23.

381   Smith, R. D. P., "The changing urban hierarchy in Scotland". *Regional Studies* 12:3 (1978), pp. 330-51.

382   Srivastna, S. R., "The Asian community in Glasgow". Ph.D. thesis, Glasgow University, 1975, 429pp.

383   Stewart, G. T., *The health of Glasgow and Strathclyde: a proposal for the correction of urban decay*. Glasgow University: Department of Community Medicine, 1976, 18pp.

384   Strathclyde Area Survey, *Community councils in Scotland*. Glasgow, 1978, 72 leaves.

385   Strathclyde Regional Council, *Housing plans in Strathclyde 1977: a review*. Glasgow, 1978, 15pp.

386   *Regional planning papers 1: housing studies; changes in the private sector*. Glasgow, 1978.

387   *Regional planning papers 2: housing studies; access to housing, the role of the District Council*. Glasgow, 1978.

388   *Strathclyde transport policies and programmes 1979-84.* Glasgow, 1979.

389   *Structure Plan: Vol. 1 Written statement; Vol. 2: Consultation report; Vol. 3: Key diagram.* Glasgow, 1979.

389a Tait, B., Maxwell, S., *What now, Scotland?* Edinburgh: What now Scotland Conference Committee, 1979, 11pp.

390   Taylor, P. et al., *Evidence of deprivation in Glasgow*. Glasgow College of Technology Policy Analysis Research Unit Discussion Paper 1, 1977, 15pp.

391   Tayside Regional Council, *Regional report 1978*. Dundee, 1978.

391a *Transport policies and programmes 1979-84*. Dundee, 1979.

392   Thompson, F. G., *The Highlands and Islands Advisory Panel: a review of its activities and influences*. Stornoway: the author, 1978, 50pp.

393   Thompson, W., "The New Left in Scotland". *Essays in Scottish labour history*. (Ed. by MacDougall). pp. 207-24.

394   Thomson, J. K., *Import substitution: case studies*. Edinburgh: Scottish Council Research Institute, 1978, 27pp.

395   Thwaites, A. T., "Technological change, mobile plants and regional development". *Regional Studies* 12:4 (1978), pp. 445-61.

396   Trade Union Research (Scotland) Unit, *Scottish Trade Union Review*. Glasgow, No. 1 (1978).

397 Transport Users Consultative Committee for Scotland, *Annual Report to the Secretary of State for Scotland . . . year ending 31/12/1978*. Edinburgh: HMSO, 1979.

398 Turnock, D., *Industrial Britain: the new Scotland*. Newton Abbott: David & Charles, 1979, 168pp.

399 "Oil-related developments in North Scotland". *Geoform* 8:4 (1977), pp. 183-200.

400 Urban Renewal Unit (Scottish Development Department), *Area based policies approach to urban deprivation*. Edinburgh, 1978.

401 Wannop, U., "Strathclyde". *Town and Country Planning* 46 (1978), pp. 503-506.

402 Watt, D., "The March 1st referendum". *Political Quarterly* 50:1 (1979), pp. 145-47.

403 Weir, I., *Regional budget, regional strategy and devolution*. Newcastle University Centre for Urban and Regional Development Studies, 1977, 16pp.

404 Western Isles Islands Council, *Housing plan 1979-84*. Stornoway, 1978.

405 White, D., "Glasgow belongs to whom?". *New Society* 26/4/79, pp. 188-91.

406 White, S. & Dickson, J. W., "The politics of Scottish self-government: an exercise in futurology". *Scottish Journal of Sociology* 2:1 (1977), pp. 1-10.

407 Williamson, N., "Ten years after: the revolutionary left in Scotland". *The Scottish Government Yearbook 1979*. Edinburgh: Paul Harris, 1978, pp. 61-77.

408 Wilson, J., *Devolution and voluntary organisations*. Edinburgh: SCSS, 1978, 10pp.

409 Young, R. and Jay, C., "Officer-member groups in Strathclyde". *Social Work Today* 27/2/1979, pp. 13-19.

PART II: SHORT ITEMS

500 Anonymous, Opinion Polls: Voting intentions: *Glasgow Herald*, 12/6/78; 10/7/78; 14/8/78; 11/9/78; 9/10/78; 11/12/78; 25/1/79; 12/2/79; 27/2/79; 4/4/79; 1/5/79; *The Scotsman*, 19/2/79; 25/4/79; 30/4/79. Devolution: *Glasgow Herald*, 25/1/79; 12/2/79; 27/2/79; *Daily Record*, 23/2/79; *The Scotsman*, 16/2/79; 19-20/2/79; 26/4/79; *Scottish Daily Express*, 1/3/79; *The Daily Telegraph*, 27/2/79; *Weekend World* (ITV), 25/2/79. Other matters: *The Scotsman*, 25/4-1/5/79.

501 "Aye for Scotland, No for Wales". *The Economist*, 24/2/79, pp. 17-23.

502 "Comment: devolution debate". *Scolag Bulletin* 27 (1978), p. 238.

503 "CC spotlight: Burntisland". *CCN* 21 (1979), pp. 26-27.

504 "Devolution: an opportunity to be grasped". *Scolag Bulletin* 29 (1979), p. 18.

505 "Election 79". *Shet. T.,* 27/4/79, pp. 15-18.

506 "Election round-up/Election spotlight". *WHFP,* 20/4-4/5/79.

507   "Election: the four candidates' views". *Orc.*, 19/4/79, p. 1.
508   "Key seats". *GH*, 16/4-1/5/79.
509   "Not so many are better off". *Shet. T.*, 10/11/78, p. 3.
510   "Profile: Peter Balfour". *Business Scotland*, March 1979, p. 36.
511   "Scotland 79", *S*, 23/2/79, supplement, 10pp.
512   "Scotland: a special report". *The Times*, 21/8/78, 4pp.
513   "Scotland: go forth and devolve". *Financial Post* (Toronto), 24/6/78, p. 49.
514   "Taking stock after the election". *Scolag Bulletin* 32 (1979), p. 70.
515   "Ten vital questions you want answered". *GH*, 28/2/79, p. 6.
516   "The referendum". *Journal of the Law Society of Scotland* 24:2 (1979), p. 45.
517   Able, L., "Shetland and oil: why island life may never be the same again". *North* 7:31 (1979), pp. 25-27.
518   Allan, L., "Highlands hoping for lasting cure". *GH*, 9/6/78, p. 7.
519   Ancrum, M., "The pitfalls of referenda". *S*, 30/11/78, p. 13.
520   Ascherson, N., "A gleam in the North for the Yes-men". *S*, 28/2/79, p. 13.
521   "All too Scottish". *Spec.*, 12/5/79, pp. 14-15.
522   "Analysing the Mackintosh factor". *S*, 26/10/78, p. 13.
523   "Beware the butt of the big baddies". *S*, 12/9/78, p. 9.
523a "Corridors of power after devolution". *S*, 22/1/79, p. 9.
524   "Day of reckoning for Tory 'revival' ". *S*, 25/10/78, p. 11.
525   "Devolution stushie in the Kirk". *S*, 23/2/79, p. 13.
526   "Eerie contest in the shadow of Mackintosh". *S*, 19/10/78, p. 11.
527   "Excitement has gone from the Scottish political scene". *The Scotsman Half Yearly Review*, 27/7/78, p. 1.
528   "Flower wilts but is not dead". *S*, 24/4/79, p. 11.
529   "From here, we are on our own". *S*, 28/7/78, p. 13.
530   "Future imperfect". *New Edinburgh Review* 44 (1978), pp. 25-28.
531   "Labour have Nationalists in their sights". *S*, 26/7/78, p. 13.
532   "Labour on the up and up in Scotland". *S*, 7/11/79, p. 11.
533   "Liberals sniff a change in the wind". *S*, 22/6/78, p. 15.
534   "Nationalism dissected". *S*, 10/11/78, p. 13.
535   "No easy return for Tories". *S*, 30/4/79, p. 4.
536   " 'No' vote might not mean the axe for devolution". *S*, 23/2/79, supplement p. 1.
537   "Perthshire in the balance". *S*, 21/2/79, p. 11.
538   "Political craft". *S*, 11/7/78, p. 8.
539   "Putting the party on the right track". *S*, 13/3/79, p. 11.
540   "Pym harks back to "quasifederal' theme". *S*, 13/3/79, p. 11.
541   "Referendum post-mortem for Labour". *S*, 9/3/79, p. 15.
542   "Radio Scotland: a frosted window on the world". *S*, 22/11/78, p. 13.
543   "Six vacancies for Labour candidates". *S*, 24/8/78, p. 11.
544   "SNP decide to wait and see". *S*, 5/10/78, p. 11.
545   "Steelyard blues on the campaign trail". *S*, 26/2/79, p. 9.
546   "Thatcher to thank the troops". *S*, 11/5/79, p. 15.
546a "The view from Calton Hill". *S*, 30-31/1/79; 2/2/79.
547   "Whither the Nationalists?". *S*, 6-7/6/78, p. 11.

548 "Whither now the SNP?". *S*, 14/11/78, p. 11.
549 Ashton, J., "Scotland now". *Scottish Marxist* 17 (1978), pp. 11-16.
550 Baggott, M., "Economy well geared to meet challenge of the 80s", *S*, 24/5/79, supplement p. i.
551 "Incoming industry cannot solve unemployment problems". *The Scotsman Half Yearly Review*, 27/7/78, p. iii.
552 Ballantrae (Lord), "Devolution for Scotland". *The Times*, 5/6/78, p. 17 (letter).
553 Banel, R., Convener looks back on his first year in office". *S*, 26/3/78, supplement p. 2.
554 "Industrial growth is still Scottish Council's objective". *S*, 24/5/79, supplement, p. ii.
555 "North Sea oil has proved to be a mixed blessing". *S*, 25/4/79, pp. 6-7.
556 "The Western Isles". *S*, 20/2/79, pp. 14-15.
557 Bateman, C., "Who pays the ferryman?". *G*, 2/4/79, p. 14.
558 Baur, C., "Agents looking for a clue". *S*, 26/10/78, p. 13.
559 "A referendum for Christmas". *S*, 26/9/78, p. 10.
560 "A time to lay down referendum rules". *S*, 16/3/79, p. 12.
560a "Battle to have the last word". *S*, 26/1/79, p. 8.
561 "Constituencies are facing a political carve-up". *S*, 28/5/79, p. 7.
562 "Councils seek more financial autonomy". *S*, 27/11/78, p. 7.
562a "Estimates shackle Assembly's feet". *S*, 18/1/79, p. 9.
563 "How the No-men were handed a 300,000 start". *S*, 12/2/79, p. 7.
564 "In search of a political identity". *S*, 15/12/78, p. 11.
564a "Labour's Yes-men drag their feet". *S*, 16/1/79, p. 6.
565 "No Conservative fetters on SDA". *S*, 26/10/78, p. 13.
565a "No-men gamble with a loaded dice". *S*, 17/1/79, p. 8.
566 "Politics and the pulpit". *S*, 27/2/79, p. 11.
567 "Poll prizes can come in unexpected ways". *S*, 24/4/79, p. 11.
568 "Public concern over council's private income". *S*, 29/11/78, p. 13.
569 "SNP hawks and doves in conflict". *S*, 27/9/78, p. 10.
570 "SNP may have lost a case but gained a point". *S*, 19/4/79, p. 13.
571 "The manifestos". *S*, 14/4/79, p. 4.
572 "The Yes-No road show". *S*, 20/2/79, p. 13.
573 "Tories ready to turn the tables on SNP". *S*, 30/3/79, p. 15.
574 "Varied cross-section of contests". *S*, 2/5/79, p. 8.
575 "Why marginals become pressure points". *S*, 28/3/79, p. 13.
576 Bayne, I., "The radical heritage of Scottish nationalism". *Crann Tara* 3 (1978), pp. 8-9.
577 Bell, C., "Assembly's £2000M problem". *S*, 29/9/78, p. 11.
578 "Europe elections: what's in them for the SNP". *SI* 97 (1979), p. 9.
579 "The decline and fall of public sector housing". *S*, 31/7/78, p. 7.
580 "Unemployment". *S*, 17-19/7/78.
581 Birt, A., "Twenty years after". *Question* 33 (1977), p. 3.
582 Bochel, J. and Denver, D., "What the Yes men are counting on". *S*, 13/2/79, p. 9.
583 Bogdanor, V., "The defeat of devolution". *Spec.*, 10/3/79, pp. 13-14.
584 Bowen, M., "Don't knows are everywhere in the see-saw seat". *Sunday Times*, 22/10/78, p. 4.

585 Brogan, C., "What price the arts when curtain rises on an Assembly?". *GH*, 17/11/78, p. 6.
586 Bruce, A., "HIDB and land: another approach". *Question* 34 (1977), pp. 4-5.
587 Buchan, N. (MP), "I'm putting my trust in the people". *GH*, 23/2/79, p. 6.
588 "The referendum and what it really means". *GH*, 5/1/79, p. 6.
589 Buchanan-Smith, A. (MP), "A chance to take a positive step". *Life & Work*, Feb. 1979, pp. 17-18.
590 Burgher, G. S., "Agriculture, mainstay of island's economy". *S*, 25/4/79, p. 8.
591 Burke, G. and Easton, J., "The forgotten islands". *GH*, 12-16/6/78.
592 Callaghan, J. (MP), "Yes". *Sunday Post*, 15/2/79, p. 10.
593 Campbell, Lord, "Removing the seeds of misunderstanding". *S*, 3/4/79, p. 8.
594 "Scottish committee system in action". *S*, 2/4/79, p. 8.
595 Campbell, B., "Between hard covers". *New Edinburgh Review* 46 (1979), pp. 38-39.
596 Campbell, D., "Scottish literature and the Scottish Assembly". *New Edinburgh Review* 45 (1979), pp. 3-5.
597 Campbell, G., "Deep down, Labour knows the cost". *SDE*, 26/2/79, p. 8.
598 "How Labour 'No' MPs can stop a double cross". *SDE*, 28/2/79, p. 9.
599 "Shorn and shamed". *SDE*, 28/7/78, p. 11.
600 Campbell, M., "News from South Knapdale". *CCN* 18 (1978), pp. 7-8.
601 Clark, W., "Berwick in the balance". *GH*, 18/10/78, p. 7.
602 "Come all ye faithful". *GH*, 14/5/79, p. 6.
603 "Could an Assembly and the regions live together?". *GH*, 19/2/79, p. 6.
604 "Last exit from Bannockburn". *GH*, 14/11/78, p. 6.
605 "Nationalists prepare for all-in bout". *GH*, 30/11/78, p. 6.
606 "One week to showdown". *GH*, 22/2/79, p. 6.
607 "State of the parties in Scotland". *GH*, 2/4/79, p. 6.
608 "The sides line up for the battle of Scotland". *GH*, 23/1/79, p. 6.
609 "Time for a bit of Scottish hard sell'. *GH*, 5/4/79, p. 7.
610 "Tories get scent of a 'famous victory' ". *GH*, 26/10/78, p. 7.
611 "Who are going to the aid of Reg?". *GH*, 11/10/78, p. 6.
612 "Who's who and where for E-day". *GH*, 30/5/79, pp. 6-7.
613 "Will all the faithful unite for the sake of the party?". *GH*, 8/3/79, p. 6.
614 Cooper, J. C. B., "An overview of the Scottish economy". *Scottish Bankers Magazine* 70:280 (1979), pp. 181-82.
615 Crainey, T., "Council house sales pay off". *S*, 17/5/79, p. 15.
616 "Darnley: from dream to debris". *S*, 20/3/79, p. 11.
617 Crawford, R., "Ideology and the SNP". *SI* 95 (1979), p. 3.
618 Crooks, H. T., "From the Butt to Rodel Pier". *Shet. T.*, 2/6/78, pp. 16-17.
619 Curran, F., "Front moves in on Scottish schools". *Sunday Mail*, 26/2/78, pp. 1, 3.

620 Dalyell, T. (MP), "A halfway house built on sand". *Life & Work*, Feb. 1979, p. 17.
621 "Defiance of Labour 'No' men". *SDE*, 1/3/79, p. 8.
622 "Will Scotland tax itself?". *The Daily Telegraph*, 17/7/78, p. 12.
623 "Your last chance to stop this juggernaut". *GH*, 15/2/79, p. 6.
624 Davidson, J., "Activists who prefer to stay and fight". *S*, 23/10/78, p. 9.
625 "Hawick raises the shackles of the Orange Order". *S*, 25/9/78, p. 8.
626 "How the parties sell themselves". *S*, 7/8/79, p. 7.
627 "Margo finds honour in defeat". *S*, 5/6/78, p. 7.
628 "Time of political reckoning for the modern Ma Broon". *S*, 19/2/79, p. 9.
629 Denver, D., "Will the SNP turkey be plucked, stuffed and roasted?". *S*, 23/4/79, p. 8.
630 Dewar, D. (MP), "Assembly will build on nation's heritage". *GH*, 17/2/79, p. 4.
631 "How the West Lothian question can be answered". *GH*, 26/7/78, p. 6.
632 "Nationalism: the unanswered question". *GH*, 9/11/78, p. 6.
633 Dowle, M., "Shetland and the devolution debate". *S*, 22/2/79, p. 15.
634 Downie, A., "Saline". *CCN* 21 (1979), pp. 12-13.
635 Drucker, H., "What the valet saw on Calton Hill". *S*, 9/3/79, p. 14.
636 Easton, N., "Who are the tartan tearaways?". *Leveller* 23 (1979), p. 27.
637 Edwards, R., "Let's put Scotland's house in order". *S*, 20/4/79, p. 16.
638 "Scots housing dissemblers". *Roof* 4:2 (1979), pp. 58-59.
639 Eglin, R., "Clearance of the lowlands?". *The Sunday Times*, 17/9/78, p. 72.
640 Elder, A., "Scotland's business chiefs have their say on Assembly". *GH*, 23/2/79, p. 10.
641 Emery, F., "Who's next for the balancing act?". *The Times*, 3/6/78, p. 14.
642 Fairgrieve, J., "Mr Cool in the hot seat". *DR*, 1/6/78, p. 15.
643 "The Orangemen's invasion". *DR*, 28/9/78, p. 7.
644 Faux, R., "SDA looks for a bigger budget". *The Times*, 19/9/78, p. 25.
645 Ferguson, R., "Geoff". *GH*, 8-10/5/79.
646 Fergusson, A., "False dawn". *Spec.* 2/7/77, p. 19.
647 "The Scots least need to prove anything to anybody". *GH*, 16/2/79, p. 6.
648 Ferris, P., "Reality behind the Scots trumpets". *Obs.*, 25/2/79, p. 11.
649 Finlay, A., "Change of reason". *GH*, 5/6/78, p. 6.
650 "Reg in the running". *GH*, 28/8/78, p. 6.
651 "Tale of brave soldiers who brought down their own castle". *GH*, 5/5/79, p. 4.
652 "The road from Winnie Ewing". *GH*, 13/2/79, p. 6.
653 Finlayson, J., "Homeless; we need a ceasefire". *EN*, 18/1/79, p. 8.
654 "Now, perhaps, they'll end all the bitter fighting". *EN*, 19/1/79, p. 10.

655   Fleming, A. A., "What the General Assembly has asked for". *Life & Work*, Feb. 1979, p. 16.
656   Fletcher, A. (MP), "The BBC's phoney war". *S*, 4/11/79, p. 8.
657   Forbes, G., "The sacked Sheriff who refuses to stay out of politics". *GH*, 26/9/78, p. 7.
658   Forgan, L., "The islands which got rich Occidentally". *G*, 12/8/78, p. 15.
659   Frame, J., "Deciding what the vote means". *EN*, 21/2/79, p. 12.
660   Fry, M., "A gaping provincial in Europe". *The Scotsman Half Yearly Review*, 27/7/78, p. i.
661   "Tourism's unimpressive balance sheet". *S*, 27/6/78, p. 11.
662   "Younger can lead Scotland into Europe". *S*, 10/5/79, p. 15.
663   Fyfe, A., "My five years of hell". *GH*, 24/5/79, p. 6.
664   Gardiner, B., "Edinburgh still drags its feet". *CCN* 19 (1978), pp. 6-7.
665   George-Brown, Lord, "Is Jim Callaghan a man of honour?". *Sunday Express*, 4/3/79, p. 16.
666   Gibbs, K., "South East England's aviation rip off". *SI* 91 (1979), pp. 4-5.
667   Gibson, J., "The rise of pressure groups in Scotland". *Question* 31 (1977), pp. 3-4.
668   Gibson, R., "The rise and ? of the SNP". *Crann Tara* 3 (1978), pp. 6-7.
669   Gilchrist, J., "Conflict in the capital". *S*, 19/8/78, p. 10.
670   Goodman, F., "Test for the PM's pay norm". *FT*, 23/10/78, p. 31.
671   Goodwin, G., "Slum isle". *Sunday Mail*, 1/4/79, p. 9.
672   Graham, C., "Why you must vote no". *SDE*, 20/2/79, p. 15.
673   Grant, S., "Battling for Scottish independence side by side". *The Daily Telegraph*, 29/3/78, p. 17.
674   Greenfield, R. H., "Scots Nats pin hopes on Margo". *The Sunday Telegraph*, 28/5/78, p. 17.
675   Grimond, J. (MP), "The Scottish Assembly: why it will not work". *Spec.*, 10/2/79, pp. 14-15.
676   "Scottish complacency". *Spec.*, 10/6/78, p. 12.
677   Hallett, D. J. H., "Land: the case for conservation". *S*, 16/5/79, p. 12.
678   Hamilton, A., "Shetland: the outstanding success story". *The Times*, 21/8/78, p. iii.
679   Hargraves, A., "Travelling the opposite way". *Question* 34 (1977), pp. 3-4.
680   Harris, P., "A publisher's polemic". *S*, 25/7/78, p. 8.
681   Hearst, D., "The late British Rail". *S*, 10-12/4/79.
682   Herron, A., "A churchman's case for voting 'No' ". *Life & Work*, Feb. 1979, p. 19.
683   "Another tier that must not be shed on Scotland". *GH*, 17/2/79, p. 6.
684   Hetherington, A., "BBC Scotland: the controller comments". *S*, 11/8/78, p. 8.
685   "My three stormy years in command of BBC Scotland". *GH*, 22/12/78, p. 7.
686   Hetherington, P., "A party puzzled by its own popularity". *G*, 11/9/78, p. 13.

RREFREFERENCE SECTIONR

687 "A touch of roots in Sillars country". *G*, 25/4/79.
688 "Easing the land away from the lairds". *G*, 1/7/78, p. 15.
689 "Eleven's hour". *G*, 1/11/78, p. 13.
690 "For Reid, read right". *G*, 28/6/78, p. 13.
691 "Hardie's annuals". *G*, 1/2/79, p. 15.
692 "House call". *G*, 26/8/78, p. 15.
693 "Modern miraculous clearances". *G*, 17/7/78, p. 11.
694 "Nats keep Labour on the hook". *G*, 6/10/78.
695 "Pay policies snare the Berwick runners". *G*, 24/10/78, p. 4.
696 " 'Personal' votes likely to tip the Berwick stakes". *G*, 9/10/78, p. 4.
697 "Perth of the blues". *G*, 14/5/79, p. 13.
698 "Popular Winnie hopes to nip in on a whisky vote". *G*, 26/4/79, p. 6.
699 "Portland Place devours its devolutionary". *G*, 22/12/78, p. 11.
700 "Scottish No-men jubilant as the gap closes". *G*, 28/2/79, p. 6.
701 "Scottish oil region cool on devolution". *G*, 12/2/79, p. 4.
702 "Scottish Tories in disarray". *G*, 28/10/78, p. 15.
703 "Scramble to unseat the confident Mrs Bain". *G*, 14/4/79, p. 3.
704 "Shetland in the 80s: an island unto itself?". *G*, 10/2/79, p. 5.
705 "SNP back to the drawing board". *G*, 2/6/78, p. 13.
706 "Steel the target as Tories launch Scottish attack". *G*, 28/8/78, p. 2.
707 "The contrasting threads which form the Nationalist tartan". *G*, 15/3/79, p. 13.
708 "The left, right victory march". *G*, 5/8/78, p. 15.
709 "The Tam and Jim roadshow's final act". *G*, 26/2/79, p. 3.
710 "Tories sporting chance". *G*, 30/4/79, p. 4.
711 "Voters were confused if not indifferent", *G*, 5/3/79.
712 "Why Labour is defending a Tory seat". *G*, 28/9/78, p. 7.
713 "Why Scotland's ayes again fear English gold". *G*, 22/1/79, p. 9.
714 "Will Scots succumb to a right-winger?". *G*, 18/5/78, p. 16.
715 Hill, B., "Oil riches and deprivation: two aspects of Scotland". *Municipal Journal*, 18/5/79, pp. 516-17.
716 Himsworth, C. M. G., "Wide horizons for Edinburgh community councils". *CCN* 15 (1978), pp. 4-5.
717 Hoffman, H., "System three and Hamilton". *GH*, 7/6/78, p. 6 (letter).
718 Hoggart, S., "Legislating more power to Scottish elbows". *G*, 6/7/78, p. 15.
719 Holmes, A., "Community that may lose its heart". *S*, 11/12/78, p. 9.
720 Home, Lord, "Why I switch to 'No' ". *SDE*, 24/2/79, p. 8.
721 Horsborough, F., "How we can make the Assembly work". *EN*, 26/2/79, p. 8.
722 "Mr 40 per cent". *EN*, 12/12/78, p. 10.
723 "The battle to become an MP". *EN*, 18/4/79, p. 12.
724 "We may see a coalition Assembly". *EN*, 21/2/79, p. 12.
725 Hulbert, J., "Eurothreat to hill farmers". *S*, 8/9/78, p. 10.
726 Hume, G., "The crumbling image of Housing Action". *S*, 16/4/79, p. 9.
727 "Improved for the demolishers". *S*, 17/4/79, p. 11.

728   Hunter, W., "Where you vote yes to say no". *GH,* 27/2/79, p. 6.
729   "Wind of change through Gaeldom". *GH,* 9/10/78, p. 7.
730   Hyndman, B., "Tom's future in the stars". *DR,* 7/7/78, p. 1.1
731   Jack, I. and Hughes, R., "A slight case of nervous breakdown". *The Sunday Times,* 11/6/78, p. 17.
732   Jackson, P., "Money: who pays the piper?". *S,* 1/2/79, p. 11.
733   Jenkins, P., "Commentary". *G,* 23/3/79, p. 19.
734   Jones, C., "Eleven Scots MPs ready to bow out". *S,* 4/8/79, p. 11.
735   Kellagher, I., "Why Arran fears for its future". *The Weekend Scotsman,* 16/9/78, p. 4.
736   Kellas, J., "Test that faces the voters". *DR,* 12/2/79, p. 7.
737   Kemp, A., "Referendum question time". *S,* 26/2/79, p. 9.
738   "Scotland closes the economic gap". *S,* 6/4/79, p. 13.
739   "Scotland's time of reckoning". *S,* 29/1/79, p. 7.
740   "State of Scotland's fourth estate". S, 26/6/78, p. 11.
741   Kennedy, G., "The far right". *Question* 31 (1977), pp. 4-5.
742   "The parliamentary road to independence". *S,* 30/10/78, p. 11.
743   "Time for SNP to grasp Irish nettle". *S,* 23/1/79, p. 6.
744   Kernohan, R. D., "First things first". *Life & Work,* April 1979, p. 5.
745   "The Kirk and its house organ". *The Weekend Scotsman,* 27/1/79, p. 1.
746   Kiernan, V. G., "Review of 'Breakaway' ". *New Edinburgh Review* 41/42 (1978), pp. 60-62.
747   Kilbrandon, Lord, "Have we got the Assembly right?". *EN,* 29/8/78, p. 8.
748   Laing, J., "King Murray's law". *DR,* 8/6/78, p. 9.
749   Langdon, J., "The dash to devolution: Labour's gravest error?". *G,* 2/3/79, p. 2.
750   Leslie, G., "EEC elections". *SI* 98 (1979), p. 6.
751   Lester, T., "The real Scottish problem". *Management Today,* Aug. 1978, p. 70.
752   Levy, G., "Scotland the shrewd". *SDE,* 10/2/79, p. 8.
753   Lindsay, N., "Aberdeen's changing politics". *Question* 31 (1977), p. 5.
754   Lindsay, S., "Flotta's crofters cash in on the new gusher". *GH,* 19/1/79, p. 7.
755   Lindsay, S. and Allan, A., "Riddle of Highland estate's new laird". *GH,* 9/11/78, p. 7.
756   Lindsay-Smith, I., "SNP's fight to show they are still alive". *Obs.,* 22/10/78, p. 6.
757   Linklater, J., "Crisis day for the future of student unions". *GH,* 4/10/78, p. 7.
758   Lithman, A., "Knitting new life into an old island". *SDE,* 8/1/79, p. 6.
759   McCartney, B., "Firm focus on Nationalists". *S,* 1/5/79, p. 5.
760   MacCormack, I., "Wanted: a fishing policy for the Isles". *WHFP,* 18/8/78, p. 3.
761   McCormick, N., "Law: judges waiting in the wings". *S,* 1/2/79, p. 11.
762   "Scottish Nationalists say 'Yes — for Scotland' ". *Shet. T.,* 9/2/79, p. 12.

763 MacDiarmid, H., "Tourism: a double-edged sword". *The Weekend S.,* 1/7/78, p. 1.
764 Macdonald, M., "Grass roots democracy: the story so far". *North 7* 29 (1978), p. 21.
765 MacGibbon, I., "Vote to put Scotland back on the political map". *S,* 31/5/79, p. 13.
766 McGurk, J., "After the nightmare — the dream". *S. Mail,* 8/10/78, pp. 24-5.
767 MacInnes, I., "Uranium: where do we stand now?". *Orc.,* 29/3/79, p. 5 (see also p. 3, and two previous numbers).
768 McKie, D., "A bid to wake the living and count the dead". *G,* 14/2/79, p. 15.
769 "Will Berwick put more nails in the Nationalist coffin?". *G,* 19/10/78, p. 15.
771 Mackintosh, J. P., "Will the Tories seek to shelve devolution?". *S,* 3/7/78, p. 9.
772 MacLachlan, S., "Cash key to the Assembly". *DR,* 2/11/78, p. 21.
773 "Labour swings back into gear". *DR,* 2/6/78, p. 15.
774 "Neck and neck". *DR,* 10/4/78, p. 4.
775 "The buck stops here". *DR,* 27/2/79, p. 7.
776 "Their hopes in your hands". *DR,* 28/4/78, pp. 14-15.
778 "Wilson is favourite". *DR,* 14/11/78, p. 7.
779 Maclaren, D., "A personal view". *Crann Tara* 6 (1978), p. 18.
780 Maclean, D. M., "Gaeldom reborn". *S,* 5/4/79, p. 10.
781 Macleod, A., "Dr No gives up his island". *S,* 10/4/79, p. 11.
782 "Getting the Mod back to its roots". *S,* 6/10/78, p. 13.
783 Macleod, A. and Dowle, M., "NATO eyes on Scotland as 'fall back' base", *S,* 20/11/79, p. 9.
784 McMillan, J., "Britain must stay united". *SDE,* 22/2/79, p. 8.
785 MacThomais, F., "Gaelic — a waking animal". *Crann Tara* 5 (1978), pp. 5-6.
786 Malone, D., "The split among the bosses". *DR,* 14/2/79, p. 7.
787 Manson, T. M. Y., "The Nevis Report: what future for Shetland?". *New Shetlander* 124 (1978), pp. 7-9.
788 Marquand, D., 'The devolution debacle". *The Listener,* 8/3/79, pp. 334-36.
789 Marshall, J., "Faces of Shetland". *The Times Educational Supplement (Scotland),* 21/7/78, p. 11.
790 Masterson, M. P., "Electing Scotland's community councils". *Local Government Chronicle,* 23/9/77, pp. 764-65 (General).
791 "Electing Scotland's community councils". *Local Government Chronicle,* 18/11/77, pp. 938-40 (N.E. Fife).
792 "Scotland forms its new councils". *Municipal Review,* March 1978, p. 374.
793 "Scottish grass roots show how its done". *Anchor,* Nov. 1977, p. 6.
794 "The youth vote for community councils: the experience of East Kilbride". *Community Education* 1, 1978, pp. 5-7.
795 Masterson, M. and Masterman, E., "Too many buried talents". *CCN* 23 (1979), pp. 11-12.

U

796 Maxwell, S., "A chance to push forward democratic frontiers". *GH*, 16/2/79, p. 6.
797 "Centralism v. localism". *Question* 33 (1977), pp. 3-4.
798 "The break-up of Britain". *Question* 31 (1977), p. 7 (review).
799 Meyer, G., "An Orkney view of the Western Isles". *Orc.*, 1/6/78, p. 4; 8/6/78, p. 5.
800 "Bigger Orkney Islands Council faces future in its new home". *Orc.*, 4/1/79; pp. 1, 7.
801 Midwinter, A. and Page, E., "Reorganisation and the rates: reality behind the rhetoric". *S*, 21/2/79, p. 11.
802 Millan B. (MP), "It's all too remote — a 'Yes' is the answer". *EN*, 23/2/79, p. 14.
803 "What went wrong?". *S, Mail*, 4/3/79, p. 24.
804 Morris, M., "The islands that unearthed an embarrassment of riches". *G*, 23/3/79, p. 19.
805 Morrison, I., "Waiting to see how the land lies". *GH*, 25/11/78, p. 4.
806 Mount, F., "The psychotics revolt". *Spec.*, 10/3/79, p. 4.
807 Munro, N. and Ross, D., "A tale of two conferences". *WHFP*, 23/2/79, p. 2.
808 Murphy, J., "After devolution, what about social work". *Municipal Journal*, 14/7/78, pp. 686, 688.
809 Nabarro, R., "Glasgow: what change with GEAR". *Architects Journal* 168 (7/7/78), pp. 27-28.
810 Nairn, T., "Nationalism and the Windsor state". *New Stat.*, 23/2/79, pp. 248-50.
811 "The clans that will live to regroup". *G*, 21/5/79, p. 8.
812 "The new exiles". *Question* 25 (1977), p. 7.
813 "What really happened in Scotland". *New Stat.*, 9/3/79, p. 313.
814 Naughtie, J., "Party divided against itself". *Macleans Magazine* 91 (6/11/78), p. 35.
815 Niven, B., "Left unity and devolution". *Labour Monthly*, March 1977, pp. 131-33.
816 Parkhouse, G., "Banana skins at Berwick". *GH*, 23/10/78, p. 6.
817 "Berwick battle lines". *GH*, 25/9/78, p. 6.
818 "Everyone is to blame". *GH*, 12/3/79, p. 6.
819 "John Smith becomes a big name". *GH*, 13/11/78, p. 6.
820 "Snow ball effect of the SNP on the confidence vote". *GH*, 26/3/79, p. 6.
820a "The man who looked a winner but failed to conquer Westminster". *GH*, 31/7/78, p. 7.
821 "The referendum recedes". *GH*, 24/7/78, p. 6.
822 "Yes, No, but what if it's maybe?". *GH*, 1/3/79, p. 6.
823 Perman, R., "A spider's web of issues". *FT*, 5/2/79.
824 "Bumpy rise for a bold Scottish enterprise". *FT*, 20/4/79.
825 "Each party waits for outcome of close battle". *FT*, 13/10/78.
826 "Exit the standard bearer". *FT*, 15/11/78, p. 11.
827 "In line for the booby prize". *FT*, 26/5/79.
828 "Lothian Region". *FT*, 5/10/78.
829 "Main parties gather strength at expense of Nationalist decline". *FT*, 3/5/79.

830 "Oil rush abates". *FT*, 19/9/78.
831 "Regional quirks will affect the fate of Scotland". *FT*, 13/2/79.
832 "Scotland". *FT*, 27/11/78, pp. 17-24.
833 "Scottish banking and finance". *FT*, 20/3/79.
834 "SNP weakens traditional allegiances", *FT*, 12/4/79.
835 "Strathclyde squares up for friendly devolution battle". *FT*, 20/2/79.
836 "Surfeit of red herring". *FT*, 26/2/79.
837 "The Council's unique writ". *FT*, 9/2/79.
838 "The fight to breathe new life into Scottish industry without proving a soft touch". *FT*, 9/6/78.
839 "Then Glasgae belongs tae me". *FT*, 6/1/79.
840 "Transports of delight". *FT*, 15/9/78.
841 "Unlikely socialist hero". *FT*, 28/10/78.
842 "When big became beautiful in the small isles". *WHFP*, 10/11/78, p. 2.
843 "Why the SNP is jubilant". *FT*, 5/3/79.
844 Perman, R. et al., "Glenrothes". *FT*, 30/6/78.
845 "Irvine". *FT*, 5/9/78.
846 Petrie, G., "Power game: clash ahead on poll plan", *EN*, 20/10/78, p. 7.
847 Prattis, I., "The West Highlands as a marginal community". *Crann Tara* 4 (1978), pp. 10-12.
848 Pym, F. (MP), "Conservative options on devolution". *S*, 1/6/78, p. 14.
849 Ramsay, C., "Socialists and the referendum". *Crann Tara* 3 (1978), pp. 4-5.
850 Rantell, K., "Matriarchy rules OK". *GH*, 6/12/78, p. 4.
851 "Race against time to save Glasgow's heart". *GH*, 10/8/78, p. 7.
852 Raphael, A., "Caper that ended in tears". *Obs.*, 4/3/79, p. 9.
853 "Referendum bait for SNP". *Obs.*, 30/7/78, p. 3.
854 Ray, J. J., "How different are the Scots and English?". *Contemporary Review*, 234 (1979), pp. 158-59.
855 Reid, G. (MP), "The Assembly: this is our big step forward". *EN*, 2/2/79, p. 14.
856 Rifkind, M. (MP), "Leadership without leaving the UK". *S*, 20/9/78, p. 10 (letter).
857 Ritchie, M., "BBC TV: what's gone wrong". *GH*, 20-21/10/78.
858 "Council houses: will they sell?". *GH*, 21/6/78, p. 7.
859 "Hannigan's Folly men build a new reputation". *GH*, 25/8/78, p. 7.
869 "Nuclear dump plan splits conservationists". *GH*, 29/8/78, p. 7.
861 "On the trail of Jim and Tam's Yes/No road show". *GH*, 10/2/79, p. 6.
862 "The Borders: No man's land". *GH*, 23/2/79, p. 7.
863 "War against the Front moves North". *GH*, 30/6/78, p. 7.
864 "Why man from Clydeside chose lighter shade of red". *GH*, 27/6/78, p. 7.
865 Robertson, G. (MP), "Wreckers in the Lords". *S*, 3/8/78, p. 8.

308   SCOTTISH GOVERNMENT YEARBOOK 1980

866   Rose, R., "Assembly: English 'no's' and Scottish 'aye's'". *GH*, 26/10/78, p. 6.
867   "Twelve months hard for Scottish voters". *GH*, 2/8/78, p. 6.
868   "What is Scotland voting about?". *New Society*, 8/2/79, pp. 294-96.
869   Ross, R., "The power an Assembly will have". *GH*, 14/2/79, p. 6.
870   Rissell, W., "Devolution's anchor man weathers storm". *GH*, 28/7/78, p. 7.
871   "In from the cold". *GH*, 7/10/78, p. 6.
872   Russell, W. and Findlay, A., "A vote for Europe". *GH*, 20/3/79, p. 6.
873   *Scotsman, The*, "An assessment of the Scottish constituencies". *S*, 10-30/4/79.
874   "Scotland 78". *S*, 22/3/78, supplement, 10pp.
875   Scott, D., "Authorities uneasy about tenants' charter". *S*, 10/11/78, p. 13.
876   "Growth rate of Glenrothes meets with criticism". *The Scotsman Half Yearly Review*, 27/7/78, p. iv.
877   "It's all moving for travelling folks". *S*, 20/10/78, p. 15.
878   " 'Quango' system under fire". *S*, 4/8/78, p. 11.
879   "Rates increases breach government guidelines". *S*, 14/3/79, p. 12.
880   "Review of local government expected". *S*, 24/5/79, supplement, pp. i, iii.
881   "The dilemma of open government". *S*, 1/6/78, p. 15.
882   "The quango tree just keeps on spreading". *S*, 6/12/78, p. 11.
883   "The view from Calton Hill". *S*, 5-8/2/79.
884   "The who's who of Scotland's quangos". *S*, 5/12/78, p. 11.
885   "Time of reckoning for COSLA". *S*, 23/3/79, p. 14.
886   "Which path will Shetland follow?". *S*, 19/6/78, p. 9.
887   "Younger stresses need for open government", *S*, 8/5/79, p. 7.
888   Scottish Information Office, *Scottish Office: devolution digest No. 1*. Edinburgh, 1977, 3pp.
889   *Scottish Socialist*, "The splitters of the SLP". Scottish Socialist, Nov. 1976 (Special issue), 4pp.
890   Sillars, J. (MP), "Searchlight of public concern". *S*, 8/12/78, p. 15.
891   "The future is ours to shape". *GH*, 15/2/79, p. 6.
892   "Where we go from here". *S. Mail*, 4/3/79, p. 25.
893   Silk, P., "Codes of practice". *CCN* 17 (1978), pp. 4-5, and 18 (1978), pp. 4-6.
894   Simpson, A., "At 86 it's a lively yes from staunch patriot Wendy". *GH*, 28/2/79, p. 4.
895   Simpson, D., "Case for abolishing rates". *S*, 5/3/79, p. 11.
896   Smart, K., "The power to rule a nation". *EN*, 20/2/79, p. 10.
897   Smith D., "Frustration: barrier of silence". *CCN* 15 (1978), p. 24.
898   Smith, G., "The Scotland Bill: a problem of accommodation". *The Times*, 3/7/78, p. 14.
899   Smith, J., "Crucial arena for the SNP". *S*, 27/4/79, p. 8.
900   Smith, J. (MP), "The final say". *DR*, 28/2/79, p. 7.
901   Spens, M., "Future of Shetland". *S*, 1/6/78, p. 14 (letter).
902   "Greenland, Aland and the Faroes: the lessons for Shetland". *New Shetlander* 127 (1979), pp. 18-21.

903 Sproat, I. (MP), "Just why do these sinister people want a 'Yes' vote?". *SDE*, 25/2/79, p. 16.
904 Steel, D. (MP), "A Grand Committee is the answer now". *GH*, 23/3/79, p. 6.
905 "High time we had control". *GH*, 23/2/79, p. 6.
906 "Why we should say yes on March 1". *GH*, 24/11/78, p. 6.
907 Stewart, D. (MP), "Now's the day and now's the hour". *GH*, 23/2/79, p. 6.
908 "Why I'll play the waiting game". *DR*, 29/9/78, p. 11.
909 Stewart, J. D., "Have the Scots a lesson to teach?". *Municipal and Public Services Journal*, 19/1/77.
910 Stewart, W., "Battle of Britain". *Macleans Magazine*, 7/8/78, pp. 33-36.
911 Stokes, J., "The swings and roundabouts of devolution". *The Daily Telegraph*, 14/11/78, p. 18.
912 Taylor, T. (MP), "A constitutional nonsense which will blow up in our face". *GH*, 23/2/79, p. 6.
914 "Inside story of how the laws are passed". *GH*, 2/2/79, p. 6.
915 "The final say". *DR*, 28/2/79, p. 7.
916 "Union blues". *G*, 20/11/78, p. 12.
917 "Why we should boot out the 'costly monster' ". *EN*, 22/2/79, p. 10.
918 Taylor, W., "Made to measure". *S*, 19/2/79, p. 8.
919 "Signing the pledge for Scotland". *S*, 12/3/79, p. 9.
920 "The aide of the party". *S*, 16/4/79, p. 8; 23/4/79, p. 8; 30/4/79, p. 8.
921 Thatcher, M. (MP), "No". *Sunday Post*, 25/2/79, p. 11.
922 "What we plan for Scotland". *GH*, 1/5/79, p. 6.
923 'Theseus', "Referendum diary". *S*, 16/2/79; 23/2/79; 1/3/79.
924 Thomson, J. K., "What future for the SDA?". *S*, 21/8/78, p. 6.
925 Towers, R., "Conflict on uranium isle". *GH*, 19/3/79, p. 7.
926 "The island that turned a tide of decay". *GH*, 4/12/78, p. 7.
927 Trevor-Roper, H., "Labour's shabby project". *Spec.*, 24/2/79, pp. 8-9.
928 Trotter, S., "Face to face with the devolution pilot". *GH*, 20/2/79, p. 6.
929 "Heads that could roll on the swingometer". *GH*, 21/4/79, p. 6.
930 Tucker, A., "Could Scotland become a nuclear graveyard?". *G*, 22/8/78, p. 15.
931 Van Der Vat, D., "Glasgow is not dead yet". *The Times*, 28/1/78, p. 14.
932 "More than a match for the North Sea pipedream". *The Times*, 10/10/78, p. 14.
933 Waller, I. and Berrington, H., "When 'Yes' means 'No' ". *The Sunday Telegraph*, 4/3/79.
934 Webster, J., "The lady says 'no' ". *SDE*, 23/2/79, pp. 20-21.
935 Wheen, F., "What's under the Tory kilt?". *New Stat.*, 27/4/79, pp. 582-83.
936 Whitton, D., "Bulk of area should be taken as red". *S*, 2/5/79, p. 8.
937 Wilson, B., "How Labour beat blizzard and SNP". *Obs.*, 16/4/78.
938 "Labour set to pick Reid". *Obs.*, 18/6/78.

939   "Skye jobs plight — 20% on the dole". *GH*, 22/12/78, p. 7.
940   "The appeasement of nationalism is a misguided exercise". *WHFP*,
       23/2/79, p. 2.
941   "The trials of Roddy". *WHFP*, 23/6/78, p. 2.
942   "Town rules are OK for towns — but not in the Islands". *G*,
       26/2/79, p. 9.
943   Wilson J., "Anatomy of a Scottish executive". *S*, 31/10/-2/11/78.
944   Wishart, B., "Looking back at last year". *Shet. T.* 5/1/79, pp. 4-13;
       12/1/79, pp. 4, 8.
945   Wishart, R., "It's make your mind up time". *S*. Mail, 14/1/79, pp.
       10-11.
946   "Teddy's law". *S. Mail*, 1/4/79, p. 11.
947   "What will it really cost?". *S. Mail*, 28/1/79, p. 13.
948   Wishart, R. and Calder, J., "Plain man's guide to the Assembly".
       S. Mail, 4/2/79, p. 10.
494   Wolfe, W., "Discipline and justice in the SNP". *S*, 9/11/78, p. 13
       (letter).
950   "No more betrayal: the SNP puts you first". *EN*, 25/4/79, p. 12.
951   "SNP 'No' to pact". *S*, 13/9/78, p. 8. (letter).
952   Wyllie, C. D. and Affleck, C. I., "Waiting in the wings: the crisis
       in the SNP". *New Edinburgh Review* 43 (1978), pp. 7-8.

INDEX TO SECTION 17

REFERENCE SECTION

THE SCOTTISH GOVERNMENT YEARBOOK 1976-7

Ed. by M. G. Clarke and H. M. Drucker

CONTENTS

REFERENCE SECTION

REFERENCE SECTION

THE SCOTTISH GOVERNMENT YEARBOOK 1978

Ed. by H. M. Drucker and M. G. Clarke

CONTENTS

APPENDICES

REFERENCE SECTION

THE SCOTTISH GOVERNMENT YEARBOOK 1979

Ed. by N. Drucker and H. M. Drucker

CONTENTS

REFERENCE SECTION